The Golden Pastime

A NEW HISTORY OF YACHTING

BOOKS BY JOHN ROUSMANIERE

A Glossary of Modern Sailing Terms (1976)

No Excuse to Lose (with Dennis Conner, 1978)

The Enduring Great Lakes (editor, 1979)

"Fastnet, Force 10" (1980)

The Luxury Yachts (1981)

America's Cup Book, 1851-1983 (1983)

The Annapolis Book of Seamanship (1983)

*The Student and Instructor Workbook
for The Annapolis Book of Seamanship* (1984)

The Sailing Lifestyle (1985)

*Desirable and Undesirable Characteristics
of Offshore Yachts* (editor, 1986)

The Dolphin Book Club Log Book (1986)

The Golden Pastime (1986)

Copyright © 1986 John Rousmaniere

All rights reserved.
Published simultaneously in Canada by Penguin Books Canada Ltd.,
 2801 John Street, Markham, Ontario L3R 1B4.

Edited by Joseph Gribbins
Designed by Clare Cunningham
Produced by Walter Fuller Jr.
Printed in the United States of America by Taylor Publishing Company,
 Dallas, Texas.
The text of this book is composed in 9/12 Century Schoolbook,
 with captions set in 9/10 Baskerville Italic.

First Edition

Custom edition published and distributed by The Fine Books Division of
 Taylor Publishing Company, Dallas, Texas.

Portions of this book appeared originally in Nautical Quarterly magazine.

ISBN 0-393-03317-1

W.W. Norton & Company, Inc., 500 Fifth Avenue, New York, NY 10110
W.W. Norton & Company Ltd., 37 Great Russell Street,
 London WC1B 3NU

1 2 3 4 5 6 7 8 9 0

A NEW HISTORY OF YACHTING

BY JOHN ROUSMANIERE

A NAUTICAL QUARTERLY BOOK

W.W. NORTON & COMPANY
NEW YORK   LONDON

THE FINE BOOKS DIVISION OF TAYLOR PUBLISHING COMPANY
DALLAS

4

Foreword

Searching my heart for its true sorrow,
This is the way that I find to be:
That I am weary of words and people,
Sick of the city, wanting the sea....

I should be happy — that was happy
All day long on the coast of Maine!
I have a need to hold and handle
Shells and anchors and ships again!

I should be happy, that am happy
Never at all since I came here.
I am too long away from water.
I have a need of water near.

— Edna St. Vincent Millay, "Exiled"

The nine essays in this history of yachting concern more than three centuries of dreamers who have had a need of water near, around, and under. Tycoons and teachers, racers and cruisers, they are people who would echo E.B. White's confession, "With me, I cannot not sail." How and why they have sailed for pleasure despite immense sacrifices of time, energy, and money are questions that run through these essays.

The commonplace answer to these questions, of course, is that we sail because sailing is *fun*. Although it may be true in some instances, that answer is false as a generalization; as anybody who has done a bit of sailing knows and is sufficiently honest to admit, lighthearted enjoyment and yachting do not always go hand in hand. Anyway, if the attraction were merely the fun that sailing offered, only sybarites would buy boats. Others will say that the true enjoyment comes in the technical challenges of getting a boat from here to there — navigation, steering, setting sails, all the rest. That, too, is part of the answer; but if sailing's appeal were merely technical, only technicians would go to sea. Since many other types of people besides technicians and sybarites pursue the pastime, we must look elsewhere, beyond pure pleasure and technical challenge, to understand what motivates people to sail voluntarily.

I can think of two motivations. While they will be illustrated by the stories and biographies in these pages, it's not letting the cat out of the bag to say an introductory word or two about them before we head off on our voyage of discovery through the history of yachting. Simply put, yachtsmen and yachtswomen have been trying to impress other people, or have been searching for meaning in life, or have been caught ambivalently between the two. The best summary of the first reason is the phrase "conspicuous consumption," which the American sociologist Thorstein Veblen invented and publicized in his book, *The Theory of the Leisure Class*, published in 1899: when they are made highly visible and materialistic, leisure and consumption are tools whose sole purpose is to win the world's esteem. "Esteem," wrote Veblen, "is awarded only on evidence." When it is simply conspicuous consumption, yachting is the *gilded pastime*: all flash and little substance. (What Veblen did not anticipate is a counterculture that awards esteem on the evidence of conspicuous *non*-consumption, which can produce reverse snobbery. That variation will not concern us until our story gets to Joshua Slocum, Bernard Moitessier, and other hairshirt singlehanded voyagers.)

The other reason for sailing for pleasure can loosely be described as spiritual. This motivation has to do with finding personal or even religious meaning by pushing the limits of a beautiful but potentially dangerous world. Allow me to attempt an analogy: For centuries, the pleasure sailor taking a yacht to sea has performed an act that in courage (or foolhardiness) could be duplicated today only by a private citizen blasting off into space in his or her own space shuttle. Until space shuttles are within private means, people venturing beyond the horizon on their own must continue to make do with yachts. These adventures — always passionate, sometimes quixotic or even foolish — make up the rich core of what I call the *golden pastime*, and they and the fascinating people and vessels that accomplished them are the subject matter of this book.

Acknowledgments

Blessing on the child who is surrounded by strange books and wondrous family traditions. This project has been in the making since the day almost thirty years ago when, while I was rummaging through the rows of sailing books in my father's library, my fingertips first slid over the gold inlays on the cover of *The Lawson History of the America's Cup.* Pressed to explain it and its neighbors, my father opened up a rich new world in the stories of his boyhood: of cruising on his uncle Nathaniel Ayer's big Herreshoff schooners, *Queen Mab* and *Lynx,* of racing with Harold Vanderbilt and Rod Stephens, of sailing a Six-Meter up the East River before movie cameras to provide action for a Carole Lombard film. Sometimes they seemed like tall tales (especially the one about the movie); but I absorbed their romance and suspended judgment until time proved them true. (Only last year I saw a 1937 film called *Nothing Sacred,* in which Frederic March seems to be steering a Six-Meter under the Brooklyn Bridge with a winsome Carole Lombard — my father in a wig — handling the jib sheets. Children, believe your elders.)

When I was fourteen, I got a glimpse of the larger context of all this history when I heard Briggs Cunningham, fresh from winning the 1958 America's Cup match, state very clearly and publicly in the model room of the New York Yacht Club that he hoped that a foreign challenger would soon win the Cup. The commodore standing at his elbow flushed and assured us that Mr. Cunningham surely was exaggerating. My sense of irony was immature, but I could tell that something fascinating was going on and deserved further attention. Yet it was not until 1971 that I could give yachting history that attention. As a second lieutenant assigned to teach history during the academic year at the United States Military Academy, at West Point, I had a summer free for reading. This came about for the simple reason that, not knowing what to do with a mere second lieutenant, the academy gave me only one duty that summer, which was to count golf balls at the country club. That chore taking only an afternoon, I was free to read every word written for publication by the great boating journalist and *Yachting* columnist Alfred F. Loomis, using scrap-books and books kindly loaned me by Mrs. Loomis. The long essay about Alf Loomis that grew out of that delightful summer could not be published until there was an outlet for it, boating magazines at the time being interested only in cruise narratives, racing journalism, and instructional articles on subjects such as how to trim sails and how to avoid running into things.

Enter the remarkable *Nautical Quarterly,* whose editor, Joseph Gribbins, published my Loomis piece in 1979 and, over the next six years, ran ten more articles that I wrote on yachting history between bouts of churning out books about how to trim sails and avoid running into things. Much of this book is a flourishing of those eleven seedlings. That it is not a jungle is due to Joe Gribbins, one of those editors all authors dream about but rarely encounter: encouraging, always available, flexible about deadlines and word counts, interested in the topic, and never failing to come up with the right word or phrase when the original falls flat.

I wish to thank Walter Fuller Jr., Clarence S. Lovelace, and Eric Swenson for helping to get this book on track to publication; Sohei Hohri, librarian and curator of the New York Yacht Club, for his assistance and encouragement over the years; Benjamin Fuller and Elizabeth Parker, of the Mystic Seaport Museum, for tracking down paintings and photographs; Clare Cunningham, for her handsome design; deLancey Funsten, for constant good cheer and administrative efficiency in moments of chaos; Karen Kratzer, for so precisely pasting up these pages; Rebecca Smith, for editorial assistance with the original articles; Victoria Harwood, for sharing the burden of reading proofs; Halsey Herreshoff and Carlton J. Pinheiro, of the Herreshoff Museum, for providing some important information on short notice; and Roderick Stephens, Jr., for his memory of a visit to Nat Herreshoff.

This book is dedicated with love to my brothers James Ayer Rousmaniere, Jr. and Peter Farwell Rousmaniere, who enjoy a good story.

John Rousmaniere
Stamford, Connecticut
February 27, 1986

Contents

I

The First Yachts and Yachtsmen

"God would not damn a man for a little irregular pleasure."

eisure and love of luxury, two of the prime components of yachting, are popularly regarded as creations of the warm climate and genial outlook of southern Europe; but yachting as we know it sprang out of the chilly North Sea, and it was shaped by the fierce commercial and religious tensions of Reformation Holland and England. Although very different sorts of people, the mercantilist Dutch burghers and the melancholy Stuart King, Charles II, seized upon the idea of using ships for pleasure in quite similar ways, and so took leisure to sea. They were the first yachtsmen, and we are their heirs.

Each group built and conspicuously used pleasure boats, partly as instruments of the state but mainly as personal tools of enjoyment and fulfillment. The major difference between the way they used their yachts and the way twentieth-century yachtsmen use theirs is that, three centuries ago, yachting was much more intimately bound up with people's serious lives ashore — with commerce and religion, politics and science. This change is exemplified in the ways the word "yacht" has been defined over the centuries. Today, most people would define a yacht as a well-constructed, relatively large boat used solely for pleasure; but in 1789, in his definitive *Universal Dictionary of the Marine*, perhaps the first dictionary of English nautical terms, William Falconer provided three very different meanings that fairly summarize the limited history of yachting until then, and indicate the pastime's interrelationship with the rest of life. A look at Falconer's definitions will provide us with a format for a sketchy survey of the history of yachting before the golden pastime's great boom in seventeenth-century northern Europe.

The first of these meanings is that a yacht is a state vessel "usually employed to convey princes, ambassadors, or other great personages from one kingdom to another." By that definition, there were yachts some five thousand years ago, when a Mesopotamian scribe signified "nobleman" with a glyph that showed a man standing in the bow of a reed boat. Much later, in the three centuries before the common era began, the Greek Ptolemies who ruled Egypt after the death of Alexander the Great kept as many as eight hundred houseboats called *thalamegoi* moored at Alexandria to convey themselves and their officials on work and pleasure

rounds. Some of these were remarkable vessels. Ptolemy IV, otherwise best known for marrying his sister and slaughtering his mother, brother, and uncle, commissioned the construction of a four-thousand-oared catamaran stretching three hundred feet in length and forty-five feet in beam, and towering sixty feet above the surface of the Nile. The Romans who overthrew the Ptolemies were not fooled by claims to the boats' official status; they called these vessels *lusoriae*, "pleasure boats." With a cynicism in which Thorstein Veblen would have delighted, the poet Horace wrote of their owners:

> They change their sky, not their soul
> Who run across the sea.
> We work hard at doing nothing;
> We seek happiness in yachts.

These floating pleasure palaces must have served some political need, for at one stage the Roman statesman Seneca the younger suggested that the best way to solve a vexing state controversy was to send not war ships but "pleasure boats and houseboats and the playthings that kings use for disporting themselves on the sea." (As we will see throughout this history, yachts were often tools of diplomacy.)

Falconer's second definition of "yacht," after the traveling ship of state, is that of a royal boat "reserved for the sovereign" and "nobly ornamented with sculpture." Cleopatra's famous barge, whose namesake will appear in all her quixotic glory in the next chapter, fits this definition neatly. According to Plutarch, the vessel's stern was layered with gold and the oars with silver, and the sails were colored purple (or crimson, some scholars say) with dye made from ground mollusks raised in specially protected beds in the Mediterranean off the Phoenician city of Tyre. For the next sixteen centuries, kings, queens, and their offspring luxuriated, were carried, and sometimes were buried in such splendid vessels of many sizes, most built with the utmost care. Since they were usually funded from royal purses and not state exchequers, they served to enhance the monarch's own personal power while providing him (or her) with private and safe transportation. So valuable were these ships that monarchs used them as bribes when

On page 8, the first British royal yacht, Charles II's fifty-two foot Mary, is shown sailing up the Thames in 1660, flying the hoy rig, with a boomless mainsail, two jibs, and a squaresail. This Leslie Wilcox painting is owned by Dr. Beppe Croce, the President of the International Yacht Racing Union, which governs all of yacht racing. The Van de Velde sketches on the opposite page show the evolution of the first yachts. Above is a Dutch Staten Jaght, or official vessel, similar to Mary. The gun was a realistic concession to the intermittent Anglo-Dutch naval wars; the leeboard could be lowered to improve sailing ability in deep water and raised (as shown here) to allow for safe navigation in the shallow Zuider Zee; the huge aftercastle provided privacy for passengers. Below is the English royal yacht Charlotte, which is quite different in some details. Her gun ports were purely decorative; the deeper waters of the Thames allowed her to be built with a keel instead of leeboards; and the more commodious hull that the keel allowed meant that the aftercastle could be dispensed with.

negotiating treaties.

The first royal ship built for pleasure, and not for transport or presence, may have been a vessel with the extraordinary name of *Rat o' Wight,* which, reportedly, was constructed for Queen Elizabeth I at Cowes on the Isle of Wight to celebrate the victory over the Spanish Armada in 1588. So little is known about *Rat o' Wight,* however, that it is safer to identify the tiny *Disdain,* commissioned by the Stuart King James I, as the first true royal pleasure boat. A miniature of the warship *Ark Royal,* she was built for James' ten-year-old heir, Prince Henry. According to her builder, the master shipwright Phineas Pett, the goal was educational: *Disdain* was built for Henry in order "to disport himself in about London Bridge and acquaint his Grace with shipping and the manner of that element." She was only twenty-five feet long in the contemporary way of measuring, "by the keel" (that is, along the length of her keel; overall lengths were about ten percent greater). Pett described her as "garnished with painting and carving, both within board and without, very curiously according to his Lordship's directions." Since "curiously" meant "carefully" at that time, Pett had no complaints. *Disdain* was enrolled in the Royal Navy's list, from which she was removed in 1618, six years after the prince's death, which left James's son Charles next in line — unluckily, as it turned out. We will return to royal yachting with Charles's son.

Finally, Falconer's third definition of "yacht" is the one that most corresponds with ours; yachts are smaller ships used either by government officials or "as pleasure-vessels by private gentlemen." It is this definition that best describes the first fleet of trim little pleasure ships that cruised and raced upon Amsterdam's Ij River, and that gave our sport and pastime its name.

The golden pastime, satisfyingly, was born in a golden age. Following on its declaration of independence from Spanish rule in 1581, the Netherlands experienced two centuries of extraordinary commercial success that historians have called the Golden Age of the Dutch Republic. This spot of land that had been painfully won, inch by inch, from the North Sea was the home of a powerful navy and a great merchant fleet, of the first successful capitalistic state, of an intellectual and artistic blossoming in Spinoza and Rembrandt. Many years of struggle against the sea and invaders had honed the Dutch into a serious, independent people whose experience and world view made them immediately receptive to the hard pragmatic theology of John Calvin's Reformation. Sir William Petty, an English scientist and writer, once described the Dutch as "for the most part thinking, sober men, and such as believe that Labour and Industry is their duty toward God." In his famous study of the ideology of money-making, *The Protestant Ethic and the Spirit of Capitalism*, the German sociologist Max Weber identified this bond between faith and worldly ambition as the primary cause of northern Europe's commercial success; the mere pursuit of wealth for its own sake was not countenanced. Weber's thesis has been accused of being too simplistic; but it was sometimes difficult to sort out Dutch piety from Dutch mercantilism: *"Voilà votre religion!,"* Sweden's King Charles X, holding up a coin, once declared to a Dutch diplomat. Still, no one could accuse the Dutch of being conspicuous consumers on the scale, say, of a George Crowninshield or a James Gordon Bennett Jr., whose excesses will be outlined in later chapters. One British visitor to Amsterdam during this period observed:

> *Never any country traded so much, and consumed so little; they buy infinitely, but 'tis to sell again, either upon improvement of the commodity, or at a better market. They are the great masters of the Indian spices, and of the Persian silks; but wear plain woolens, and feed upon their own cloth to France, and buy coarse out of England for their own wear.*

By 1662, the seven United Provinces of the Netherlands were packed with some two million people, many of them Jewish, Protestant, and Catholic refugees fleeing from one persecution or another and welcomed by the Dutch, whose natural tolerance was enhanced by a practical interest in recruiting new talent. The population density of the tiny country was great for the day — about one hundred thirty-five people per square mile (one and one-half times that of England and Wales at the time, and equal to that of the state of Virginia in 1980). It was a heavily urban culture; ten percent of Netherlanders lived in Amsterdam (by contrast, teeming London contained six percent of all Englishmen). Almost everybody else lived in Rotterdam, Haarlem, and the other cities and large towns. Water was the country's lifeline. An elaborate

1 2

Charles II, surrounded by royal finery and symbols, moodily sits for an official portrait. During his twenty-five years as king, he worked long and hard in trying to escape monarchical pressures, and one of his routes was to go sailing. Samuel Pepys once wrote of Charles that "Two leagues travel at sea was more pleasure to him than twenty by land."

system of natural rivers and engineered canals funneled boats, people, and goods. Horse-drawn passenger ferries kept regular schedules (sometimes at night). On holidays, the canal boats carried the populace into the country, as burghers, housewives, tradesmen, and prostitutes cheerfully elbowed each other with a Brueghelian vulgarity.

Crowded Amsterdam became Europe's busiest port, as important to the Atlantic Ocean as Tyre had been to the ancient Mediterranean and as Salem, Massachusetts, would be to all oceans a century and a half later. Amsterdam was a great hive of commerce where river traffic met sea traffic at the busy wharves of the Dutch East and West India Companies to exchange goods, silver, marks of credit, and news. All eyes and ears were turned toward the sea: to reports about vessels on the eight-month voyage to Japan, where of all Europeans only the Dutch were permitted to trade until the mid-nineteenth century; to gossip about the Malayan spice harvests; to accounts of battles during the three great naval wars the Dutch fought against the British in 1652-54, 1665-67, and 1672-74.

While the India Companies' great merchantmen challenged Portuguese, Spanish, and English traders in speed and bulk, Dutch naval architects favored trimness in their other vessels. The warships that escorted their merchantmen were usually smaller than the enemy's men-of-war due to the restrictions of the shallow Zuider Zee and, the naval historian David Howarth suggests, because there was no absolute monarch to insist on the conceit of massiveness. Perhaps, too, the Dutch, like many experienced mariners, saw the advantage in battle of a quick, maneuverable ship. From this model the navy and merchant commands of Holland developed a fast all-purpose vessel called a *Jaght Schip,* the ancestor of the yacht.

With its hard guttural and its "j" pronounced half-way between "y" and "h," *jaght* was derived from the verb *Jaghen,* meaning to tow with horses, hunt, or pursue. At first, the term *Jaght Schip* described one of those horse-drawn canal boats on which the Dutch commuted; but by the early seventeenth century it came to mean a fast, relatively small boat, much the way *Jaght Vogel, Jaght Peerd,* and *Jaght Hond* meant a hawk, horse, and dog used in the hunt. While most *Jaght Schips* were probably in the forty-

to sixty-foot range, these slippery vessels came in many sizes, from the twenty-foot privately-owned *Boeyers* to the huge one hundred twenty-foot India Company traders and packets. Modeled after the bluff-bowed, flat-bottom *flutes* (so-called because their round sides made them look like huge musical flutes), these vessels were fast and seaworthy, their large leaf-shaped retractable leeboards providing shallow draft in shoal water as well as great weatherliness in most offshore conditions. In 1598, two *Jaghts* survived a violent storm off the Cape of Good Hope to reach India; eleven years later, the English mariner Henry Hudson sailed a *Jaght* called *Halve Moene,* which probably was no larger than fifty feet, across the Atlantic to explore the northeast coast of the New World. By the mid-seventeenth century, these capable sloops were serving a wide variety of official functions. In war, they were courier boats and tenders for the admirals, and they also fought — in a battle near the Straits of Magellan in 1615 a *Jaght* sank the Spanish flagship. In peace, they were in government or India Company service, chasing smugglers, collecting customs duties, and ferrying officials about Amsterdam.

The very largest *Jaght Schips* were ship-rigged; the others were sloops. A few sloops carried the old-fashioned boomless spritsail rig, in which a long sprit running from the mainsail tack to the leech supported the sail. Most, however, flew either the bezan rig, in which there were a boomed mainsail with a short club gaff and two headsails, or the hoy rig, which consisted of a boomless mainsail under a long gaff (also called the "half sprit"), a small square topsail, and two headsails. When the vessel was at rest, the battenless mainsail was brailed in at the mast rather than doused. The bezan rig and, indeed, the powerful *Jaght Schip* hull itself survive today in the Dutch *Tjalk* yachts that are seen around the North Sea and, occasionally, in North America. But whether a modern version could be as handsomely decorated as an original is open to question. Even the smallest *Jaght* was smothered in gilded carvings. The towering aftercastles on the larger vessels, like those on Dutch warships, were interwoven with glittering seaweed, mermaids, rampant lions, sea serpents, sea gods, and other pagan images that, John Calvin or no John Calvin, no self-respecting seaman would sail without. Forward, on the snub bow, a lion or unicorn might be lunging from a delicately carved platform to tame onrushing seas. Although only some vessels were armed, almost all *Jaghts* were built with gun ports surrounded by gilt wreaths. Judging from contemporary paintings and etchings by the two William Van de Veldes, they flew immense flags, presumably to declare their owners' status and the day's itinerary.

Relatively secure in its borders and prosperous in its commerce, the Netherlands gradually took on the trappings of what we would call a middle-class country, among them some sporting accoutrements. Eventually, some *Jaght Schips* ended up in the hands of wealthy individuals. Even a workaholic Hollander occasionally took some leisure, and company and private *Jaghts* often cruised, raced, or engaged in highly visible mock battles between squadrons of boats. The pleasure boat had come of age.

One indication of Dutch influence in nautical matters is that when the members of the world's first yacht club, the Water Club of the Harbour of Cork, Ireland, engaged in their own elaborate fleet maneuvers in the eighteenth century, the flags they used as signals were called "Dutch colors." Another, and — to our purposes here — most valuable effect of Dutch seamanship and naval architecture was its influence on an English refugee whose lifeline also extended to the sea. This man took the Dutch *Jaght Schip* and, freeing its ties to commerce, transformed pleasure sailing into a pastime with an identity all its own. He was Charles Stuart, the future King Charles II of England and Scotland.

He was, first of all, a man of the wrong century. Better had this royal humanist lived in the reasonable 1700s than to be imprisoned in the one century since ancient times when most things that were considered important were defined with cut-throat intensity by radically differing views of how humans relate to the absolute. When monarchy was restored to England in 1660 after the Puritan interlude, and he accepted Parliament's invitation to return and reign, Charles was only thirty years old. Eighteen of those years he had spent either in civil war, in flight, or in poverty-stricken exile, despairing of a people that had cut off the head of their king, his father. There were times when sailing in small boats in one place of exile or another seemed to give him his only escape from gloom. Sailing saved Charles' life, too, for he had several times made good narrow escapes from Oliver Cromwell's Roundheads in small ships. In 1651, he had last seen England from an ignominious, but

Jachts in Action — 1697

Every Martinmas, on November 11, huge crowds would pack the banks of the River Ij to watch four or five hundred boats in action. If we are to believe an account of one mock battle between *Jaght Schips,* held in honor of Czar Peter the Great of Russia in 1697, these maneuvers had the potential of becoming painfully realistic. Peter had come to Amsterdam *incognito* in order to learn the shipwright's trade and carry the skill back to St. Petersburg and create a Russian navy. When the Dutch finally discovered the czar's presence — reportedly, the first diplomatic approach was made by an official climbing up a frigate's ratlines to where Peter was tarring a mast — they insisted on honoring him with a grand mock battle. Peter was safely installed on a spectator boat to watch the two squadrons of *Jaghts* sail in formations signaled from the admiral's flagship. The sailors' self-discipline quickly broke down, and the two lines disintegrated into a massive tangle where the crews cheerfully blasted away at each other with house-rattling bursts of blank musket and cannon fire. Peter rapidly worked himself into "a state of rapture difficult to describe," in the words of a companion. Wild-eyed with excitement, the czar ordered his astonished hosts to sail into the fight and let him join in.

While not as gaudily decorated as the great Staten Jaghts, *the small gentleman's yachts owned by Dutch* burghers *had one or two elegant carvings and flew large flags and streamers when assembled for maneuvers and mock battles.*

secure, perch on the deck of a thirty-five foot coal barge called *Surprise,* which carried him to France, whence he made his way to the Netherlands, where his dear sister Mary was married to William of Orange. There Charles did enough sailing to reveal his passion to his hosts. While passing through Amsterdam on his way to the restoration, he was presented with a fifty-two foot *Jaght* by the Burgermaster, who, no doubt, hoped to alleviate international tensions. In his response to the presentation speech, Charles diplomatically waffled. Nevertheless, several months later, on August 15, 1660, the perspicacious gadabout and Navy official Samuel Pepys noted in his diary, "I found the King gone this morning by five of the clock to see a Dutch pleasure-boat below bridge." The bridge was London Bridge, the only crossing of the Thames in the city until the mid-eighteenth century, and the pleasure-boat, now Charles's, was that Dutch fifty-two footer, which the king obligingly named after Mary.

By all accounts a natural and accomplished sailor, King Charles was apparently happiest aboard a boat. "Two leagues travel at sea was more pleasure to him than twenty by land," Pepys observed. Charles's friend the Duke of Buckingham went further to say that sailing was the king's *only* joy. This comment may surprise those who have heard of the "merry monarch" and his passions for fine clothes, high-stakes gambling, vigorous hunts, and glamorous women. But, as Antonia Fraser stresses in her biography, *Royal Charles,* there was more to this man than glitter and games. Charles was, at heart, a melancholy, almost desperate man who never quite seemed, since his return, to be himself. It was a plague of the times. His contemporary Pepys mourned a day when "a man cannot live without playing the knave and dissimulation" (likewise, in a study of seventeenth-century English literature, T.S. Eliot wrote of the time's widespread "dissociation of sensibility"). It was a tumultuous age with few certainties; it was a century like ours, full of disillusionment and viciousness. The end of medieval certainties, violent revolution, religious reformation that never seemed to gain sufficient security to be universally and consistently tolerant — all had left people struggling for some sense of comfort that refused to come.

Charles Stuart had suffered more than most. In 1557, Queen Elizabeth I had signed the death warrant for his great-grandmother, the Catholic Mary Queen of Scots, with the tacit approval of Mary's son and his grandfather, James I. His father, Charles I (brother of the owner of *Disdain*), had also been decapitated, not by royalty but by commoners sitting in the revolutionary Puritan Parliament. Now Charles II, if not a closet Catholic at least a Catholic sympathizer, had to preside over the English monarchy's rapid submission to another Protestant, but less radical, Parliament. By turns analytical and flippant, sensitive and libidinous, elegant and uncouth, passive and aggressive, Charles exhibited the brinkmanship of the doctrinaire fatalist. He threw his money, women, and ministers around as though there were no tomorrow, and his aimlessness was so apparently undisciplined that the Bishop of Salisbury described Charles as "not knowing how to get around the day." The Bishop elaborated:

> He was during the active part of his life given up to sloth and lewdness, to such a degree that he hated business, and could not bear the engaging in anything that gave him much trouble, or put him under any constraint . . .

In a more secular age two hundred years later, Thorstein Veblen described the conspicuous consumer in a remarkably similar way: "The characteristic feature of leisure-class life," he wrote, "is a conspicuous exemption from all useful employment." Elsewhere he added a scathing bit of sarcasm: "The pervading principle and abiding test of good breeding is the requirement of a substantial and patent waste of time." After almost twenty years in which his daily concern was survival, Charles in the 1660s faced a responsibility that was quickly eroding into that of a figurehead, a task for which he was greatly over-qualified. Soon we will see how other people have dealt with similar quandaries. Here we will speculate that Charles's headlong pursuit of pleasure was a means to gain distance from a reality so painful that, at times, it may have threatened his sanity.

His justification was terse and quotable: "God would not damn a man for a little irregular pleasure." Irregular pleasure he did enjoy and conspicuous consumer he was. Compulsively acquisitive — "Charles never discarded, he only added to his hand," it was said of his accumulation of mistresses — he built at least twenty-

16

six luxury yachts for his own use during his twenty-five year reign, and openly named many of them for his paramours. *Cleveland* honored Barbara Villiers, Duchess of Cleveland, who mothered five of his bastard children. Louise de Kéroualle inspired two yachts, *Portsmouth* because she was Duchess of Portsmouth, and *Fubbs* because she had baby fat and was "fubby" or "tubby." *Monmouth* was named for his eldest bastard son, James, Duke of Mon-

At left is the face (and chubby body) that inspired two royal yachts. This is Louise de Kéroualle, the Duchess of Portsmouth, for whom Charles II named his Portsmouth *and* Fubbs. *Perhaps intending to suggest an exoticism that is not apparent in her firm gaze, the portraitist showed her with a smiling black slave offering a cornucopia of pearls. Seen opposite is Samuel Pepys (pronounced "peeps"), whose enormous diary — which he kept in cipher — provides an intimate view of Restoration England and her remarkable king. As a clerk in the Navy office and later as Secretary to the Admiralty, Pepys often sailed in the early yachts.*

"The Dutch have too much trade, and the English are resolved to take it from them." For the same mercantilist reason, he took advantage of his position as patron of the Royal Society to urge scientists to drop basic research and put their energies into designing faster ships and better navigation systems. When told that astronomical observations were needed, he reportedly replied that he "certainly did not want his ship-owners to be deprived of any help the Heavens could supply," and authorized the construction of the renowned Greenwich Observatory and appointed the first royal astronomer.

The love of sailing, the passion for luxury and pleasure, the sensuality, the sporadic but keen brilliance, the concern for practicality, and (perhaps above all) the burgeoning eagerness to escape shoreside responsibility — all these traits of character and mind combined naturally in Charles's fascination with yachts. So pleased was he by the Dutch-built *Mary* that he and his brother James, Duke of York, almost immediately ordered English-built pleasure boats from Peter and Christopher Pett, two brothers in the country's greatest family of shipwrights. The results were Charles's forty-nine foot *Catherine,* named for his fiancée, and James's fifty-two foot *Anne,* named for his wife. The new boats were similar to the typical Dutch *Jaght Schip* except in one significant detail: because the waters of the Thames are deeper than those of the Ij and Zuider Zee, each had a keel and a deep draft of seven feet rather than the leeboards and three feet of draft of the Dutch yacht that Charles named *Mary.*

Though vastly different in temperament, the two brothers — one playful, the other somber — had found one interest in common. What happened was inevitable. On May 21, 1661, *Catherine* beat *Anne* in the first recorded yacht race. A few months later, the first race narrative was written. "The King lost it going, the wind being contrary," the writer John Evelyn noted in his diary after a thirty-five mile race from Greenwich to Gravesend and return, "but [did] save stakes in returning." *Catherine,* apparently something of a downwind flyer, won £ 100. Evelyn went on to report that the two yachts were attended by a "kitchen-boat," which was a barge that sent over food and drink during the long race. These little sporting ships that were so new to England, Evelyn concluded, made "very excellent sailing vessels." When he wasn't racing,

mouth. Neither did he neglect his legal relatives, for there were two *Henrietta*s and two *Mary*s for his favorite niece and sister, and two *Catherine*s for his patient wife.

On the other hand, Charles should not be dismissed with Veblenesque cynicism. Extremely intelligent, he was also capable of great bursts of energy. Complained Pepys soon after the restoration, "The King do tire all his people that are about him with early rising since he come." He was especially excited about maritime affairs, and continued the build-up of the navy and merchant marine begun under Cromwell because, a contemporary observed,

A Floating Palace of the Seventeenth Century

In his vessels, Charles II must have felt at palatial home. He certainly spent sizeable fortunes on the boats and their upkeep. Royal yachts cost about twice as much per ton to build as a man-of-war, and three times as much per ton as a merchantman. From some account books, we know that of the £ 1200 that Charles spent on one yacht, more than half went toward luxury items: £ 120 on silk signal flags; £ 300 to £ 450 on carvings and paint; £ 200 on painting alone; and £ 100 on guns. Furnishings aren't mentioned, probably because they were borrowed from palace inventories. On board, there were thick quilts, gilt leather, crimson damask hangings, pewter chamber pots, feather beds, and velvet cushions (on which Pepys once slept off a "supper mighty merry," as he colorfully described a floating drinking bout). As all this royal luxury had to be supported in a royal style, each yacht carried a crew of thirty to forty men — about one man per foot of length — whose annual wages came to about £ 1500 or more than the cost of the yacht herself. Since Charles regularly overspent his income on these luxuries, which included dogs, horses, and women, he struggled to convince Pepys and other Navy officials of the justice of using government funds to pay his crews or even buy his yachts. His success, however, was limited.

Yacht racing and the first yachts appeared almost simultaneously in England, thanks to Stuart competitiveness. Here, Charles's second Mary, *built in 1677, pounds through a lumpy sea with her jib and squaresail luffing. To windward, near some onlooking ships, is another yacht, perhaps* Charlotte, *owned by the king's brother James, the Duke of York.* Mary *was still afloat in 1816.*

Charles used his yachts to carry him on inspections of the Royal Navy or simply to help him relax. Sometimes he brought along Queen Catherine, who was a sufficiently good sailor to own her own yacht. They would dine together on one vessel and, it appears, retire to separate beds — on separate yachts.

Charles was highly accomplished as a seaman and owner. "He possessed a transcendent mastery of all maritime knowledge," said Pepys, who knew boats and was no sycophant. A skillful helmsman who often steered during races, an able deckhand eager to hand and reef sails, and blessed with a strong stomach, Charles especially enjoyed sailing in rough weather, which some of his friends did not. (Pepys, in his diary, reported that during one cruise "I was overcome with sea-sickness so that I began to spew soundly, and so continued for a good while.") Charles also had an understanding of the principles of naval architecture, and pressed his builders hard. At the king's specific request, the first ketch rig was installed in *Fubbs*. Despite her triumph in that early race in 1661, he was disappointed by the first *Catherine* and sent her back to the yard for four more tons of musket-shot ballast and a complete new set of sails made of Holland Duck. Later, two centuries before lead ballast came into common use, Christopher Pett recommended putting it in the royal yacht *Henrietta* because, as he explained in a letter asking for the approval of the Navy Commissioners, to have sufficient ballast with a less dense material, such as stones, would require half-filling the cabin, and the boat would still heel so far that she would "run to leeward."

A fascinating indication of English technical advance at sea is the admiring report of an inspection by the Burgermaster of Amsterdam, Nicholas Witsen, of Charles's first *Catherine,* captured in 1673 during the third Anglo-Dutch War. She was "very costly," Witsen began, and also very beautiful, with a figurehead that consisted of a yellow painted head surrounded by sea nymphs and goddesses, rails covered with "gold painted carvings of grotesque figures and plants," and many flags, among them a great silk streamer that draped from the masthead to the water. The hull was constructed of a ruddy Irish wood, "the finest wood to be found in Europe" that, because it resisted rot, was left unpainted and untarred along the topsides, contrary to Dutch custom. Witsen observed that, in shape, *Catherine* was sharper in the bow,

rounder in the stern, and flatter along the sides than the *flute*-like *Jaght Schips.* Witsen made an interesting reference to a moveable mast step that could be adjusted "to seek sailing power"; to a sailor, this suggests a means for adjusting the mast's position or rake in order to balance the helm, which would be a sophisticated device on any modern racing sloop.

Charles's willingness to experiment met its limits with the ingenious work in naval architecture conducted by Sir William Petty. Trained in medicine, this energetic polymath was a prominent member of the Royal Society and the Oxford Experimental Science Club, under whose auspices he conducted research in anatomy. He was well known for reviving a hanged woman whom he presumed to be dead and was about to cut open when she began to breathe. In that day of generalists and maritime commerce, this anatomist put much thought into the theory of hydrodynamics. In 1662, he gained and proclaimed the fundamental insight that, all else being equal, a long narrow hull makes less resistance in the water than a short wide one. As he put it, "Length hindereth not as doth breadth." Since wide hulls are more stable than narrow ones, he concluded that to provide high speed and high stability, the boat should be constructed of two parallel, narrow hulls spaced far apart by crossbeams. He called this vessel a "double-bottomed" boat; we call it a catamaran. He built four such boats, the first two of which were remarkably successful: in a race off Ireland, the aptly named *Innovation,* a twenty-footer, soundly trounced three monohulled boats; later, over the sixty-five mile run between Holyhead and Dublin, her successor, *Innovation II,* outsailed the packet boat by fully fifteen hours in heavy weather.

Impressed by Petty's accomplishments, Samuel Pepys openmindedly concluded that naval architecture would be improved only through experiment. A special committee of investigation of the Royal Society, while noting some structural problems with *Innovation,* concluded that she was fast, seaworthy, and weatherly. All the same, King Charles made fun of Petty and what he called his "fantastical double-bottom machine." Still, Petty had the satisfaction of knowing that one of his papers on "double-bottom" boats had been locked up as a state secret. The first but (as we shall see in our discussion of Nathanael Herreshoff) hardly the last designer of multihulls to be scorned by authority, Petty was stung.

In 1665 he built a new boat called *Experiment* and sent her out into the Bay of Biscay in search of the gale that, he was sure, would test and ultimately prove her seaworthiness. She found the storm, which unfortunately sank her with all hands. Although fifteen normal boats went down in the same gale, whatever momentum Petty's ingenious idea had was lost. He went on to other brainstorms, among them the double writing machine, which automatically made a copy of a letter while the original was being written. By 1684, his interest was again excited, and telling a friend, "the fits of the Double-Bottom do return fiercely upon me," he produced a fourth catamaran, *St. Michael,* to do battle with Charles's skepticism. Apparently she was a failure, and the king did not change his opinion of multihulls.

Charles II died in 1685 soon after being formally received into the Roman Catholic Church, and with the name of his last mistress, Nell Gwynne, on his lips. He was succeeded by his dour Catholic brother, James, the second yachtsman. The bastard Monmouth tried to ignite a Protestant uprising but, true to Stuart family tradition, he was decapitated by his uncle, who in turn was overthrown in the bloodless Glorious Revolution of 1688 and was succeeded, at Parliament's invitation, by his daughter Mary and her husband, the Dutch Stadholder William III of Orange, son of Charles's sister Mary. With the reign of William and Mary, the last trappings of absolute monarchy disappeared in Britain. Despite attempted returns by pretenders for the next half century, Stuart rule and the vicious religious struggle also ended.

Besides passing on Navy and merchant fleets that were many times larger than the ones he had inherited (as well as England's first national debt), Charles left behind a trend. The word *jaght* had entered the English language in a variety of spellings that reflected problems with the Germanic guttural, among them *yeagh, yoath, yaugh, yought, yott,* and *yatch.* Aristocrats and even well-to-do commoners were cruising up and down the Thames and into the Channel, and potential owners were so eager for their boats that Christopher Pett threatened to charge a special fee for entertaining them in his yard. Of the more than two dozen Stuart royal yachts, William and Mary inherited a fleet of eight or more, whose two hundred fifty crewmembers annually drained £13,000 in salaries and upkeep. Time and rot gradually pared the fleet

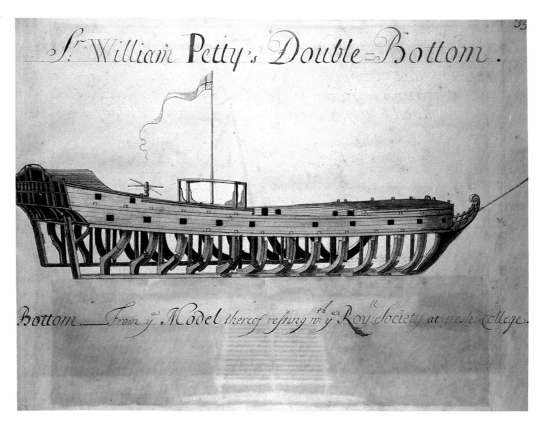

Above, plans for Sir William Petty's "double bottom" Experiment, *the first catamaran built in Europe. Like the highly popular Hobie Cats of our day, she had asymmetrical hulls — both hulls were flat on the inner sides and curved on the outer sides.* Experiment *suffered the fate of many boats of her type: though fast, she was derided by the authorities (in her case, Charles II) and the idea did not catch on. As we will see in Chapter Seven,*

Nathanael Herreshoff's catamarans met with the same reaction. Right, King William III and Queen Mary, James's daughter, receive a royal salute from a fleet of yachts and galleys as they board a royal yacht at Gosport some time after their joint accession to the English throne in 1688.

20

This engraving of the entrance to the Medway River, at the mouth of the Thames, shows a typical English Channel maritime scene in the eighteenth and early nineteenth centuries. English waters were packed with thousands of yachts, work boats, pilot boats, and small ships. All were built to essentially the same design, which had hardly changed from that of the first English Jaght Schips of the 1660s. Not until the 1830s did yachts take on a distinctive appearance, and it wasn't until the 1870s that a naval architect could make a living by designing pleasure vessels.

down, but William and his Hanover successors, no matter how little they shared in Charles's seafaring interest, always wanted yachts at hand to carry them across the North Sea from one of their realms to another. Some of Charles's yachts were remarkably long-lived. While the first *Mary,* the Dutch gift, was wrecked in 1675, her successor, built in 1677, was not broken up until 1816, only three years before the birth of Queen Victoria. The second *Catherine* reminded people of Charles's long-suffering wife until 1801; there is justice somewhere in the fact that she outlasted that hussy *Fubbs* by two years.

And fittingly, considering the two-nation origin of the golden pastime, the Stuart yacht that has the most interesting story is the Anglo-Dutch *Princess Mary,* which William III of Orange built for his bride Mary Stuart in 1677, and brought across when they became king and queen of England. After she was dropped from the royal fleet in 1714, the Royal Navy sold her to a trading company, which renamed her *Betsy Cairns.* For sixty years she was a West Indies trader and privateer. In 1810, in her one hundred thirty-third year, the Navy chartered her back to transport troops to fight Napoleon in the Peninsular War; for a brief time she regained a touch of royalty as the floating headquarters of the Royal Artillary during the siege of Cadiz. The Napoleonic Wars over, *Betsy Cairns* was returned to civilian life to lug coal. Her long history eventually became known, and soon before she broke up in a gale in 1827, in her one hundred fiftieth year, a Dr. Sheldon McKenzie set down an ironic couplet about her:

Behold the fate of sublunary things,
She exports coal which once imported kings.

Charles might have seen the humor in it, for nearly two hundred years earlier he had fled his homeland in another coal carrier only to return to England with a yacht like her.

II

Cleopatra's Barge and the Daring George Crowninshield

"He appears so happy with himself, much as our boys are with their new sled."

round the time that the last of the Stuart royal yachts were breaking up into flotsam, the first true American yacht that we know about, *Cleopatra's Barge,* was built in 1816. Until then, American maritime history says almost nothing about pleasure sailing. In his scholarly study, *The Fore-and-Aft Rig in America,* E.P. Morris devoted four pages to a survey of terms used between 1620 and 1790 to describe New England sailing vessels, and although he came up with many uses of the general terms "boat" and "ship," and quite a few of rig-specific terms such as "sloop" and "ketch," he found but one mention of "pleasure boat" and none at all of "yacht." Morris suggested one reason:

In the earlier periods, through the seventeenth century, vessels were not built in the young Colonies for a specific service; the same boats were used indiscriminately for fishing, for the coasting trade, for long sea-voyages, and the use that was made of a particular boat or kind of boat seldom justifies definite inference in regard to either the hull or the rig.

Granted, down in New Amsterdam, that outpost of the Dutch East India Company, there was a *Jaght Schip* called *Onrust,* which the Dutch explorer Adrian Block built in 1613 and sailed east on the voyage in which he encountered the island that was eventually named for him. Later, depending upon water for transportation as greatly as did the residents of Amsterdam and London, the English merchants and gentry who took over Manhattan Island and its harbor from the Dutch soon developed their own fleet of rowing barges and pleasure sailboats, which were known to be fitted with luxury items such as damask curtains. They also engaged in competition. In an engraving published by William Burgis in 1717 and often duplicated today, we see two smallish, bezan-rigged, cabinless sloops without leeboards sailing close-hauled side by side off New York. A label accompanying the engraving reads: "Colonel Morris's *Fancy,* turning to windward with a sloop of common mould." Apparently, these two boats of similar design (but, notably, an unspecified type) were having at it just as a couple of modern one-designs might test their speed and weatherliness.

The fact that *Fancy's* owner was Colonel Lewis Morris, an important colonial official and master of the great manor of Morrisania, in the Bronx, suggests that, however undefined pleasure sailing may have been in colonial New York, it attracted the rich and powerful, just as it did in the Old World. Still, the simple *Fancy* could not be considered a yacht by English or Dutch standards, and while she may have shared an anchorage with some other vessels that were fitted out for comfort or occasionally used for pleasure — say, a merchantman with a pleasant cabin — they should not count, either. Tight finances and revolutionary national purpose naturally dictated that shipbuilders direct their energies toward developing a strong merchant marine, not a fleet of leisure vessels. So it is not surprising that the most reliable authority on early yachts, Captain Arthur H. Clark, who gave the subject considerable research, stated succinctly in *The History of Yachting, 1600-1815,* "we find no record of yachts built or owned in the United States until the beginning of the nineteenth century."

Inevitably, somebody acquired enough cash and leisure time to introduce yachting to this new, insecure country. That somebody was the unforgettable Captain George Crowninshield Jr., of Salem, Massachusetts, the master of the fantastic *Cleopatra's Barge* and the leader of one of the strangest odysseys in history.

It is said that every soul contains the seed of at least one adventure, and may not pass contentedly without allowing it to sprout and flourish. So when the soul of George Crowninshield fled his body on November 26, 1817, it can only have been with joy. So energetically had he lived, so lively had been his passion for heroic action, that his neighbors stood watch over his corpse and expected his imminent resurrection. His pastor, Dr. William Bentley, had no such hopes, but even this rationalist of the Enlightenment was appalled by the wall between Crowninshield's life and death. "What an awful contrast when I sat with a shimmering taper by the body of my friend in the place which once gave him so much pleasure and now had become his tomb!" Bentley reported. "What a contradiction between the gayest apartment I ever beheld and death!"

That "gayest apartment," the place of George Crowninshield's wake, was the ultimate product of his fifty-two years of daring: the gilt and green and varnished cabin of his incredibly expensive one hundred-foot brigantine, *Cleopatra's Barge,* the first luxury yacht

*T*he great nineteenth-century
shipping and transportation fortunes
that gave birth to the golden pastime
were themselves offspring of the
marriage of city and sea, as the
painting of a trading ship tied up to a
busy commercial wharf near the Tower
of London suggests on page 24. To
meet the demands of growing
populations, hard-driving merchant
captains developed ever-faster vessels.
The resulting wealth allowed for
leisure, which in turn led to yachts
such as Cleopatra's Barge.
Opposite, William Burgis's 1717
engraving shows a variety of vessels
sailing near New York's Manhattan
Island. In the right center, the hoy-
rigged sloop flying two large flags is
Colonel Lewis Morris's Fancy,
"turning to windward" against a
sistership whose bow is just visible.
The number of landings, wharves, and
boatyards indicates how greatly our
ancestors depended on waterborne
transportation. One hundred years later,
American shipping had become a much
larger and more centralized operation,
as the 1806 painting on pages 28-29,
of Crowninshield's Wharf in Salem,
Massachusetts, proves. The outermost
of the nine Crowninshield East
Indiamen at the immense wharf is the
America, *the most successful privateer
in the War of 1812.*

in the United States. In her, Crowninshield had sailed to Italy and back, his advertised goal, as Bentley had said of the voyage, being "the display of our naval architecture & of our ability to combine in the ships not only all the convenience, but all the luxuries of home." As we will see, that may not have been George's only purpose. Not until John Cox Stevens sent *America* to Cowes in 1851 would another Yankee yacht sail to Europe.

George Crowninshield was a partner in one of the most successful merchant companies in one of the most successful shipping ports in the world — Salem, Massachusetts. In 1684, three generations back, a German named Johannes Kaspar Richter von Kronenscheldt landed in Boston, claimed to be a nobleman fleeing a tragic duel, and became a respected doctor. His grandson George — our George's father — had made a sizeable fortune in the old-fashioned way of Salem, through privateering and smuggling and shipping. He had married the sister of America's first millionaire, Elias Hasket Derby, a merchant prince known as "King" Derby for his wealth, regal appearance, and arrogance. When old George's sister married the "King" himself, the men became double brothers-in-law. Nevertheless, they were perpetually at each other's throats about dock space, politics, and every other grievance they could concoct. Old George had six sons, of whom George Jr. was the eldest, and he gave them all the same mariner's training: school until the age of eleven, and then a year's thorough training in navigation by Nathaniel Bowditch and other masters before heading off as cabin boys in Crowninshield ships. Most Crowninshields had commands by their twenties. Year after year, they conned family brigs packed with New England's manufactures, gold coins, and such odd products as ginseng and butter half-way around the world to the Orient, where they traded for whatever product would bring an outrageous profit back in Salem. Their fast ships, daring seamanship, and keen ability to sniff out the slightest trade advantage became legendary. In 1796, commanding their *Belisarius* ("one of the fastest sailing ships that swam the seas," said a contemporary naval architect), twenty-nine-year-old George Jr. made a successful round trip in only seven and one-half months; in 1800, he sailed the family's seven-hundred tonner *America* back from Calcutta in a record one hundred three days. In 1801 alone, two Crowninshield ships brought in one million

pounds of pepper from Sumatra. Expanding their trade from "our pepper gardens" (as they called that Indonesian island), they imported Indian and Arabian coffee, the great fad of the late eighteenth century. "Coffee, coffee is the stuff," boasted brother Benjamin. "Salem rolls in riches with every tide, and every ship plank is bound for India." Brother Jacob once returned to Salem with an elephant, reportedly the first ever seen in the United States. After making some money displaying it to paying customers, he sold the animal for $10,000, reaping a solid profit.

Yet even Salem's "restless, enterprising merchants and captains" (to quote one historian) tired of sea duty after a decade or two. When the Crowninshield boys yearned for dry socks, they came ashore as partners in the family shipping empire, and the old man placed most of them where they would do the most good for the firm in counting houses around the world. Young George, however, was installed on the family's India and Crowninshield Wharfs in Salem, where he rigged and provisioned the family fleet of twelve ships for their long, arduous trips. Some Crowninshields ended up in politics in the Republican Party of Thomas Jefferson, not the cautious Federalism of established New England. In 1798, they refused to help pay for the frigate *Essex,* which the Federalists built to fight in the undeclared war against the French, and soon after brother Jacob upset the arch-Federalist Timothy Pickering in a race for the national House of Representatives. The family founded their own Republican newspaper, which, to tease the Federalists, hammered away in favor of the radical doctrine of social equality. A few years after, Jefferson appointed Jacob Secretary of the Navy, and James Madison later awarded the same post to brother Benjamin. Although they criticized Jefferson's embargo on foreign trade, a not-too-successful attempt to isolate the new nation from the unending European wars, the Crowninshields did not completely break with him despite the embargo's damage to Salem's economy. The family was making a pretty profit smuggling West Indies coffee.

When war against England came in 1812, the Crowninshields dared their neighbors not only by supporting it (at the Hartford Convention, many prominent New England Federalists seriously debated seceding from the Union in protest) but also by reviving an old family tradition. As the Tory historian of Salem, James

Duncan Phillips, put it, "the Jeffersonian group headed by the Crowninshields rushed precipitately into privateering." Young George's swift little thirty-five foot sloop *Jefferson* and a couple of other family vessels were put to productive use chasing down British merchantmen, and they caught a total of eighty-two of them with cargos that ranged from Bibles to women's dresses. By one account (no doubt exaggerated), the family cleared two million dollars off the war.

Although their sudden success allowed Salem to enjoy the highest income of any town in America, the benefits of this wealth were not wasted on conspicuous consumption. Much of the pepper and privateering profit was salted away in local banks and later stimulated New England's great manufacturing boom of the mid-nineteenth century. The successful merchantmen of Salem were still guided, as their less-wealthy ancestors had been, by the discipline of Puritanism. Their devotion to practicality, guilt, and relative modesty is neatly summarized in the fiscally conservative commandment, "Never touch the principal." What few luxuries they allowed themselves were, on the whole, subtle and constructive ones. To house their huge families they built handsome Samuel McIntire mansions; to shelter the mounds of Oriental curiosities they brought home in their ships they formed the educational East India Marine Society (now the Peabody Museum). It was a stable, self-examining community, this turn-of-century Salem.

But it wasn't young George Crowninshield's way to follow such cautious norms. He was decidedly a rebel. Not for him the modest values of family, home, and church. He never married, and never even settled down with the same lady friend. He loved having a good time, rejoiced in showing off, and did not collapse from guilt when he spent a lot of money to do either. For example, instead of a simple one-horse buggy, George drove a bright yellow curricle behind two horses; instead of somber black jacket and breeches he wore an outfit that included gold-tasseled boots, a colorful checked waistcoat, a foppish pigtail, and a high-crowned beaver-skin hat. Besides dandyish clothes, George also enjoyed playing with children, who followed him everywhere.

Most of all, George loved being a hero. He often risked his neck to save somebody's life, rescuing children from burning buildings, non-swimmers from Salem Harbor, and sailors from shipwrecks on Massachusetts Bay. On a smaller but certainly no less important scale, every Christmas he helped the poor get through another cold winter by personally handing out firewood — an act of social decency of which few, if any, of the other leading characters in this book were capable. His rewards were general adulation, glowing editorials in the family newspaper, and a medal from the Massachusetts Humane Society.

During the War of 1812, George even rescued a hero's corpse from the British. On June 1, 1813, in full view of crowds standing on the shore of Massachusetts Bay, the British frigate *Shannon* engaged and half-destroyed the American *Chesapeake*, killing her captain, James Lawrence, who died with the celebrated instruction, "Don't give up the ship!," on his lips. The British towed their badly pummeled conquest to Halifax, Nova Scotia, where they buried Lawrence with full honors. Crowninshield gathered a crew of sea captains and, in one of the family traders, sailed to Halifax under a white flag and recovered the captain's body — but not to general applause. So angry was Federalist Salem's opposition to the war, which by cutting off most shipping was decimating the New England economy, that no minister of Lawrence's church, which was Episcopal, could be persuaded to read the funeral service. Crowninshield's tolerant Unitarian pastor, William Bentley, volunteered and did the duty.

I will digress here to discuss two remarkable men who, in different ways, play important roles in the story of Crowninshield and *Cleopatra's Barge,* one as a commentator and the other as a role model. We have just encountered the first. Like his friend Thomas Jefferson, William Bentley, D.D., was both an astonishing polymath and a Republican, a man who broke down barriers rather than built them (his ecumenism extended to participating in Roman Catholic services — an act of no small courage in those days). Able to read twenty different languages, he was sometimes called on by the federal government to translate diplomatic papers. He was also a prolific church historian and omnicurious natural scientist who kept careful track of shooting stars, earthquakes, sea monsters, and other phenomena. Though not a systematic theologian, Bentley was a prominent spokesman for the liberal humanism that was gradually taking over New England religion, and often felt the barbs of criticism. Yet for all his accomplishments, Bentley believed that his true vocation was to be a small-town pastor. Resisting many attempts to win him away to grander callings — Jefferson asked him to be the first President of the University of Virginia, and Madison wanted him to be the Congressional chaplain — Bentley was content to spend his entire thirty-six-year career in Salem's impecunious, controversy-ridden East Church, somehow finding free moments for his intellectual interests between preaching sermons (two every Sunday), baptizing babies, marrying the young, and burying the dead.

We know all this, as well as an extraordinary amount about his time, because from 1784 to his death in 1819 Bentley kept a meticulous diary that totaled some two million words. In printed form it takes up four volumes and two thousand, three hundred pages. Besides being a treasure house of facts, both trivial and significant, about the early United States, *The Diary of William Bentley* offers a wonderful insight into the heart, mind, and soul of a man of conscience in a controversial day. Although it lacks the literary grace of Samuel Pepys's great diary of the 1660s, which is such an important source for early English yachting, it offers many delights for a patient reader willing to wade through Bentley's meticulous observations about the weather, the shipping news, and his own teetering finances. For example, on his dissent from orthodox Christianity:

I have adopted many opinions abhorrent of my early prejudices, & am still ready to receive truth upon proper evidence from whatever quarter it may come. I think more honor done to God in rejecting Xtianity itself in obedience to my convictions, than in any fever, which is pretended, towards it., & I hope that, no poverty which I can dread, or hope I can entertain, will weaken my resolutions to act upon my convictions. The only evidence I wish to have of my integrity is a good life, & as to faith, his can't be wrong whose life is in the right. (April 22, 1788)

And this charming New Year's resolution:

Rules for the next year, to give opinions with caution, & to quote authorities with the same, to have as little confidence in the world as possible & as much benevolence. (December 31, 1792)

*"T*he first in every enterprise, the most fearless of danger," William Bentley wrote of the heroic Captain George Crowninshield Jr., shown opposite in a painting ascribed to Samuel F.B. Morse. A man of the Napoleonic age, George may even have dreamed of rescuing the exiled emperor. Typically, his eyes are distracted by a distant goal; his telescope is at hand to bring it closer. At the right is William Bentley, D.D., himself: pastor, diarist, historian, linguist, political propagandist, scientist, and longtime observer of George's quixotic activities.*

As his diary testifies at length, Bentley was a friend to almost everybody in Salem, but especially to George Crowninshield Jr., whose Republican political views he shared and with whose cousin Benjamin he boarded. The relationship was not without strain — Bentley was often left holding the bag for church repairs that George impulsively promised but failed to pay for, and the minister wished his seaman friend were more observant and sensitive. They had little else in common except their confirmed bachelorhood and short height (Bentley at about five feet and Crowninshield some five inches taller). But each seemed to fill some need in

the other: the hyperactive, daring George was surrogate extrovert for the intellectual, cautious preacher, who in exchange satisfied the wild man's need for reflection.

Of the two, Crowninshield best represented his times. Action — energetic *doing*—filled the air in this day when the American Revolution was part of the memory of anybody in middle or old age, and a few of its heroes still walked the earth. But for many in the first decades of the nineteenth century the heroic example of the American Founding Fathers paled before that of the other extraordinary character who plays a more distant role in this story. Any understanding of the early nineteenth century must begin with the reputation of Napoleon Bonaparte.

A childhood hero to people as different (and as complex) as Sigmund Freud and J. Pierpont Morgan, Napoleon has inspired more ambivalent passion than any other man in the world's recent history. Beethoven worshipfully dedicated his third symphony, the "Eroica," to him, then changed his mind upon hearing of Napoleon's self-appointment as Emperor. "His presence on the field made the difference of forty thousand men," said the Duke of Wellington. "This scourge of the world . . . a Robin Hood of the big breed," said Jefferson. In his outsized military campaigns, love affairs, and statements, Napoleon — even, or perhaps especially, when he languished in British captivity on the island of St. Helena — touched many of the most profound and contradictory human emotions and desires: liberty and fate, race pride and nationalism, autonomy and exile, selfishness and self-sacrifice, and above all pure action, no matter how misconceived. Napoleon is the role model for anybody who feels in him- or herself the potential of romantic, fated heroism, the possibility of becoming the *unusual person.*

Napoleonic in drama if not scope, young George Crowninshield's heroics were all those years underwritten by his tight-fisted father. He was forty-nine when the old man finally died on June 16, 1815; but the patriarchal fetters remained strong. The will insisted that his son's plaything *Jefferson* be sold off. This last assertion of paternal prerogative left George boatless. But he was rich, for the old man left $200,000 to be shared by his sons, each of whom had roughly an equal fortune of his own. With the family firm broken up and the brothers finally allowed to go their own way, George bade farewell to Salem and headed west. Bentley thought he had seen the last of him, but only five months later George was back, having covered some two-thousand miles through the wilds of Kentucky, down the Mississippi River, and back on conveyances no faster than steamboats — a sprint, relatively speaking. That his report was disappointingly skimpy is clear enough in Bentley's diary entry on April 16, 1816: "His taste and education found little to love in the wilds . . . So ended the Western Tour, of which enthusiasm has nothing to record."

A series of later diary entries through the summer and fall of 1816 reveals that George's enthusiasm had been directed back to the sea. On June 10, Bentley notes, "The timber is preparing for the Brig to be built below Crowninshield's wharf," and ten days later, "Becket preparing for a raising." This was Retire Becket, builder of some of Salem's best ships. He was about to elevate the new vessel's frames in preparation for planking. The summer passes without mention of the ship, but on September 9 Bentley records, "A man lost his life this week by falling from the stages of the vessel belonging to G. Crowninshield." On the twenty-fifth, a premature announcement that the ship at Becket's is "ready for launching nearly." Then on November 22 Bentley reports that the ship is a hermaphrodite brig and is costing George "a fortune." He also gives us a hint of his friend's ambitions: George "is preparing for a visit to Europe, in a manner to us before unknown as to expence and project." Finally, on December 9:

> *By invitation I visited the hermaphrodite brig* Concordia *lately built by Capt. G. Crowninshield and now fitted for sea in a manner never before observed in this town. Her model is excellent and her naval architecture the best . . . The expence must have been very great but the aid to improvement and enquiry is great and extensive. Nothing has been suffered to enter, [which is] not in the highest style of excellence. I should have been very glad to have had an inventory of the contents of this vessel.*

Bentley's admiration was not isolated. *Car of Concordia,* as George proposed to name her, was the talk not only of Salem but of the entire East Coast. With the flair of a modern press agent, George had publicized her widely while she was still on Becket's

blocks, and after she was launched in December, friends, journalists, and the merely curious were invited aboard to inspect her under her owner's proud supervision. "You would be astonished to see the multitudes that visit my brig — or yacht — as they call her," George wrote his brother Benjamin, in Washington, on December 29. The size of the audience for his drama amazed him: "I have had one thousand nine hundred women and seven hundred men in one day, and an average of over nine hundred a day for the past two weeks."

From a distance — a long distance — she looked like any well-built one-hundred foot Salem trading schooner with a brigantine, or hermaphrodite, rig (squaresails on her forward mast and fore-and-aft on her after mast). But up close she was like no East Indies trader ever built. Most obviously, her paint scheme was asymmetrical — the starboard topsides covered with bright stripes, the port ones with colorful herringbones. Then there were the multicolored velvet ropes around the cockpit. And even more strangely, nailed to her deck was a life-size wooden Indian. His bow and arrows complemented the twelve gun ports, out of which stuck nine-inchers and small carronades, ready for business nobody could explain, considering the peaceful implications of the vessel's name.

Down below, she was breathtaking. Her many cabins had the eye-popping luxuriousness of one of Charles II's royal yachts. Among her radically non-Puritan features were First Empire-style furniture, inlaid mahogany soles and paneling, gilt mirrors, a chandelier, false windows, gilded beams, velvet lines to grab in rough weather, and a mansion's inventory of silver service, glassware and chinaware (all of which was stowed in special hidden lockers). Under only moderate pressure, George discussed his expenses. The lyre-backed, gold-fringed sofas cost $400, the chandelier $150. Soon the word was about that, *in toto,* he had spent $50,000 on the yacht.

George's intentions were unclear; the only thing certain was that he was leaving Salem in search of international adventure. At one time or another, he spoke of cruising to Greece and Italy, then to Spitzbergen, Russia, and South America. The government, perhaps at the request of brother Benjamin, the Navy Secretary, covered every eventuality by providing more than three hundred letters of introduction to (George boasted) "all the consuls in Europe and to all the Commanders in the fleets as well." A banker took his ambitions so seriously that he arranged for a letter of credit totaling $30,000 despite George's assurance that $5,000 was plenty. But there was no limit to George's horizons; on the official customs form, under "destination," his clerk filled in the following:

To one or more ports, places, cities, islands, townes, boroughs, villages, bays, harbours, basins, rivers, creeks, lakes, inlets, outlets, situated in the known world, between the latitude of the Cape of Good Hope and the Arctic Circle, one or more times.

Exactly why George's "hobby" (as he referred to her) was so gaudily luxurious nobody ventured to suggest in print. Perhaps the reason was that his situation was so obvious. Even cautious Salem could understand the energy of a rich fifty-year-old bachelor finally busting out of the family mold. No doubt George saw the projected "voyage of amusement and travels" (as the *Salem Gazette* described it) at least partly as an escape from stifling Salem. Like the protagonist in John Marquand's novel about the confinements of privilege, *The Late George Apley,* he knew all too well that "memory and tradition are the tyrants of our environment." It was natural that this man-boy, who throughout his life had been pushing the limits of respectability, would declare his independence with playful and grand ambition. His sister-in-law Mary, Benjamin's wife, seemed to understand this. "He appears so happy with himself, much as our boys are with their new sled," she wrote her husband. "I envy him his feelings." Others were less sympathetic. Brother John and sister Sarah became so obnoxiously sarcastic that George cut them off with $10 each in an addendum to his will. After George changed the yacht's name from the staid and diplomatic *Car of Concordia* to the more racy *Cleopatra's Barge,* Benjamin sniffed from Washington that he was not surprised that his brother would choose "some foolish name that would be laughed at." Perhaps he harbored fears that George would introduce himself to royalty by rolling out of a rug, as the Egyptian beauty was presented to Mark Antony.

There did seem to be a sense of purpose that, though at first clumsy and vague in its articulation, spurred George on through most of his adventure: he would impress Europe's leaders with the best products of American democracy, not with the trivial purpose of trade and profit, but in an atmosphere of friendly ease. When he predicted to a sightseer that the King of Naples would soon hang his hat on one of a row of custom-made gilt pins in the main saloon, he hinted at his dreams and ambitions: the King of Naples, whom he hoped to host, had until a year or so earlier been Napoleon's lieutenant, Joachim Murat. *Cleopatra's Barge* overflowed with Bonapartist symbols: gilded Napoleonic eagles hung everywhere, and the cabin boys and steward were outfitted in imperial gold and green. The imperial theme extended even to Pompey, the golden ship's cat that napped upon the huge bed in the owner's stateroom.

In late 1816, George chose his crew. His cousin Benjamin, William Bentley's landlord and an experienced Indiaman, was named as captain and brought along his moody son of the same name as a guest (and, as it turned out, navigator). To distinguish them, they were called "Sailor Ben" and "Philosopher Ben," respectively. Almost every American male who had heard of the *Barge* and could write his own name had applied for the job as clerk; but George chose an old friend, the consumptive Samuel Curren Ward. Besides those four, there were two mates, eight seamen, four cabin boys, a freed slave named Hanson Posey as steward, and the black cook William Chapman, who could do celestial navigation, and who claimed not only to have sailed with Captain Cook but to have watched an Hawaiian, thinking he was eating pig's guts, dine on the massacred explorer's intestines.

In early January of 1817, *Cleopatra's Barge* took a successful trial run to Cape Ann and return; then she was frozen in by one of the harshest winters within memory. While the unemployed were put to work attempting to chop Salem Harbor clear of ice, George handed out firewood to the poor and ran out to his vessel in a sleigh. And he gave a dinner to celebrate the inauguration of President James Monroe. Bentley was a guest, one of the few men in mainly Federalist Massachusetts who agreed with George that the event deserved special attention. Although the harbor began to open up in early March, George equivocated about his adventure to the point where Bentley wondered if he had changed his mind entirely. Sister-in-law Mary Crowninshield wrote her husband that the moral was clear: "So not even the celebrated *Cleopatra's*

bove is "Philosopher Ben"
Crowninshield, George's waspish
cousin, who was navigator for most of
the voyage of adventure. His journal is
an important and insightful source of
information about the trip, yet even he
could not explain some of George's
strange activities. Opposite, this
painting of the one hundred-foot
hermaphrodite brig Cleopatra's
Barge *does not do full justice to her*
eccentricity; it shows only her
herringboned port side and neglects both
the wide-striped starboard side and the
wooden Indian standing on deck.
However, the artist did accurately
represent her straight, almost flat sheer.

Barge confers happiness — indeed where is it to be found?"

George finally shed his doubts. On the morning of Sunday, March 30, 1817, the docking lines were cast off. Apparently, crew problems had led George to limit his ambitions for this voyage, or so Mary reported to Benjamin. "He told me he should not stay away long — would return and go again. He did not offer to get us any pretty things," she added waspishly, "and I did not ask him."

The initial destination was the Azores, a popular rest stop on any cruise to the Mediterranean, and *Cleopatra's Barge* made Fayal in a quick sixteen days, experiencing some snowy gales but no trouble except that the captain had some difficulty understanding the owner, who had developed a few curious ideas about seamanship during his fifteen years on the beach. George's weather sense was guided more by his dreams than by more traditional indicators. For example, when he awoke from a dream about wild horses he ordered Benjamin to batten down in preparation for a gale, ignoring the clear sky and stable barometer. They reached Fayal on April 15, and after some initial confusion about whether they were pirates, were welcomed eagerly by the American consul, a man named Dabney, and the Portuguese gentry.

Except for George, who couldn't have cared less which people came aboard just so long as there were lots of them and they liked his boat, the naive Yankees were keenly disappointed by the southern European culture they found at Fayal and, later, in Spain and Italy. Someone wrote in the log: "Of all nations, kindred and tongues [foreign], I never met with such a miserable set of beings as here offered themselves to our view, filthy, ragged, and uncouth." To the regret of the snobbish young Ben (who was anything but a philosopher when he wrote about the guests in his journal), George welcomed everybody. "We are full of ladies and gentlemen, in their best bibs and tuckers, drinking our health in bumpers, and [taking] a pleasant tour of *Cleopatra's Barge,*" Philosopher Ben wrote. Ladies became so seasick that "none of them could walk upright" and were sent ashore by their husbands in an open boat through a rain squall. "So much for politeness," concluded the social critic, who despite his professed chivalry made no effort to help the women. (A New Yorker from another vessel volunteered.) Meanwhile, the Portuguese men were "charmed with our accommodations and fascinated with our wine" and "poured

their libations to Bacchus, and at dark left us in good humor." The story was much the same at Madeira, where a dozen or more boats brought hundreds of tourists, "intermixed with hes and shes, all sea-sick, rolling from side to side, drinking wine and running to and fro from the after cabin to the cook's room, presenting a scene of confusion that I am altogether unable to give an adequate description of." The crew's meals became irregular, and perhaps in retaliation they announced, to the annoyance of a local order of mendicant friars, that the wooden Indian was an American priest. Young Ben delighted in the dismay this caused among the brothers, whom he called "this lazy and worthless class. . . [who] are not, like our shaking Quakers, a community for good."

George carried on east toward the Mediterranean, and enjoyed the satisfaction of helping to rescue a cabin boy who fell overboard near the Straits of Gibraltar. After an eye-opening stopover in Moslem Tangier ("Everything we see reminds us that we are no longer among a people whose modes of thinking are like our own," young Ben wrote in his journal), they crossed over to Gibraltar and, with relief, to English faces and language. While the exhausted crew repaired the ravages of the visiting crowds by touching up scuffed paint, George, reviving his intentions of being received by royalty, began to inquire as to the whereabouts of Caroline, the Princess of Wales, who had been cast off by her husband, the Prince Regent. She was, he learned, in Italy, and perhaps his disappointment was assuaged by the attention he received from the Governor and some American naval officers, to one of whom he loaned $1500.

For the next few weeks, during a meandering hop-scotch along the European coast of the Mediterranean, *Cleopatra's Barge* played a mixed role as floating museum, bar and grill, and entertainment center. George hunted up the United States Naval Squadron at Majorca, exchanged entertainments with some bored American officers, and handily beat the frigate *United States* in an informal race to Barcelona. There, his crew's worst social and religious prejudices were revived. While the yacht had been aswarm with sightseers throughout her short life, there had been nothing like the crowds at this Spanish city. As young Ben described the phenomenon, "If a supernatural being had descended from heaven to work miracles; if an archangel had landed on this earth; such things could not have been more wonderful than the arrival of the *Cleopatra's Barge* at Barcelona." An estimated twenty thousand people poured aboard in only five days. The crowd was so great, rude, and dirty that even George agreed to allow entry only to people who had been issued passes by the American consulate. But the system broke down almost as soon as it was implemented. "Everybody is made to think himself at home," complained Philosopher Ben, whose own cabin was packed from dawn to midnight with "friars with thick hoods and fat bellies, generals, colonels, etc., etc., dressed for the occasion, priests in black robes, and hats of three feet in diameter, and ladies, aye of every sort, colour, and size, under heaven. Never was there such a group, never such a crowd, and smell, since the days of Noah's Arc. Charybdis was not more dangerous to ancient navigators." When a storm rolled the boat, fifteen or twenty people were draped over the rails in the throes of seasickness. A Spanish army officer became so impatient to board that he brandished his pistol and ploughed through the crowd jamming the gangway, and so determined was one woman that she ignored the lateness of her term of pregnancy and went into labor in the main cabin and had to be carried ashore.

If some of the Americans were unhappy with the Europeans, their doubts were paralleled by their Spanish hosts' unreadiness to believe that such a glory as *Cleopatra's Barge* could be produced by a people who they believed were close to savages. Like the visitors of Salem, they wanted everything explained to them: the advantages of bird's eye maple in cabinetwork, the price of each object, the details of the American diet. Of course, George was eager to please. Meanwhile, the Americans were undergoing a similar challenge as they witnessed stately holy day processions toward the city's cathedrals. If we are to believe young Ben's diary, their anti-Catholicism was modified almost as much as the Spaniards' anti-Americanism — but not so much that the sailors could resist one temptation: they proclaimed the sainthood of the Indian and urged their visitors to kiss its wooden feet.

The extravanganza moved on to Toulon and Marseilles, France, as the crew, already fatigued by their endless duties as none-too-cheerful hosts, repainted the scarred woodwork for the second time in forty days. George serenely lectured some visiting French army and naval officers on the glories of American life and the injustice done by exiling Napoleon to St. Helena. The Frenchmen, no doubt looking over their shoulders for Bourbon spies, reacted with quiet enthusiasm to this sympathy with their fallen hero. Reads a log entry:

They whisper his name in the most expressive manner; they look at the eagles which adorn our cabin, put their hands upon them with the greatest affection, turn their eyes up to heaven, and oftentimes breathe a sigh which melts the heart. At the sound of his name they start with enthusiasm; and, if you reciprocate their assertions, they seize your hands, clap you on the shoulder, and even embrace you.

Praise for the vessel was universal: "Far superior to any yacht he had ever seen," according to a paraphrase of some comments by a Lieutenant Tilley, Royal Navy, master of an English yacht moored in Marseilles; "this magnificent palace of Neptune," gushed a German astronomer named Baron de Zach. In Genoa, the aged English Baron Carrington was so impressed that he insisted on calling George "my lord." Perhaps Carrington, said to be the first tradesman ennobled by George III (as thanks for bailing a prime minister out of a financial embarrassment), recognized something of himself in the freewheeling American adventurer. George's delight with the pretension was so obvious that his sailors found that calling him by this sobriquet would lead to a large tip. Encouraged by this attention, and inspired by the spirit of Bonapartism that hung over southern Europe, George paid due respect by writing a letter to his brother Benjamin in favor of a former secretary of the emperor, an Italian banker named Casati who lived in New York. De Zach gave him a letter of introduction to the Governor of Elba, the island where Napoleon had lived in exile for a few months until his escape two years earlier, in March of 1815, had led to Waterloo and a more secure imprisonment on the South Atlantic island of St. Helena.

From here on, the voyage of *Cleopatra's Barge* becomes increasingly mysterious, if not conspiratorial. Later, Philosopher Ben would bitterly accuse George of secretly arranging the trip solely to lure aboard a noble person — he mentioned the Princess of Wales and Lucien Bonaparte, Napoleon's most talented and unlucky brother — in order to impress his neighbors on his return to America. Writing after he left the yacht, Ben claimed that George was " the greatest lump of deception in the whole world of man. His conduct is so extraordinary, and is so contradictory and absurd, that no man, under an acquaintance of two or three months, would be able to unravel it." The reasons for the young hothead's rage are unclear. Perhaps he was disappointed at not being let in on his cousin's plans (whatever they may have been), or maybe the plot (if there was one) was poorly managed.

That George could have dreamed up a scheme to rescue one of the noble castoffs of the Napoleonic Age is, given his temperament and the spirit of the day, pretty likely. Where Ben could have been wrong was in identifying George's true goal. An addictive celebrity who would build a palatial yacht and name her after one of the most romantic figures in history does not aim for mere princes. If Captain George Crowninshield of Salem ever actually conspired to rescue anybody, it most certainly was the hero of heroes, then surrounded by British soldiers on a rock of an island in the South Atlantic. If so, he was not alone. Between July 15, 1815, when Napoleon surrendered aboard the English frigate *Bellerophon* in Rochefort, and May 5, 1821, when he died on St. Helena at the age of fifty-two, plots to rescue him were rumored just about everywhere. Many of them revolved around America, in which Napoleon had expressed an interest in living in quiet exile.

Such was the former emperor's aura that, with a logic that from this distance appears contorted, many of his contemporaries believed that his conquerers owed him a free old age. Guided more by passion than by political realism, these people reached this conclusion despite Napoleon's proven history as an aggressor during nineteen years of intermittent warfare (whose casualties numbered more than nine hundred thousand people on all sides), his violation of many treaties, and his escape from Elba and bloody march of reconquest that ended at Waterloo. Regardless of all available evidence that his nature was less than peaceable and trustworthy, Napoleon's defenders, and romantics in general, had been shocked in 1815 when the English did not grant him liberty — say, on a country estate — but instead had packed him off to St. Helena under a large and heavily armed guard. That in doing so the English had surely saved him from instant decapitation by the French Bourbons was not something generally acknowledged in Bonapartist circles.

For better or worse, certain men have attracted reputations that, by admitting neither of mortality nor of limitation, breed conspiracies. Conspiracy revolved around Napoleon, and still revolves if we are to believe a recent book that repeats in a new guise an old claim that he was poisoned. One writer has argued that the Napoleon who died on St. Helena was a double, and the real emperor lived happily into old age in America. Whether or not a rescue was attempted, at least four efforts are reliably known to have been undertaken to provide an American haven for Napoleon and his followers. Joseph Bonaparte, who had escaped to New Jersey under an assumed name after the cause was shattered at Waterloo, on June 18, 1815, purchased one hundred fifty thousand acres of land in western New York where his brother might find safety and friends. Farther south, a couple of dozen Bonapartists and creoles secured a safe house in New Orleans. A few hundred miles away, a loose group called the Vine and Olive Society settled on land in Alabama partly to produce wine and partly to provide a haven for their leader. Finally, on Texas's Trinity River, a favorite general of Napoleon's, Baron Charles Lallemand, attempted to establish a utopian community of exiles that he called the Field of Refuge. Lallemand, of all the conspirators, may have been the most talented as well as the potential savior on the most intimate terms with the great man. After Waterloo, he had advised Napoleon against surrendering, and had personally asked *Bellerophon*'s captain to carry the emperor to the New World, declaring, "There is no liberty for the Emperor except in the United States of America." Interestingly, Lallemand met with William Bentley during a visit to Salem in April of 1817, several weeks after *Cleopatra's Barge* headed east to Europe. In his diary, Bentley said of Lallemand, "I found in him all I might expect from the firm friend of Napoleon. His person good, his system like his mind [prepared] for ready action, at home everywhere, free, cheerful, interesting."

How the rescue would be effected was the stuff of less careful preparations. At one time, the Caribbean pirate and hero of the Battle of New Orleans, Jean Laffite, blithely volunteered to save the exile, and there was talk of a large payoff to an unnamed American, sometimes identified as a U.S. naval officer, sometimes as a

Hudson River merchant. There was no question that any raid on St. Helena — one thousand miles off the African coast and deep in the southeast trade winds — would demand superb seamanship as well as an excellent vessel.

And this leads us back to George Crowninshield. Goethe once said of Napoleon's life that it was like the Book of Revelation: "We all feel there must be something more in it, but we do not know what." The same could be said of the hero of our story. Regardless of the ubiquitous conspiracies, the shadowy details of his voyage, his romantic affection for Napoleon, and his obvious qualifications for the rescue, George Crowninshield and *Cleopa-*

tra's Barge would never sail within four thousand miles of St. Helena, and Napoleon would never set foot off it.

Before leaving Genoa on July 14, George loudly announced to his crew that he was going in search of a princess, and he engaged a musician and two language instructors, one Italian and the other French, apparently with the motive of aiding in that goal. The worst gale of the trip quickly blew the yacht to Leghorn, where he and Sailor Ben left the yacht and went inland to Florence to attempt to meet Napoleon's wife, Marie Louise. Not only were his notes and letters of introduction not acknowledged, but he somehow sprained his ankle, and when he hobbled back to Leghorn, neither he nor his cousin had much to say before heading off to the island of Elba. There, they visited the modest house of exile, and chatted with a hermit who claimed to have twice met Napoleon and with a former imperial servant, who gave George a sealed packet of letters for Joseph Bonaparte (an indication as much of the tight security around the old Bonapartists as of George's sympathies). George came away with some mementoes collected with such passion that they might be called relics: a piece of carpet from his hero's bedroom and some tiles from his bathroom; fruit from his vines and apple trees; and some objects actually used by Napoleon: a book of maps, a leather cup, and a pair of riding boots that the Emperor had found were too small.

Finally, they were off to Rome — for millenia the end of religious and imperial pilgrimages and now the focus of one that seemed to have qualities of both — for here were the Bonapartes. Enriched by their relative's plundering and appointments, they now lived in conspicuous luxury as they halfheartedly complained of the injustice done their benefactor. The exception to this familial hypocrisy was Napoleon's mother, Letitia. The stark "Madame Mére" dressed in black and financed any adventurer who promised a reunion with her son. On August 8, George, Sailor Ben, and the ship's musician went up to Rome from Civita Vecchia, one of the ancient ports of the great city, and between then and August 17, George somehow became friendly with and, apparently, trusted by the Bonapartes. We know this not because he described their meetings (in fact, for the first time during the trip George wrote no letters home), but because of the several intimate presents and seemingly important responsibilities he was granted. The gifts

Opposite, the sad-eyed "Sailor Ben" Crowninshield, the paid master for the voyage, is seen in a classic New England sea captain's portrait, with one of his commands, Prudent, *in the distant background. Right, "the gayest apartment I ever beheld," according to William Bentley, was the luxurious saloon of* Cleopatra's Barge, *a reconstruction of which is on permanent display at the Peabody Museum, in Salem, Massachusetts. On the table are the open ship's log and a portrait of the yacht. George Crowninshield did not mind announcing that he paid $400 for the sofa with the lyre-shaped carvings and that the entire vessel cost some $50,000. Note the velvet grab lines for steadying one's progress forward or aft.*

included a picture of the Emperor given him by old Letitia Bonaparte (who claimed it was her favorite), a lock of hair cut from her own head by Napoleon's promiscuous sister Pauline, a tortoiseshell snuff box, and a ring with Pauline's likeness. The duties were to carry to safety two men, said to be the captain of the ship on which Napoleon fled from Elba on the way to Waterloo and a young man who claimed to be the exiled emperor's own adopted son. The yacht's crew, who had put up with the usual hoard of visitors (including many peasants from inland villages), received instructions from George to be prepared to sail on a moment's notice. The new seriousness of the cruise was suggested by the arrival of a French man-of-war, which dropped anchor close by and, it seemed, spied on *Cleopatra's Barge.*

George and Sailor Ben returned on the seventeenth with the musician and the two Frenchmen, who were quickly joined by two compatriots. The next morning they headed toward the Strait of

Bonifacio, between Sardinia and Corsica. Perhaps they intended to land at the Bonaparte homeland — given George's Napoleomania, it would be surprising if they did not — but when the warship from Civita Vecchia was sighted astern and a couple of others were seen ahead, they turned the yacht's bow west toward Gibraltar. Having accomplished their apparent purpose by keeping strangers, and possible troublemakers, away from a volatile situation, the French ships disappeared astern. The normal ship's routine was disrupted in favor of the new guests, who ate at the captain's table with George and Sailor Ben while Philosopher Ben and the clerk, Ward, were exiled, seething, to another. Perhaps this was a cause of the young man's pique at George; but there was another result: somewhere during the thirteen-day trip, George got wind that Napoleon's "adopted son" was not who he had claimed he was. After *Cleopatra's Barge* dropped anchor in Gibraltar, for whatever reason, the young man and some of the other guests went ashore on September 1, and the ever-bitter Philosopher Ben soon followed. Two days later, the yacht weighed anchor and headed back to Salem.

The return voyage was slow, and *Cleopatra's Barge* did not tie up at Crowninshield's Wharf until October 3. The remaining Frenchmen left, the sailors were paid off, and George and Hanson Posey stayed to live alone in the yacht's sumptuous cabins. As before, when George foreshortened his western trip, William Bentley was disappointed in his friend's imagination and commitment. "Mr. C. has all the habits of a seaman," he complained the day the yacht returned, using "seaman" to mean unreliable and impulsive. "Thus an immense sum has been expended for an excursion which might have been made by working a passage to these several known marts familiar to our seamen and visited almost daily by our vessels."

Back in Salem, George complained of heart pains and shortness of breath. November came, and after going inland for ten days on unknown business, he returned to the yacht on November 24. On the twenty-seventh, he spent the day playing games with his nieces and nephews and planning greater and longer-legged yachting adventures with his friends. At nine that evening he complained of faintness, and while Posey was pouring him a gin, he collapsed and died. Strangely, Samuel Ward, his clerk, expired at almost exactly the same moment ten miles away.

He was mourned. On hearing the news, his old friend and sometime critic Bentley described George in his diary as " the first in every enterprise, the most fearless of danger, and never sparing of himself in any labour he undertook." Although his pastor accepted it, much of Salem was not ready to see George Crowninshield die. Not simply a surprise — an especially sad one for the poor, who depended on his generosity — his passing was quite unbelievable to those who were stimulated by his quixotic energy. As it was widely believed that he was in a trance, the body was not allowed to be moved from the yacht until putrification set in, and then a watch was kept for a while over the grave to await the dead man's return. Bentley was appalled by these superstitions. "A thousand tales, a thousand fears, have marked this event," he despaired.

The people were right. Crowninshield did not die, in spirit at least. For years after *Cleopatra's Barge* returned home, it was generally believed that he had intended all along to rescue Napoleon Bonaparte, and actually took preliminary steps to do so. The details of secret adventure surfaced in print from time to time. To paraphrase one such article, published in a local newspaper in 1898: While in Rome George was recruited by Letitia Bonaparte to sail to St. Helena with the captain who had managed the Elba rescue and her son's doctor, who would be put ashore to approach Napoleon and organize the escape. Sailing in a hurricane near Corsica, *Cleopatra's Barge* was chased and fired on by three French men-of-war. Signaling the French, "Catch me first, then I'll surrender," George piled on so much sail that the first mate protested that the topmast would soon break. "It must be done," declared George. "Yankee honor is at stake." Yet the enemy continued to gain, and soon put a cannonball clean through the yacht's mainmast, disabling her. When the French approached, George demanded an explanation. "We have undoubted proof that the object of your voyage is to provide succor for an enemy of France," was the response. The warships escorted him back to Civita Vecchia, where the plot was cancelled. George considered pressing charges on the French but, finally deciding that he was technically guilty, repaired the damage and — so this fanciful tale concluded — sailed for home.

While his reputation for heroism grew ever more mythical, his "hobby" did not long outlive him. George's brother Richard bought *Cleopatra's Barge,* but soon went bankrupt. He stripped her of her furnishings (which he sold for $7,000), and, in July of 1818 auctioned her off for $15,400. For a few years she carried cargo and passengers to Rio de Janeiro and Charleston, and then she voyaged around the Horn to the Sandwich Islands. King Kamehameha bought her for six thousand piculs of sandalwood for use as his royal yacht. On April 5, 1824, while the King was touring England (where he soon contracted measles and died), a drunken crew ran her ashore on the island of Kauai, and she broke up. Somebody dug a sample of her woodwork out of the sand and sent it to be displayed as an artifact of Hawaiian history in the Bishop Museum in Honolulu.

George died just as Salem's and his family's fortunes began to decline. The harbor channel was too narrow and shallow for the big, deep clipper ships that came to dominate American trade, and the next generations of Crowninshields were too unimaginative or unambitious to join other merchant families in shifting venturous attention to railroads and textiles. In the twentieth century, three great-grandsons of brother Benjamin met with minor success. Frank Crowninshield, the best known, was editor of *Vanity Fair* magazine in the 'twenties, and his cousin Bowdoin designed yachts (among them Thomas W. Lawson's unsuccessful America's Cup contender *Independence*). Bowdoin's brother Francis honored the memory of his great-great uncle by publishing letters, journals, and log entries concerning the "voyage of amusement" in a handsome leather-bound volume; he also named his one hundred-nine-foot Herreshoff schooner *Cleopatra's Barge II,* and he donated to Salem's Peabody Museum an accurate reconstruction of the original yacht's maple and mahogany main saloon, in which you can today see Napoleon's boots and cup, Pauline Bonaparte's locks of hair, and the other relics.

George Crowninshield's adventures have left us with a nagging question: Why did he bring *Cleopatra's Barge* home so soon? Perhaps unloading the foreigners at Gibraltar had been the plan all along; maybe, as one writer has suggested, the "son" was a discarded lover of Pauline Bonaparte's that had to be got out of Rome, and George was an easy mark. *That* George Crowninshield certainly was, especially when somebody needed saving; but this cannot be the whole answer. I prefer to believe that he did indeed have grand ambitions, which might well have included taking part in a plot to rescue Napoleon, but that a more important responsibility interfered, probably in connection with his failing health.

What that responsibility was became clear after his death, when a young woman named Elizabeth Rowell, a native of Marblehead, produced a will signed by George that acknowledged and benefited their bastard seven-year-old daughter, Clarissa. Elizabeth declared that George had long before paid another man to be the titular father, and, before departing for Europe, had written a will leaving them both some money. However, since his return from Europe, he had shown new interest in the girl, and during a ten-day visit with them in November had rewritten the will to double the legacy to approximately $16,000.

His relatives had known of this mistress; but the child was shocking news and a blot on their reputations, especially should she keep the Crowninshield name. Although they inherited the vast majority of his fortune of $350,000, the brothers and sisters challenged the will, unsuccessfully as it turned out. William Bentley was aghast at the family's behavior — "Than this act nothing could be more shameful."

Her inheritance allowed Clara Crowninshield (as she came to call herself) a better education and broader upbringing than Salem could have offered. After a childhood friend, a sickly Maine girl named Mary Storer Potter, married the poet Henry Wadsworth Longfellow, they asked the pretty, lively Clara to accompany them on a tour of Europe in 1835. It did not turn out well. Clara first watched her friend Mary fade away and die painfully in Rotterdam, then was rejected by the widower for a wealthier woman of more respectable New England parentage. Clara later married a German art scholar, and in 1866 they moved from Boston to Dresden, where she long outlived her husband, Longfellow, their children, and her grandchild. Clara finally died in 1907 — ninety-seven years after George Crowninshield fathered her, ninety years after the wondrous voyage of *Cleopatra's Barge,* and seven years after the end of the century of Napoleon. Of all three, father and yacht and century, what Longfellow once said about Clara Crowninshield certainly applies: "Clara is always well and always mysterious, like the heroine in a French novel."

III

The Squadron, the Stevens Brothers, and the America Adventure

"He was in every way typical of his generation: hard living, hard riding, and hard swearing, he was yet kind-hearted and extremely hospitable."

he most celebrated event in the history of yachting occurred on August 22, 1851. On that day, a one hundred and two foot schooner yacht named *America,* owned by a syndicate that was headed by Commodore John Cox Stevens of the New York Yacht Club and including his brother Edwin, beat some cutters and schooners in the fleet of the Royal Yacht Squadron in their home waters. The Americans thereby took possession of a rather ugly bottomless ewer that was originally called the Hundred Guinea Cup and was eventually named for its winner. In more recent yachting history, the only event that comes near to matching it is the 1983 triumph of *Australia II,* the first challenger to win the America's Cup from the New York Yacht Club after twenty-four failed challenges over a century and one-third.

Then and now, that single race in 1851 has been seen as a turning point in history — the athletic equivalent of, say, the Boston Tea Party or the defeat of the Spanish Armada — where an upstart nation upsets an older power. Mourned an Englishman, "We have had 'Brittania rules the waves' over our door for a long time, but I think we must now take down the sign." An American who was in England at Cowes at the time of the race wrote in a letter to the New York sports periodical *The National Police Gazette:*

> America's *achievements will form — indeed have already formed — an era in our history. They attest the excellence of our mechanics, the skill of our mariners, the enterprise of our national character, and the liberality and taste of two gentlemen [Stevens and his brother Edwin] who have done very much to advance our prosperity and reputation as a Maritime People.*

Euphoria swept the United States. Hearing the result as he was speaking on the floor of the Massachusetts House of Representatives, the great orator Daniel Webster proclaimed, "Like Jupiter among the Gods, America is first and there is no second!" A far less jingoistic observer in New York City, George Templeton Strong, complained in his diary: "Quite creditable to Yankee shipbuilding, certainly, but not worth the intolerable vainglorious vaporings that make every newspaper I take up now ridiculous. One would think that yacht-building were the end of man's exis-

tence on earth."

In this chapter, we will look at the men and institutions and yachts that figured prominently in the period leading up to that race off Cowes. First, we will see how a group of English and Irish landed aristocrats, some of them wonderfully colorful, shaped the pastime from a variety of naval, commercial, and sporting traditions. Then we'll see how a generation of steel-eyed gamblers and businessmen founded American yachting. Finally, we will hear how the two groups came together when the Americans tested their mettle by taking *America* to England.

1: The Glorious Royal Yacht Squadron

This tale is that of the early yacht clubs, and especially of the origins, formation, and influence of the Royal Yacht Squadron, which, while not the first English yacht club, was certainly the most influential. The chance to race against the Squadron's fleet was one of the main reasons for the construction of *America,* and the Squadron's august reputation was the reason her victory was so astonishing on both shores. During the first half of the nineteenth century, the Squadron reached a pinnacle of fashionableness through a combination of its members' wealth, position, eccentricity, and interest in sailing, plus (last but clearly not least) the mixed blessing of patronage by a decidedly mixed-up royal family.

That there were any clubs anywhere in Britain was due to coffee, political tolerance, and the growth of leisure. First made available in the mid-seventeenth century, coffee quickly became the addiction that it has since remained. In the liberating atmosphere of post-1688 England, where one's head was no longer always in jeopardy in political debate, the gentry and aristocracy were lured to coffee houses to soak up both caffeine and Parliamentary gossip. Human nature being what it was (and still is), people of like interests tended to congregate together, convincing the shop owners to restrict the access of one or two rooms so that particular groups could chat in privacy. The clergy gathered at Child's, conveniently located in St. Paul's churchyard; Jacobites schemed at the Cocoa Tree; Samuel Johnson performed at center stage in Will's; even women met at Almack's; and because the gentry talked money at

White's, this club soon became the most exclusive of all. And finally, in 1770, there were a sufficient number of Thames pleasure sailors to form a sailing club at the White Swan Tavern, in Chelsea.

While that club (which we'll return to in a moment) was the first English yachting organization, Ireland's Water Club of the Harbour of Cork preceded it by fifty years. We do not know for certain who the founders of the Water Club were, but it is safe to guess that they came from the ruling class of Protestant Anglo-Irish merchants who, a historian later wrote, were "delicately sensitive to any infringement of class or position." In a place where class and position were rigidly defined by increasingly harsh anti-Catholic laws, the Water Club may have been one of those barricades behind which an insecure elite retreats from real or imagined threats by the great unwashed. Such a colonial outpost would be at home in Forster's *Passage to India* or Orwell's *Burmese Days.* Hearkening ever toward London, the Water Club's twenty-five members sailed vessels gilded in the style of England's royal yachts in elaborate, pseudo-naval maneuvers. Ashore, twenty-seven Rules and Orders regulated almost every moment in a club life chockablock with ceremony and gargantuan feasts — the otherwise all-powerful Admiral was allowed to bring a mere two dozen bottles of wine to club dinners. The most telling remark about this imperial ghetto ostensibly devoted to the water is its Rule 14: "Resolved, That such members of the Club, or others, as shall talk of sailing after dinner be fined a bumper."

In England, meanwhile, there were a few people who gammed about boats after dinner. One of these was the writer Roger North, whose cruising career began in the days of the Stuart kings and ran well into the 18th century, and who could rhapsodize about sailing with self-conscious charm: "For the day proved cool, the gale brisk, the air clear, and no inconvenience to molest us, nor wants to trouble our thoughts, neither business to importune, nor formalities to tease us; so that we came nearer to perfection of life there than I was ever sensible of otherwise . . ."

Among the few English pleasure-sailors in the late seventeenth and early eighteenth century there was also "young Berry in the yacht *Anne*" whom Samuel Pepys chanced upon in Cadiz, Spain, in 1684. But the long-legged cruises of Berry and North were not, it seems, duplicated by many others. Most pleasure sailors congregated on the placid, winding Thames in little sloops or fancy rowing barges. There they joined the Hanovers to hear concerti by Handel, whose "Water Music" was played, literally, on the water, and to watch and wager on rowing races.

In the eighteenth century, gentlemen's sports were sedentary, and first among them was betting. Men bet huge sums on the smallest matters: on card draws and professional boxing matches and cock fights and barmaids' brawls; on the longevity of mutual friends and who would next walk through the door; on races between crippled beggars, between horses, between ferrymen. Observing all this inactivity, as well as the fashion of pouring huge sums into barely-used country villas, Henry Fielding, the author of *Tom Jones,* wondered why more people were not pursuing "the highest degree of amusement" by "the sailing ourselves in little vessels of our own." Fielding, who himself cruised to Portugal, concluded that sailing's pleasures were unknown only because few people had tried them.

When pleasure sailing was finally introduced to British sportsmen, neither North's lyricism nor Fielding's chiding had much to do with it. The agent was our old friend the wager, spurred along by a dissolute duke. Watching the rowing races on the Thames from their little sloops, the men who founded the sailing club at the White Swan Tavern began to feel the first twitch of participatory competitiveness and inevitably engaged in short brushes along the sidelines of the sprints, no doubt with sizeable bets as encouragement. The final catalyst for the formation of a club was one of the more notorious characters in English history, the feckless Henry Frederick, Duke of Cumberland.

The historian of the yacht club that carried Cumberland's name tactfully refers to him as "a man of taste as well as more boisterous pleasures," but "that foolish sot" satisfies another writer. When he was twenty-five, he had been found guilty as a correspondent in a sensational divorce case and fined £ 10,000. Soon after, he came across a young widow of easy reputation who had, it was reported, "the most amorous eyes in the world and eyelashes a yard long." The Duke tripped over the eyelashes and, after a week's frantic courting, married the lady. Both actions drove his brother King George III to an apoplectic frenzy that ended only when the duke left England in exile. After five years spent tearing up the conti-

nent, Cumberland returned to London and, perhaps desiring to curry favor with the gentry, offered his patronage to the sailing group at the White Swan. Why these presumably respectable merchants accepted his offer is one of those mysteries whose solution probably lies in a marriage of convenience between ambition and snobbery: better a debauched duke than no duke at all. We should recall, too, that public behavior was not yet regulated by Queen Victoria's gimlet-eyed propriety, and that every kind of wildness was tolerated so long as a man was productive. For example, Charles James Fox, the great liberal politician who stood at the center of every important public issue from 1768 until his death in 1807, was as famous for his drunken orgies as for his golden-voiced orations.

With Cumberland's patronage, the White Swan group became the Cumberland Sailing Society, and by 1775 they were racing on the Thames as well as cruising up and down the river in company. The year's highlight was the race for a cup presented by the Duke himself. Only boats not let out to hire were eligible, and newspaper advertisements invited "all gentlemen proprietors of pleasure sailing boats within the British dominions" to compete — although, apparently, these boats could be steered by professionals. The new club came up with an "aquatic uniform" for its members, who seem to have had no other special privileges.

On race-day morning, the crews gathered at the White Swan to draw lots for starting positions. With that, any semblance of order quickly disappeared as the narrow twenty-footers elbowed each other around the twelve-mile river course, their three-man crews working harder at pushing opponents back than at sailing their own boats forward. Cutlasses slashed at sheets and rigging, handspikes thumped on heads. When this sailing brawl finally staggered to its bruised finish, the crews crawled back to the White Swan for the awards ceremony at which the winner and the Duke of Cumberland took turns sipping claret from the silver cup as the losers cheered and fired off cannon. This went on for seven years until the Duke got bored and stopped showing up. He had other fish to fry, such as tutoring his teen-age nephew the Prince of Wales in the niceties of dice-rolling and whoring; but he left his patronage behind. The Cumberland Society soon became the Cumberland Fleet; later the name was changed to the Royal

Thames Yacht Club.

It was great fun, but it was great fun on a small scale. The industrial revolution and a growing empire spawned a whole new level of wealth that would not deign to sail in twenty-foot four-tonners. Those whose purses could accommodate bigger yachts took to salt water — first at Brighton, where the Prince of Wales held court in his fantastic pavilion, and later at Cowes.

Meanwhile, London club life underwent a strange and painful transformation. What had begun as a reasonably democratic means for people to enjoy each other's company was transformed around 1805 into a savage jungle of snobbery. The agents of change belonged to a tribe of fops calling themselves the Dandies. Their leader was one George Bryan "Beau" Brummell, a witty, charismatic wastrel whose friendship with the Prince of Wales allowed him to set the standards of high fashion and low behavior. Because old George III had been lapsing in and out of insanity since 1788, his eldest son was more or less considered to be the country's leader, a responsibility that he shouldered with less rather than more devotion. He had already matched his uncle Cumberland by marrying against the king's wishes, but by choosing a twice-widowed Roman Catholic, a Mrs. Fitzherbert, he had invited prompt annulment, since by the Act of Succession of 1701 any English monarch had to be untouched by popery. Only after Parliament paid off his huge debts did he legally marry Caroline of Brunswick in 1795. Once Caroline was safely delivered of an heir, which was all that Parliament had desired, the prince cast her off for a string of mistresses and, later, all but ignored his daughter, Charlotte. (This story ended as miserably as it began: Charlotte died in childbirth in 1817 and, after the prince became George IV in 1820, Caroline sued for her rights as queen only to see her less-than-pristine morals dragged through court and the streets. Surviving all this Hanover misery was the prince's niece, Victoria, who promised to be good and did so.)

No wonder early nineteenth-century Britain worshipped her naval and military heroes, for few of the realm's Royals deserved much respect. No wonder, too, that in this vacuum Beau Brummell and the Dandies could take over White's and the other elite men's clubs simply by using a member's right to turn down applicants with a single black ball. In elections, voters would signify

Why a Yacht Club's Chief Officer Is Called "Commodore"

The term "commodore" has designated the president of a yacht club since the formation of the Cumberland Society in the late eighteenth century. Before then, the head of the first yacht club — the Water Club of the Harbour of Cork — was called "admiral," a name of equal naval pedigree but higher rank. Exactly why "commodore" won out over "admiral" is not known for certain, but we can speculate that "commodore" appealed because it suggested responsibilities less onerous and permanent than did "admiral." Until the nineteenth century, when it became a specific rank between Captain and Admiral, "commodore" meant one of two things in the Royal (and, later, U.S.) Navy. Either it was a temporary title given to an officer of any rank who took over command of a detached squadron, or it was an honorary title granted officers of especially commanding presence and ability, as in "Commodore John Paul Jones" (and, in the civilian world, "Commodore Cornelius Vanderbilt"). "Admiral," on the other hand, always meant "the commander of the seas," which suggests an enormous burden of permanent responsibility that hardly describes somebody in titular charge of a yacht club for a two- or three-year term.

Alongside both "captain," which has always been used to identify the owner of a yacht, and the blue-jacketed, brass-buttoned outfit that has been every pleasure sailor's uniform, the yachtsman's use of "commodore" reveals the strong role that naval traditions have played in the pastime. Today, this influence surfaces in many ways. One small example is the prefix "the" that some yachtsmen apply to the names of their yachts, as in "I'm cruising aboard the *Morning Watch* next weekend." Strictly speaking, the prefix comes only before the names of naval ships, as in "the *Intrepid*." More noticeable is the rigid routine that

The perfect model of a turn-of-century yachtsman, Cornelius Vanderbilt III poses aboard his two hundred forty-seven foot steam yacht North Star around the time that he was elected Commodore of the New York Yacht Club in 1906, when he was only thirty-three years old. He has all the panoply and accessories of a well-found turn-of-century yachtsman and commodore, including a telescope with which to keep track of his racing sailboats in the distance. This Vanderbilt was a great-grandson and namesake of the legendary "Commodore," whose ruthless acquisition of shipping and railroad monopolies founded the family fortune.

dominates many modern yacht clubs. Like the navy, they ceremonially mark the changing of command from one commodore to another, and they appoint official fleet surgeons and clergy, who bless the squadron during an elaborate opening-day parade. As on a ship, officers of the day are assigned to take charge of the yacht club when the commodore, rear-commodore, and vice-commodore are not present. When these top-ranking officers make their appearance, they are granted all sorts of privileges, just like naval officers. Yachting commodores leave their automobiles in specially designated parking places, are greeted by the raising of official flags on the club's flagpole, and are universally called "commodore" by club members and employees alike. (However, they are probably not allowed to display a "commodore's privilege" — in old Navy slang, an open fly.)

After his or her tour of duty, a former yacht club commodore always retains the title as an honorific. This was first impressed on me many years ago when I crewed on board a racing yacht owned by a former commodore of the New York Yacht Club, a gentleman then in his late fifties who, in the same way that George Crowninshield responded to "Lord," enjoyed being called "Commodore." One morning, while entering the harbor after the finish of a long-distance race, we spied an anchored schooner owned by one of my skipper's predecessors in that distinguished position. Our commodore steered his boat in a slow circle around the schooner until one of her crew called below to *his* commodore. Their commodore came on deck and, with a grace that belied his old age, skipped to the after deck. Simultaneously, each man bowed respectfully toward the other, doffed his blue yachting cap, and intoned, "Commodore!" After a moment, they straightened up and put their hats back on, and then we went on our way. That was the only word exchanged during the entire encounter.

approval or disapproval by placing a white ball or a black ball in a box. Usually, only one or two black balls would mean automatic rejection. When it worked, this system was meant to support Doctor Johnson's definition of "club" — "An assembly of good fellows, meeting under certain conditions." Good fellowship should include being around people that you like. But when the system was carried to extremes, it tended to undermine both the assembly and its relationships. The Dandies cheerfully exploited the blackball by using it to reject just about anybody for just about any reason. "It will do him good" was a typical explanation, although people would also be turned down for wearing what the Dandies felt was the wrong color tie. Lord Castlereagh, the Foreign Secretary, was blackballed from White's, where he had every good reason to expect to be admitted, and apparently the reason was that he was the Foreign Secretary. One patient soul was blackballed twenty times before the Dandies were convinced that it had done him enough good.

Much of this undoubtedly was a twitch in the generation gap: young men trashing their parents' friends, values, and institutions. It was social Luddism: at the same time that unemployed handworkers were tearing down the power looms that had put them out of work, the Dandies were tampering with society's gears. In England, where a man's club has always been a large part of his identity, this was serious business. After a few years of this foolishness, the old gentry and aristocracy learned a lesson, and founded new clubs without the Dandies (many of whom eventually ran out of money and fled to Europe — Brummell himself died in a French insane asylum). Due to a rising interest in participant sports around the end of the Napoleonic wars, some of these new groups were athletic clubs. A tennis club was being planned in 1819, rugby football clubs were muddying fields, and there were local hunts. And there was, inevitably, the Yacht Club, which we know today as the Royal Yacht Squadron.

On June 1, 1815, several owners of big yachts met at the Thatched House Tavern, on London's St. James's Street, to form their own sailing club. Among the forty-two founding members were two marquises, three earls, four viscounts, four barons, and five baronets, which should indicate what kind of club they had in mind. The rules that they drew up were as simple as the organization's title: the Yacht Club. Members were required to own yachts of at least ten tons burden, which probably could be satisfied by a little twenty-five footer; the initiation fee was £ 3 (about $150 today); and dues were £ 2. The club was to be a kind of nautical mutual-aid society, for "although the parties may be personally unacquainted," any member in trouble should be able to count on help from another member, the minutes insisted. Money was set aside to facilitate communications through special club signal books. Finally, semi-annual members' dinners would be held at the Thatched Roof in winter and "the hotel in East Cowes" during the summer.

Once a major ship-building port, Cowes had recently joined Brighton as one of England's most fashionable watering holes. Isolated from the mainland by the swift-flowing Solent and infrequent ferry service, Cowes had been attracting visitors such as Emma Hamilton, Nelson's mistress, and the Dukes of Bedford and Clarence since 1800. From time to time, a couple of yacht owners might race around the Isle of Wight for high stakes, or the "fashionables" might sponsor a fishermen's race, but Cowes didn't become a yachting center until after Waterloo. "Sea bathing" in the warm water of Cowes Roads and the Medina River was the main attraction, at least until the main attraction became the visitors themselves.

Undoubtedly hoping to be allowed to doze peacefully out of sight of both royalty and the public, the Yacht Club's founders were rudely awakened by a quick series of events. First a large number of retired and half-pay naval officers at loose ends after almost a generation of warfare asked to be admitted. They were, and the financial security that resulted briefly allowed the elimination of annual dues. Then the Prince of Wales, Beau Brummell's old patron and now Prince Regent in place of his lunatic father, came knocking. Always entranced by the sea, George had the captain of the royal yacht, *Royal George,* notify the club of his interest in joining. He was, of course, admitted, and soon after came his brothers the Duke of Gloucester and the Duke of Clarence, a navy veteran who spoke movingly of having been converted to the Christian faith during a gale at sea. The immediate effect of the admission of royal members was on the Yacht Club's finances: so expensive were the special red morocco signal books presented to the Prince

Opposite, in an 1880 painting, the much disputed white ensign flies over the Royal Yacht Squadron's clubhouse in the old castle — or "cow" — at Cowes. In the foreground, a yacht's professional crew rows a sail ashore while another crew works on a mooring buoy. In the background, two people in a rowboat sail a model yacht that looks a lot like America, *as does the sharp-bowed black schooner flying the white ensign. Before 1851, English yachts had bulbous bows and narrow sterns; but after the triumph of* America, *with her hollow (concave) forward sections, British sailors realized (to quote the Marquis of Anglesey) that they had been "sailing stern foremost" and began building a whole new family of fine-bowed, wide-sterned yachts. On the right is the Prince of Wales, later the Prince Regent and King George IV, who added to the prestige and fashionability of the Yacht Club by granting it a royal warrant, the first ever given to an English club.*

Regent that annual dues were reinstated. Another result was an instant clamor for membership that led to the lifting of the minimum size limit of yachts from ten to twenty tons (and, in 1825, thirty tons). And when George finally became king in 1820, he allowed the club to add the prefix "Royal" to its name, thereby setting a precedent for all English clubs. This dramatic gesture symbolized the monarch's interest in the sea as well as his willingness to join his subjects in their leisure activities; and it also elevated yachting above almost all other interests. When George IV sailed over to Cowes in triumph a year after his accession, three Royal Yacht Club vessels were given the honor of escorting the royal yacht to her mooring as the chubby old womanizer bowed deeply to ladies waving to him from a nearby ferry.

Under royal sponsorship, and especially under the sponsorship of this king, Cowes, yachting, and fashion quickly came to be mentioned in one breath. A local newspaper of the time challenged "any watering-place in England to compete with Cowes or to produce a collection of such brilliant stars of fashion as at present illumine our hemisphere." A lady remembered a week at Cowes consisting of "sails around the island, champagne luncheons, a very pleasant archery meeting at Carisbrooke, and a final wind-up with the Royal Yacht Squadron ball, unusually gay and certainly the most amusing one at which I ever had the good fortune to be present." In its tenth year, the club had two hundred regular and honorary members who owned five thousand tons of vessels and employed five hundred local seamen.

The Royal Yacht Club (and, later, Squadron) had as its purpose, in the felicitous phrasing of the most recent of its four historians, Ian Dear, "to be a convivial focus for a seaborne community." The club's early members worked hard at events that brought them together rather than those — racing is the best example — that might tear them apart. They sponsored mock-naval reviews, processions, balls (some of which were held on the yachts themselves), and cross-Channel cruises to buy wine in France. If these gatherings were to be successful, good communication was everything. The original 1817 signal book had three thousand signals — which you would think might suffice. But by 1831 the club's signal vocabulary had been expanded to include more than sixty-five hundred words, nine hundred names, and two thousand sentences, includ-

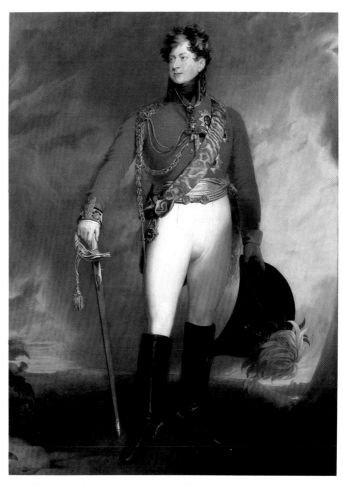

ing "Can you lend me your band?", "Have you any ladies on board?", and ways to order prawns, soup tureens, and any of fourteen different varieties of wine.

Supporting this elaborate style of life was a community of professional seamen whose morals and behavior were carefully supervised by the owners. One early English yachtsman printed up a booklet titled, "Rules and Regulations of the *Yida* to be observed by the men," which specified neatness, church attendance, hours of meals, and the authority of the professional captain. Since professionals were so important, for many years the Yacht Club's members kept track of untrustworthy seamen in a record book described as "An Account of Seamen discharged from yachts belonging to the Royal Yacht Squadron for disorderly Conduct, etc." Everybody had an interest in such a record; by the 1850s, English yachts employed some sixteen hundred paid hands, and a seaside village's economy would rise and fall on the reputation of its sailors. Eventually, in 1874, seamen were issued certificates of good conduct which they were expected to present to potential employers, like present-day letters of reference.

Image was important to the yachtsmen themselves, and they were soon faced with two problems involving their public identity, one with practical implications and the other purely a matter of status. The first difficulty stemmed from the fact that, until the 1830s (and later in the United States), there was no distinctive design for yachts. Revenue cutters, smugglers, fast fishing boats, cross-Channel passenger vessels, and yachts all came from the same designs produced by the same builders. A yacht would be maintained at a brighter gloss, and she might carry more luxurious furniture below; but in every other respect she was just another vessel of the coast. So when a member of the Yacht Club cruised over to La Rochelle to pick up a couple of hogsheads of Bordeaux, all that prevented French port captains from sticking him with a steep tariff on commercial traffic was his claim to be a pleasure sailor — a claim that, naturally enough, captains of trading, fishing, and passenger boats were quick to make once they saw its economic benefits. Such was the influence of the Yacht Club's members that the Duke of Wellington wrote a letter in their behalf to a French official asking that special cruising permits be issued to the English yachtsmen. The permits were made out, but the problem did not go away entirely.

The second problem concerned the color of the national flag that the club's yachts were permitted to fly by the British Admiralty, the department in charge of naval and other maritime affairs. Apparently, nothing nagged early British yachtsmen more than this seemingly inconsequential matter, which had much less to do with patriotism than it did with private conceits. The story of the battle of the white ensign is long, complicated, and frequently hilarious.

Three distinct ensigns were used on ships in the early days of the Royal Yacht Club: red, white, and blue. The red ensign was flown by merchant ships as well as by the naval squadron that was under the command of the most senior admiral in the fleet; the white and blue ensigns were flown indiscriminately by navy ships. Originally, and for no apparent special reason, the club used the white ensign. In 1821 it switched to red, perhaps unwillingly since the Admiralty then classed yachts as merchant ships, and merchantmen were subject to special tonnage dues and, as we have seen, to foreign tariffs. Eight years later, the club successfully applied for a warrant to be allowed to fly the white ensign, the reason no doubt being that yachts were continuing to be charged commercial duties.

So long as they were the only people allowed to use the white ensign (or any one of the three ensigns, for that matter), the Royal Yacht Club's members were content. There were other yacht clubs, but each also had its own privileged use of an ensign, the Royal Northern Yacht Club of Scotland and northern Ireland having been granted use of the blue ensign, and the Royal Cork in Ireland (successor to the Water Club of the Harbour of Cork) having the red one. Any new club, therefore, had to endure the indignity of flying the same color ensign used by another. That new club was the Royal Western Yacht Club of Ireland. Its representative, one Maurice O'Connell, saw a way around the impasse. In 1832, he asked the Admiralty to grant the Royal Western the privilege of flying a *green* ensign. The Admiralty turned him down on the grounds that "their Lordships cannot sanction the introduction of a new colour to be worn by British ships." The disappointed Irish yachtsmen had to make do with the white ensign, which of course infringed on the older club's sense of peerlessness. The problem was quickly solved in part in 1833, when, by royal decree, King William IV changed the Royal Yacht Club's name to the Royal Yacht *Squadron* — a name full of official naval implications — and granted it the right to place on the white ensign a grandly monarchial coat of arms that included a royal motto, a rampant lion, and a unicorn.

Then or since, no other yacht club was graced with that combination of special favors. Nonetheless, the members of the now-Squadron had an insatiable appetite for privilege, and in 1844 the commodore, the Earl of Yarborough, asked the Admiralty to withdraw the warrant for the use of the white ensign from the other six clubs that by then were using it. The Admiralty complied and so informed those clubs — except, for some reason, the Royal Western of Ireland. Communications across the Irish Sea must have been slow, for it wasn't until 1849 that news of the Admiralty's new rule made its way to the members of the Royal Western. They complained, and the ever-compliant Admiralty began issuing them individual warrants to fly the white ensign. Soon, of course, other clubs were applying for the right to use it, too. The inevitable Squadron protest was sufficiently strong to end up in the House of Commons. To describe the official response, I can do no better than to quote Ian Dear, who devotes seven pages to this amazing dispute: "The spokesman for the government, however, by what might be mildly called dissimulation, managed to avoid the relevant papers being laid before the House, and the Admiralty's decision stood."

Obviously, the issue had nothing at all to do with the color of the flag; "blue, green, pink, or purple ensign, there would have been the same struggle," somebody commented. The Royal Yacht Squadron wanted special treatment, and so did everybody else. Finally, in 1858, after some thirty years of bickering, the exhausted Admiralty decided in favor of the Squadron. Despite an intense lobbying effort by the Irish (who rounded up the support of thirty-six Members of Parliament), the matter ended with the Squadron in full possession of civilian rights to fly the white ensign, which before long was also the sole ensign of the Royal Navy.

Long before the battle of the white ensign was won, the club was absorbing public criticism, mainly for the apparent timidity of its members. One newspaper said that the members were not true sailors but rather "Nab-Nelsons" who stuck their bows out no farther than the Nab Lightship, at the eastern end of the Isle of Wight. One member was called "A yachting gilt-bespangled dandy." Wrote one acerbic critic:

The so-called yachtsmen of Cowes, it seems, have champagne lunches on the Solent, and then spread canvas and take a two-hours' run when the breeze is fair and light. They meet the same people at Cowes as they meet later on at the grouse [hunt], and this life which they make to resemble Heaven must be a live fac-

simile of Hell. Different clothes and the same well-fed, carefully exercised bodies, the same bored minds tired of wondering whether passion will ever come their way.

Perhaps due to this and other criticisms, but more likely because it could no longer hold back the waves of competition, the Yacht Club pulled aside the velvet veil and allowed yacht racing. It was not unknown at Cowes. Some members already engaged in private matches; the first race around the Isle of Wight, in 1824, was one of these. Two years later, the club put up a £ 100 gold cup for a race. The yachts started at moorings, which they cast off when the commodores fired a gun from a yacht anchored off Cowes Castle. A problem was that there was great disparity in the size of the boats in the fleet. The only handicapping system used in the early races was to split the fleet into divisions by tonnage and offer a trophy for each division, and it was not until 1841 that the club began to experiment with a system of time allowances that allowed one second per mile for each ton of measured volume. By all accounts, they were no more successful than modern-day handicappers at concocting a scheme that pleased everybody.

Given the era, it was only natural that yacht racing would unleash forces that the reputed aristocratic refinement of the Royal Yacht Club could not tame. The early nineteenth century was a wild time in Britain, little changed from the previous generation described by Fielding, although Victoria's reign, and other influences, would tame it — at least on the surface. Britain in this period, one historian has written, "was a singularly disorderly and undisciplined country." For instance, long after most countries had recognized a government responsibility for law enforcement, Englishmen continued to oppose the mere idea of a police force out of fear that it might lead to the loss of their civil liberties. Such raw individualism, such rough and ready anarchy, had always surfaced in nasty religious disputes and spectator sports like boxing, dog fighting, cock fighting, and, of course, public executions. Blood sports where men risked life and limb "tend to make the people bold, they produce a communication of notions of hardihood," claimed the reformer William Cobbett. Except for riding, though, blood sports traditionally were reserved for the lower classes; the gentry and aristocracy sat at a distance, made their bets, and kept their clothes and sensibilities clean. But by 1800 the upper classes were beginning to descend from their castles. After one brutal boxing match where a large part of the audience was aristocratic, a French newspaper sniffed, "certainly the English nobility stand alone in their taste for this singular and degrading spectacle." As class distinctions faded on the playing fields, courage, daring, and endurance came to be valued as universal "manly" virtues even by lords who earned £ 50,000 a year without lifting a finger. The sporting aristocrat had come a long way from the dice table, and although wagering and sport were still linked inextricably, risky participation came to be admired.

So once the Royal Yacht Club began to sponsor races, it stood back like those gentlemen at the boxing match and watched the blood spurt. When Lord Belfast's *Louisa* and Joseph Weld's *Lulworth* intentionally collided near the finish of the 1829 King's Cup in the dead of a night broken only by the flash of fireworks, their crews went at it with an assortment of weapons. The race committee eventually awarded the cup to *Lulworth* after deciding that "the use of axes in the cutting away of rigging was unjustifiable."

A founding member of the club widely hailed for his manliness was Horatio Ross, who on separate occasions walked ninety-seven miles nonstop, won tough steeplechase races against professional jockeys, and won a seven-mile single sculls race. His contemporary, the Marquis of Waterford, was best known for shooting out the eyes of the family portraits, but he also won acclaim for fighting all challengers, swimming after a hat that had been blown off his head during a sail and almost drowning, and finally being crushed to death under a horse that fell at a hurdle. Thomas Assheton-Smith, another early member, earned a reputation as a horseman that spread to France. On meeting him, Napoleon called him *premier chasseur d'Angleterre.* Assheton-Smith, too, was known to brawl and once beat a man whom he saw whipping a horse. But he became so discouraged by the bickering between Belfast and Weld after their 1829 set-to that he quit racing and built a steam boat. Unfortunately, this led to his resignation from the club since steamers were banned before 1843, when Queen Victoria and the Prince Consort, who was a member, bought the first *Victoria and Albert.* Since the queen had a summer house near Cowes, and since she enjoyed the sea — "I do love a ship!" she once

exclaimed — England's *premier club de yachting* could not blackball her preference for steam over sail. She was also a royal sponsor of yachting who was not a major social embarrassment (preceded as she was by Charles II, the Duke of Cumberland, and George IV), so the club was eager for her favor.

Increased respectability arrived in 1833 when William IV, formerly the pious Duke of Clarence, renamed the old club the Royal Yacht Squadron. This did not, however, dampen the members' hot spirits and eccentricities. Blood and guts racing continued with periodic summers off to patch wounds and hulls. An estimated £ 50,000 changed hands when Lord Belfast's brig *Waterwitch* beat an early fore-and-after, *Galatea,* in what might have been the first

The Marquis of Anglesey and Earl of Uxbridge has been described as "hard living, hard riding, and hard swearing, ... yet kind-hearted and extremely hospitable." Despite the loss of a leg at the Battle of Waterloo, he was one of England's most eminent all-round sportsmen in the early nineteenth century, during the first great flourishing of amateur athletics. His keen competitiveness is obvious in this portrait.

long-distance race —the Nab Tower to the Eddystone Light and back, two hundred twenty-four miles.

Some of the wildness spilled over into the election of members when, ironically (considering the Squadron's origins), the black ball became a weapon. The club's immensely high social standing had something to do with this, and the older members were left to defend the original aims laid out at the Thatched Roof back in '15. But the studied eccentricities of the British aristocracy played their entertaining part as well. One member regularly blackballed any applicant younger than fifty; another, with equal consistency, always blackballed if the wind was blowing from the east. One applicant was rejected because members thought his boat ugly.

A scandal developed out of one blackballing. The Earl of Cardigan, a contentious general, was put up by friends in 1845. Unfortunately, some deemed him unsuitable for membership not only because of his unpleasant personality but because he knew nothing about sailing. When the professional captain of his big schooner, *Enchantress,* asked one day if he would like to take the helm, Cardigan replied, "No, thank you, I never take anything between meals." The bitterness that developed over his name threatened to split the Squadron and eventually became public. "In the Squadron," a sporting weekly commented, "things are still aristocratic enough, though they are far from gentle." Compromise prevailed and Cardigan was admitted. Several years later, he had *Enchantress* sailed to the Black Sea to serve as his private barracks while his soldiers and officers froze in the trenches of the Crimea. It was he who inspired the cardigan sweater. More telling, it was also he who was responsible for one of the most famous military disasters in history, the charge of the Light Brigade.

Blackballed applicants took their rejections seriously. One, known to us only as "The Pirate," anchored his sixteen-gun black schooner off the Squadron's clubhouse and threatened to open fire if he did not receive an immediate apology from the man he believed to be the blackballer, Sir Percy Shelley, son of the poet. The infuriated Shelley at first refused; but he was quickly talked around by his dinner companion, who knew The Pirate all too well. Shelley reluctantly wrote the apology, which was rowed out to the ship. After a moment, The Pirate dipped his ensign, weighed anchor, and sailed off.

Of all the early members, the Marquis of Anglesey was the best-known and probably most-respected. Although a founder, he was unable to attend the first meeting at the Thatched Roof for the very good reason that he was leading a cavalry division in the campaign that ended at Waterloo, where he was one of the Duke of Wellington's most trusted aides. When an enemy shell took off his leg, he calmly said, "By God, I've lost my leg." Wellington responded, "Have you, by God?" And so Anglesey was known for the rest of his long life as the man who lost his leg at Waterloo. (Maldwin Drummond tells a sequel that serves as a jibe at the aristocracy's reputed ignorance: at his club one day, when a descendant of the Marquis told an acquaintance that his ancestor lost a leg at Waterloo, the other man — knowing of only one Waterloo, and that one a railroad station — politely responded, "Which platform?" The incensed story-teller stormed out of the room and, in the hall, met a second noble acquaintance to whom he vented his outrage, to which the equally dense man replied with a laugh, "As if it mattered which platform!") The severed leg was buried with full honors at a local Belgian church to which Englishmen took pilgrimages. It is reported that George IV, who rarely shed a tear over anybody, wept at the sight of the small tomb.

Despite his physical handicap, Anglesey was a vigorous sportsman. During a grouse hunt he accidentally put a bullet through a clergyman's hat and then assured the terrified divine, "Do not fear, I am a perfect master of the weapon." A ferociously competitive sailor who in the middle of a race he was losing shouted to his captain, "burn her as soon as she gets back," and who won and lost thousands of pounds in yachting wagers, Anglesey also showed a tender side that balanced the frenetic *machismo.* Although he was meticulous about the appearance of his yachts, he declined to tell his friends to take off their hard-soled varnished boots before coming aboard. Rather, he instructed a seaman to follow along behind them with a mop. In the gossipy history *Sacred Cowes,* Anthony Heckstall-Smith described him as being "typical of his generation: hard living, hard riding, and hard swearing, he was yet kind-hearted and extremely hospitable."

As Governor of the Isle of Wight, Anglesey lived in the castle on the left bank of the Medina River. Built by Henry VIII to defend the town from foreign invaders, the castle had a sweeping outlook

Gone are the days when Royal Yacht Squadron members signaled each other, "Can you lend me your band?", yet the Squadron retains its traditional ambiance of subdued elegance combined with occasional outbursts of bright display. Here the castle-clubhouse is decked out for the annual Cowes Week Regatta, whose races are started and finished from the Squadron itself. The Squadron remains one of the most prestigious yacht clubs in the world; the small membership list still includes titles, but they range alongside the names of many commoners who have made their mark in yachting, including those of some Americans.

on the Solent and the mainland. In 1858, after Anglesey died, the Squadron took over the castle, and there it has remained. Anglesey and the other characters who populate its colorful history come down to us larger than life thanks to the Squadron itself, which, far from being embarrassed by its members' singular behavior, has celebrated it in four books, the first published in 1903 under this extraordinary title: *The Royal Yacht Squadron: Memorials of its Members, with an Enquiry into the History of Yachting and its Development in the Solent; And a Complete List of Members with their Yachts from the Foundation of the Club to the Present Time for the Official Records.* Written around the time when its most prestigious member, King Edward VII of England, was still turning up at Cowes with his lady friends, and his nephew Kaiser Wilhelm of Germany was appearing in ever-larger, ever-faster racing yachts in order to whip his uncle, *Memorials* (as the history is known) became just another of the delightful records of mores, manners, and mania that added to the singular lustre of the Royal Yacht Squadron.

2: John Cox Stevens and the New York Yacht Club

Yachting became popular in the United States somewhat later than it did in Britain, and the story of the pastime's progress is shorter. It wasn't for lack of water and boats; neither was it for lack of a model. In 1784 a wealthy Englishman named Shuttleworth cruised across the Atlantic in a big ten-gun yacht named *Lively,* aided by twenty-five seamen and accompanied, Captain Arthur H. Clark tells us in his history of early yachting, by "a beautiful French woman." He cruised for fourteen months, ranging from Florida to Hudson Bay, and at one point entertained George Washington. As we saw in the previous chapter, thirty years later an American built a big pleasure vessel and sailed her to Europe. But something else was needed to spark the American version of the pastime — that blend of money, leisure, security, status-seeking, and competitiveness that had stimulated the growth of yachting in Britain. The flint for that spark was the remarkable Stevens family of Hoboken, New Jersey.

The first Stevens in America landed in New York in 1699 as a seventeen-year-old apprentice, prospered, and bought land. His son John sent trading ships to England and the West Indies, became a member of the Continental Congress, and helped bail New Jersey out of its Revolutionary War debts. His son John, born in 1749, was a revolutionary colonel, lawyer, inventor, and transportation entrepreneur. John Stevens owned the first trans-Hudson steam ferry service and developed the first ferry service from New York to Philadelphia, and *his* sons — John Cox, Edwin A., Robert L., and James — moved on from there. Robert was the inventor in the family; his products included the T-shaped railroad track, the first propeller-driven boat, and a bomb that was shot from a cannon. John Cox and Edwin were the financiers; together they developed ironclad ships, a highly profitable ferryboat line up the Hudson to Albany, and, on the family estate at Hoboken, an amusement park called Elysian Fields, which, of course, was serviced by Stevens ferries. In modern terms, the Stevens family was a bloodline conglomerate.

The brothers were among the first Americans to be called sportsmen, and they found all sorts of ways to enjoy their wealth. One outlet was the race track, where their horse Eclipse was a champion. In 1823, they bet all their cash, gold watches, and diamond stick pins on Eclipse before a famous inter-regional match race against a southern champion named Sir Henry. (Eclipse won by a nose.) And, of course, they enjoyed the water — especially the eldest brother, John Cox Stevens. In 1804, at nineteen, he was the test pilot for the first propeller boat, and soon after he built a twenty-foot pleasure sloop called *Diver* (or *Dive*) and a fifty-six foot ketch called *Trouble.* In them he chased around New York Bay in search of wagers with fishermen as to who had the faster boat. Like Charles II, John Cox Stevens was fascinated not only by sailing and yacht racing, but also by sailing theory. At one time or another, he experimented with a catamaran called *Double Trouble,* with centerboards and leeboards, with moveable ballast, and with outside lead ballast, which was smeared on the boat's bottom.

John Cox owned and raced many yachts before he built *America.* For some years, he devoted enormous energy (and over $100,000) on optimizing his one hundred ten foot centerboard sloop *Maria,* which was originally designed by brother Robert but was much altered. Carrying an enormous spread of sail — her main boom was almost as long as her hull — *Maria* was one of the first yachts to be called an "out-and-outer," which in today's parlance means "racing machine."

Maria often represented New York in the periodic races that took place with yachts from Boston. These contests followed an all but predictable script. First, a yachtsman from one city would write a letter to a newspaper proclaiming the extraordinary speed and marvelous seakindliness of his or a friend's boat as compared with the utter worthlessness of a diabolically conceived vessel from the other city. The letter would be picked up and published in the other city's papers, wherewith a prolonged, highly technical, and very public correspondence would ensue. Eventually a challenge would be made. One city's vessel would sail off to the other city, and the race would take place amid a blizzard of publicity that generated tens of thousands of dollars in wagers by the owners and the public at large. If *Maria* was the New York champion, she usually would lose or break down. The papers would then be filled with interminable letters from Stevens describing the highly unusual circumstances under which *Maria* had failed, reaffirming his continuing conviction of her inherent superiority over her New England opponent, and predicting the triumphs that lay in store when they met once again in more favorable weather conditions, should her owner, skipper, and crew exhibit greater competence. By the next summer, the whole cycle would be repeated.

Inevitably, a community of like-minded wagering yachtsmen gathered around all this fun. Many of them already belonged to a club for horsemen, the Jockey Club (one of whose presidents had been John Cox Stevens), so they had a local model. At five in the afternoon on July 30, 1844, Stevens and eight friends assembled on his fifty-one foot schooner *Gimcrack* to form the New York Yacht Club. While not the first yacht club in the United States — it was preceded by the Boston Boat Club, which was formed in the early 1830s but folded in 1837, and the Detroit Boat Club, founded in 1839 and still going strong — it quickly became the most prestigious. Today, it is as close to a national yacht club as there is in the United States.

The first commodore was the genial and ambitious John Cox Stevens — "that prince of good fellows" in the words of his friend Philip Hone, a former mayor of New York City. Three days after that formative meeting, the new club's eight-yacht fleet headed

JOHN C. STEVENS
First Commodore, 1844-1855

John Cox Stevens, the father of American yachting and "that prince of good fellows," looks down benignly from a portrait that hangs in the Commodore's Room in the New York Yacht Club, which he helped found in 1844. Stevens' competitiveness, technical knowledge, leadership ability, and wealth helped give birth to the yacht club, to the schooner yacht America, *and to the whole style of American sportsmanship. Opposite, her foresail handed, the schooner yacht* Northern Light *beats out of a typically crowded Boston Harbor in 1845. Her architect, Louis Winde, may have been the first American yacht designer, and she may have been one of the Boston yachts that challenged New York Yacht Club vessels in mid-century.*

down Long Island Sound on the first New York Yacht Club Cruise, which seems to have been modeled after the Royal Yacht Squadron's voyages in company across the English Channel to France. What were called "trials of speed" were held along the way. The destination was Newport, Rhode Island, whose glory days as a resort were far in the future; Hone, who was on this first cruise, called the town "a tolerably dull place of sojournment." At Newport, the fleet was joined by some yachts that had sailed down from Boston. Of course, well-publicized races took place. After a few days, Stevens issued a challenge against a Boston yacht for stakes between $5,000 and $20,000. For some reason, it was not picked up, and the yachts sailed home. Soon enough the new club built a small clubhouse at Elysian Fields and began organizing a program

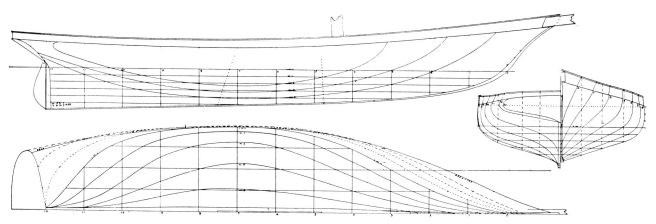

Divergent Yacht Types: U.S. and U.K.

A major barrier to international competition was that, throughout most of the nineteenth century, British and U.S. yachts were utterly dissimilar — Old World yachts being narrow and deep and New World yachts being wide and shallow. So strongly were the beamy hull and huge centerboard identified with the American character that when the Boston yacht designer Edward Burgess produced relatively narrow, deep "compromise" America's Cup defenders in the 'eighties, he was accused of being unpatriotic.

One common explanation for this divergence is that, before systematic dredging was undertaken, American yachting harbors were more shallow than English sailing areas. But this seems not to have been universally true. In the middle of the Solent — the channel separating the Isle of Wight from the mainland — lies a dangerously shallow shoal called the Brambles. At extreme low tides, it even dries out; the Cowes boatbuilder Uffa Fox enjoyed, in his playful way, using it as the field for an annual cricket match.

The most important reason for the varying national types of yachts is that, for purposes of taxing commercial vessels,

the two governments measured tonnage, or a boat's volume or carrying capacity, in strikingly different ways. The English used a formula that greatly discouraged wide beam, while the Americans had one that was neutral about width. To understand this difference, visualize two boats that have exactly the same internal volume but different shapes. One boat is long, narrow, and deep in the hold; the other is short, beamy, and shallow in the hold. Under the English rule, the first vessel would have the smallest *measured* volume. If the boats were commercial vessels — coastal traders, say — the first one would owe the lowest fees and customs duties. If they were racing yachts, under British rating rules, the deep and narrow hull would have the greatest handicap. Obviously, then, the British sailed thin yachts. It is a sign of English hospitality that the Royal Yacht Squadron did not use handicaps in computing the results of the 1851 race for the Hundred Guinea Cup. With her relatively wide, shallow hull, *America* had a small handicap compared with English yachts of similar size. If handicaps had been used, the winner certainly would have been a cutter named *Aurora*, which finished second by only a few minutes, although she was the smallest boat in the

The differences between the American and English schools of yacht design are shown clearly in these sets of lines of two boats built in 1851, the eighty-foot American centerboard sloop Sylvie, *left, and the sixty-nine foot six-inch English keel cutter* Volante, *right.* Sylvie *and* America, *both designed by George Steers, were alike in general design philosophy, but not in some particulars (*America, *for example, did not carry a centerboard). The upper drawings show buttocks, which are vertical sections taken fore and aft looking at the hull from the side; the lower drawings show waterlines, which are horizontal sections of the underbody (hull under the water) from a bird's eye view; and the small drawings show half-sections, which are taken vertically across the hull (looking from the stern on the left half and from the bow on the right half).*

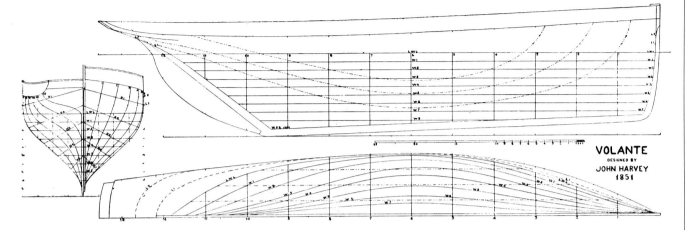

VOLANTE
DESIGNED BY
JOHN HARVEY
1851

With her shallow draft of six feet nine inches, the centerboarder Sylvie *needs a wide beam of twenty-four feet six inches to provide the stability needed to stand up to a breeze of wind. On the other hand,* Volante, *with a draft of ten feet, carries her ballast low and thus does not need wide beam for stability. Her beam is only fifteen feet.* Sylvie's *waterlines, like* America's, *are hollow forward and wide aft, while* Volante's *waterlines are straight forward. In profile, the two boats seem to be turned end-for-end: the American yacht has a plumb (vertical) rudder post and a long clipper bow, while on the English yacht the stern is raked forward sharply and the bow is plumb. In Chapter VII, we will see how these two philosophies later evolved.*

fleet and was measured at forty-seven tons to *America*'s one hundred seventy tons.

The term "cutter" was used to describe the classic single-masted English racing yacht. It referred not to the characteristics of the rig (as it does today) but rather to the shape of the hull, which was very narrow and, so she would stay upright, had a deep, heavy keel. Wide boats, on the other hand, are often sufficiently stable without a deep keel. However, they do require some lateral resistance under the water to keep them from making leeway. For this purpose, the Dutch had used two hinged boards called leeboards on their wide, shallow *Jaght Schips.* (The descendents of these boards are seen on inland lakes scows.) Several improvements were made over the centuries, culminating in "a lee board through the bottom," patented in 1811 by the brothers Jacocks, Henry, and Joshua Swain, of Cape May, New Jersey. A single largish plank was raised and lowered through a slit in the boat's bottom by a tackle. This plank was the ancestor of the centerboard. Eventually, "sloop" came to refer to the typical American single-masted centerboarder, in contrast to the English cutter.

As growing fortunes and higher ambitions encouraged the construction of ever-larger yachts, yachtbuilders adapted the two-masted, fore-and-aft schooner rig because its many sails, being smaller, were more manageable, square foot for square foot, than the few large sails carried by a sloop or cutter. A famous account of the origin of the word "schooner" has it that when the first vessel with this rig was launched at Gloucester, Massachusetts, in 1713, an observer, awed by the speed with which she slid off the stocks, shouted, "Oh, how she scoons!" — "scoons" meaning "skim over the water." Hearing this, the builder, Andrew Robinson, declared, "A scooner let her be!" It is an appealing story, but it seems to be pure invention. Several seventeenth century English and Dutch drawings show schooner rigs, and anyway, the word "scoon" appears nowhere else in the English language. The rig in its many forms did undergo its most intense development in the United States, however, and by the 1870s huge centerboard schooners made up the backbone of the New York Yacht Club's racing fleet. In England, big keel schooners were racing against cutters. As we will see in the next chapter, the design and construction of powerful centerboarders was taken dangerously far in American yacht design.

of summer races for its ever-expanding membership.

Like the Royal Yacht Squadron, the early New York Yacht Club was interested in ensigns. After a two-year campaign, in 1848 John Cox Stevens persuaded Congress to pass a law permitting yachts to enter U.S. ports without having to clear customs. To identify them, somebody connected to the yacht club designed the national yacht ensign — the U.S. flag with a fouled anchor inside a circle of stars in the upper left hand corner. It is still in use.

From time to time, English yachtsmen sailed across to race against Americans, or issued invitations for the Americans to come to Britain. In 1835, the English schooner *Gem* appeared in New York, where her owner, the Marquis of Waterford, challenged all comers to a race. Waterford was an excellent representative of the Royal Yacht Squadron: he was the one who practiced for the hunt by shooting out the eyes of the portraits of his ancestors. No race took place; but Waterford and the New York yachtsmen engaged in competition of a different sort at a formal dinner, which became so wild that the police had to break it up. Two years later, another Squadron member, Joseph Weld, bet the world at large that his cutter *Alarm* would beat any comer in a two-out-of-three match. Once again, there was no race. English and American yachtsmen finally knocked heads in 1849, when the U.S. yacht *Brenda* beat the English yacht *Pearl* by only fifty-five seconds in a race off Bermuda.

By 1850, New York had taken over from Boston as the country's financial capital. It was a booming period in which American traders seemed capable of accomplishing anything. New York clipper ships dominated the tea trade between China and Britain; American inventors had produced the telegraph, the safety pin, the rotary printing press; American railroad mileage (over Robert Stevens' tracks) was increasing by thousands of miles annually. Soon, American manufactured goods would be worth more than agricultural products — an idea as startling in 1850 as its contrary would be today.

The fortunes of John Cox Stevens expanded, and in 1848 he built himself a fantastic Greek Revival townhouse. Reported Philip Hone in his diary:

The house is, indeed, a palace. The Palace Bourbon in Paris, Buckingham Palace in London, and Sans-Souci at Berlin are little grander than this residence of a simple citizen of our republican city, a steamboat builder and proprietor; but a mighty good fellow and most hospitable host, as all who know him will testify.

In the "but" after the semi-colon, Hone, an old-line New York aristocrat, reveals some suspicions about his commercial friend's respectibility. If Stevens himself had any misgivings, he expressed them indirectly through his actions, the most extraordinary of which was about to occur.

3: The *America* Adventure

Some time in 1850, Stevens decided to build another object to challenge the Old World: a yacht to take to England to show off American shipbuilding at the time of Prince Albert's Great Exhibition of 1851. Well able to afford the adventure on his own, Stevens the clubman gathered a small syndicate of five. One was his brother Edwin, who would be the yacht club's third commodore and would found the Stevens Institute of Technology, where a century or so later yacht designers would use a sophisticated model towing tank to refine the shapes of America's Cup defenders. Two syndicate members were related to Alexander Hamilton, the founding father who did the most for American businessmen. One of these men was Hamilton's third son, James; the other was George Schuyler, James' son-in-law and the descendant of a famous Revolutionary War general.

America, as the yacht was inevitably named, was designed by George Steers along the lines of contemporary New York pilot boats. Manhattan shipbuilder William H. Brown charged $30,000 — a fantastically high price — to build her; but he promised to take her back if she was beaten during sailing trials. After her hasty launch in June of 1851, she and *Maria* sailed about evenly. This spoke well of *America;* built and rigged for an ocean crossing, she was no fragile out-and-outer. Nevertheless, Stevens claimed in long letters to the newspapers that *Maria* had once again suffered from poor handling and damage, and was clearly the faster boat. Put on the defensive by Stevens' canny use of publicity, Brown settled for $20,000. The yacht sailed east under the command of Cap-

On Friday August 22d 1851 at the Great Race for the Royal Yacht Squadron CUP at Cowes.— QUEEN VICTORIA seeing her Cousin JONATHAN VICTORIOUS, took a fancy to him and is now planning schemes how to get rid of that old Grumbler John Bull, to elope with her Cousin in his YACHT AMERICA and settle in the New Country under the Firm: "United States of Britannia & America."

America's unexpected victory let loose a torrent of patriotism typified by this cartoon showing a disappointed Queen Victoria, with Prince Albert at her side, handing over the Hundred Guinea Cup to a nose-thumbing American while the losing John Bull makes empty threats. This sort of chauvinism led one New Yorker to complain of "intolerable vainglorious vaporings that make every newspaper I take up now ridiculous. One would think that yacht-building were the end of man's existence on earth."

tain Dick Brown, an ace pilot-boat skipper, as her syndicate followed on passenger ships. She made Le Havre at a highly respectable average speed of 6.6 knots, was spruced up, and, with Stevens now on board, headed to Cowes.

By that time, *America*'s voyage had evolved far beyond a private cruise to England. "The eyes of the world are on you," Horace Greeley, the editor of the New York *Tribune* warned James Hamilton in Paris. "You will be beaten, and the country will be abused." Soon enough, the world realized that this stunning Yankee vessel might *not* be beaten. As she sailed into Cowes on the morning of July 30, she handily beat a crack racing cutter, which, however, was towing a dinghy. While the commodore of the Royal Yacht Squadron, the Earl of Wilton, had invited Stevens to use its facilities, the American was disappointed that he was not asked to race against its fleet. Even the nearby Royal Victoria Yacht Club shut him out; while they would have been pleased to let her join in if she were owned by an individual gentleman, *America*'s syndicate, its officers said, was too businesslike. Stevens tried to stir up some action with a grandiose wager: £ 10,000 — a sum equivalent to as much as $500,000 in today's currency — to the winner of a twenty-to seventy- mile race. His hosts did not budge. The London *Times* compared them to a flock of pigeons paralyzed by fear at the sight of a hawk. Where was their "pith and courage," their dedication to "our national naval spirit"?

These comments touched a tender nerve in the Squadron, with its pride in its naval connections, and Stevens was invited to participate in a race around the Isle of Wight for an "ordinary" ewer, which was called the Hundred Guinea Cup because that is what it cost. Although there was no cash prize, the English accommodated Stevens in every other way: the race would be sailed without handicap; some club rules that worked against *America* were waived; a local shipbuilder, George Ratsey, built a jib boom for her; and a local pilot was hired.

The race was started from anchor at 10 a.m. on Friday, August 22. *America*'s crew was among the slowest to get underway on the first leg, which, being a run before a light breeze, was thought to be the visiting boat's weakness. In the next hour and a half, she weaved her way between her fourteen competitors and the many spectator boats. Half-way around the Isle of Wight, *America* had a lead of more than two miles. Myth has it that Queen Victoria, watching from the royal yacht *Victoria and Albert,* asked who was in second place. "Madam," she was told, "there is no second." Finishing at 8:30 p.m. in a dying breeze, *America* was somewhere between eight and twenty-four minutes ahead of the little *Aurora* (the records vary).

Why did she win? Like all champions, she was a little lucky. Due to some confusion over the race instructions, a few of her competitors sailed a couple more miles than she did to round the Nab Lightship, which she quite legally cut. In addition, three English yachts dropped out of the race due to damage, grounding, or going to the aid of another boat. But *America* lost fifteen minutes when the new jib boom broke. Simply stated, she won because she was *fast.* Later an Englishman told an American:

That boat of yours is a wonderful creature — she beats us large [running] or to windward, and when the wind died out the other day, she actually out-drifted *us.*

America was in several ways a technological breakthrough. Her flat cotton sails were more efficient than the baggy flax sails of the British yachts, and her rig was more easily managed than theirs. Most important, as we explore in detail in Chapter Seven, she had a hull shape that, though it was not innovative (some English yachts had similar lines), was both highly unusual and ruthlessly fast. When her hosts saw her sharp bow and wide stern, which turned English boats end-for-end, they did not know what to think. The ancient Marquis of Anglesey, who had greeted her arrival with the comment, "If she is right, then all of us are wrong," leaned over the visiting yacht's after bulwark to try to spy the propeller that he was certain was under her stern. Only a quick tackle by John Cox Stevens saved him from a closer, wetter view.

On August 28, *America* sailed her second and last race under the Stevens syndicate's ownership, beating a local yacht in a gale of wind to win $500. Four days later, only a month after her arrival in Cowes, Stevens & Co. unsentimentally sold her to an Irish peer for $25,000. They then returned home to the cheers of their countrymen, having made a small profit on the expedition, all expenses paid. Would that all vacations were so rewarding.

IV

Tales of the Gilded Age

*"Men living in democratic times have
many passions, but most of these
culminate in love of wealth or derive
from it."*

achting after the Civil War in the United States took on a very different form from the pastime of John Cox Stevens. It was grander, more flamboyant, sometimes even outrageous in style and ambition. This was in keeping with the post-war period itself. Borrowing the title of a cynical novel by Mark Twain and Charles Dudley Warner, historians apply the term "The Gilded Age" to the years from 1865 to about 1900; unlike the "Golden Ages" of ancient Greece and the Renaissance, this one seemed superficial and glittery, committed more to style than substance, and especially to the style that only money could buy.

"This vigorous, turbulent realm, devoted to moneymaking by any means," as a character in Gore Vidal's novel *1876* says about the United States in its centennial year, had become a great sea of greed and, for those who were not drowned by it, of astonishing wealth. Neither income taxes nor government regulation cramped the freewheeling, and sometimes freebooting, styles of entrepreneurs feeding at the seemingly bottomless trough of America's natural resources. Statistics tell an extraordinary story of economic expansion. Between 1869 and the turn of the century, the country's population doubled, her gross national product almost tripled, and her industrial output and urban population both more than quadrupled (while farm output and rural population each merely doubled). Meanwhile, United States exports almost quintupled, railway mileage *more* than quintupled, and bank assets grew almost seven-fold.

While beneficial to some people in a material way, these tumultuous changes deeply confused others whose values had recently been disoriented by the shattering of ancient religious and philosophical certainties in the light of the discoveries of Charles Darwin. "The essential unity of ecclesiastical and secular cultural institutions was lost during the nineteenth century, to the point of senseless hostility," Albert Einstein once observed. The historian Robert H. Wiebe has described the late nineteenth-century United States as "a society without a core." Henry Adams, in his novel, *Esther,* published in 1884, called it "the rebellious age." Like the 1660s in England, it was a period of immense centrifugal energy, where the old stable institutions were being torn down and new ones were being heaved up on shaky foundations, and the gaping

cracks in the social structure that resulted were covered by a fragile patina of stylishness and sentimentality. In its instability and raw energy, the Gilded Age was fertile ground for towering social ambitions. Encompassing the greatest spurt of luxurious living since the Medici took over Rome, it was a time in America dominated by some of modern history's wealthiest and most powerful men, whose baubles included many of the most breathtakingly showy houses and (our special interest) yachts ever created. These things not only satisfied the whims of their owners, they also helped define a new and strikingly American way of life that, at first limited to the wealthier classes, half a century or more later became the standard of the rising middle class as well. "Men living in democratic times have many passions," wrote Alexis de Tocqueville in *Democracy in America,* in 1835, "but most of these culminate in love of wealth or derive from it." The great democratic royalty of bankers, steel-mill owners, stock brokers, and railroad barons found a way to advertise their success by appropriating symbols like the yacht for their own use.

1: Vanderbilt Success, Vanderbilt Misery

Spanning this period was the Vanderbilt family, whose yachting tone was set before the Civil War. In 1853, craggy Cornelius "Commodore" Vanderbilt, the roots of whose immense transportation fortune lay, as with the Stevenses, in New York ferryboats, took his two-hundred-seventy-foot paddlewheeler, *North Star,* on a breakneck four-month, twelve-thousand mile cruise to Europe and return, moving so fast that, improbable as it sounds, she was able to take in both St. Petersburg and Constantinople. The voyage was a mixed success. Like George Crowninshield, Vanderbilt tried and failed to attract the attention of English royalty. Nonetheless, he was probably satisfied with the praise of hundreds of commoners who came aboard and, like Crowninshield's guests, were amazed that a self-made American could have such grand tastes. Or so we are led to believe by the Reverend John Overton Choules's sycophantic book, *The Cruise of the Steam Yacht North Star.* The only catastrophe during the trip was the loss of a quartermaster, who fell overboard while *North Star* was sprinting around the French coast to get to the Mediterranean from Russia.

Once home, Vanderbilt promptly put *North Star* into service carrying California-bound passengers to Nicaragua, where Vanderbilt carriages would transport them across the isthmus to waiting Vanderbilt steamers, which would carry them to San Francisco.

Although the impatient old man never went on another pleasure voyage, he left his heirs enough money so that they could. And they did. The best known of them were his great-grandsons. One, William K. Vanderbilt Jr., loved engines, and the other, Harold S. Vanderbilt, loved sails. The first built "commuter boats," long arrows packed to the rails with horsepower, vehicles in which rich men from the 1880s to the 1930s roared up and down Long Island Sound to and from the New York Yacht Club's station on the East River. He once outfitted his commuter *Tarantula* with nine propellers, and she kicked up such a wake that William K. was sued for damages by people with property on the river. Later, after some time ashore to race sports cars on Long Island, where he built a long track, he installed two thousand-horsepower diesel engines in a converted English warship and cruised around the world with his wife on an oceanographic expedition, about which he wrote two rather dull books.

His younger brother, Harold, was the more remarkable of the two. Fresh out of Harvard, he won a Bermuda Race in his seventy-six foot schooner. He later donated a subchaser to the U.S. Navy and commanded it in World War I, invented contract bridge, became a superb tennis player, laid the foundation for the yacht-racing rules the whole world observes today, and defended the America's Cup three times — the last time in the one hundred thirty-seven foot J-Class cutter *Ranger,* whose design and construction he assiduously and knowledgeably supervised, and whose $600,000 cost he covered entirely out of his own pocket. His two memoirs about the America's Cup, *Enterprise* and *On the Wind's Highway,* are among the finest books on yacht racing ever written.

Finally, we consider a Vanderbilt of the Gilded Age. Harold and William Jr.'s talent and energy originated somewhere, but not with their father, Commodore Vanderbilt's grandson, William Sr. This Vanderbilt built a mammoth steamer, *Alva,* named for his wife. But the flesh and blood Alva ran off with Vanderbilt's yachting friend August Belmont, and when the yacht ran aground and sank off Martha's Vineyard, her owner left her there. Little that

he did gave him joy. All his money, he once said, only left him "with nothing to hope for, with nothing definite to seek or strive for." Inherited wealth, he declared, was "as certain death to ambition as cocaine is to morality." On any list of the saddest people in American history, he must place near the head.

2: The Rise of James Gordon Bennett

The prince of yachting's royalty in the Gilded Age was James Gordon Bennett Jr., the son of a crude Scottish immigrant who had made a fortune from his sensationalistic newspaper, the New York *Herald.* He was wealthy, ambitious, eccentric, adventurous, self-indulgent, and usually at loose ends — in short, he had all the characteristics of the classic yachtsman.

"Jamie" Bennett first appeared on the yachting scene in 1857, the year the New York Yacht Club was given the America's Cup by John Cox Stevens' syndicate. At the improbable age of only sixteen, he showed up on the Club's annual cruise in titular command of some twenty-two crew on his seventy-two foot centerboard sloop *Rebecca.* Consisting of a series of day races between New England harbors, this event was and ever has been a "cruise" in name only. In those days, it was quite informal. A dozen or so members would rendezvous with their yachts at some harbor near New York, agree on a course, and hop-scotch east for a week or so, improvising an itinerary as they went along until they got tired or had to get back to their businesses. Sometimes there was a glamorous ball in Newport. Although *Rebecca* did not win any races in the 1857 cruise, the precocious youngster must have exhibited the requisite fierce competitiveness and hard-drinking amiability, for the club's officers (ignoring his controversial father's lack of social standing) elected him a member of the club on August 12 during a special meeting aboard Commodore William Edgar's flagship *Widgeon,* anchored in New Bedford harbor.

Bennett quickly lived up to the promise he had shown on his first cruise. The next year, he entered *Rebecca* against seven boats in a race that was started off Staten Island in New York Harbor and proceeded counterclockwise around Long Island to be finished off Throgs Neck: an "ocean race" it was called by those pioneers, who did almost all their sailing in sheltered water. *Rebecca* won by five hours but was successfully protested by a competitor for saving some distance by sailing through Plum Gut, a channel at the eastern end of Long Island Sound, rather than proceeding as prescribed through another channel, the Race. "This annoyed Bennett," Jack Parkinson reports with typical understatement in his *History of the New York Yacht Club,* "and some nasty accusations appeared in the press between the two skippers concerning the use of sweeps during the calm hours of darkness."

In those days, "fair play" was a relative value, in yachting as in business. To quote W.P. Stephens, the best yachting writer at the turn of the century, "The general conditions and ethics of yachting were in a nebulous condition." Cheating — with oars, short cuts, rough and tumble tactics, whatever — was so prevalent that race sponsors normally appointed an umpire to supervise the contest and judges to hear any protests. Privacy, too, was relative. The disputes that accompanied the gentry's competitions were good copy for an aggressive press whose interest in yachting and riding was akin to that of a gossip columnist covering a celebrity ball. The New York newspapers sent out a hoard of social and technical writers to cover races, launchings, and club meetings. From time to time, they were rewarded with juicy gossip or even a scandal. In 1859, it was discovered that a New York Yacht Club member, William C. Corrie, had illegally smuggled slaves into the United States from Africa with the club burgee flying from his big schooner *Wanderer.* Corrie had evaded a British blockade after distracting its officers with good food and drink and an informal race, which *Wanderer* won. The resolution heaving Corrie out of the club accused him of "being engaged in a traffic repugnant to humanity and to the moral sense of this Association."

Ever enthralled by yachting, Bennett entered more races, and had some success (meaning he won some bets). In August of 1860, for stakes of $250, he lost a match race whose conditions even then were curious. *Rebecca* and James M. Waterbury's *Julia* started not from anchor, as was usual, but under tow behind a steamboat powering into the wind. At a signal, both towlines were dropped and the boats headed off on separate tacks. Four minutes later, the race officially began. The course consisted entirely of a twenty-mile leg dead to windward to the anchored race committee boat.

Soon after Fort Sumter was fired upon, Bennett, now all of

On page 68, a Frederic S. Cozzens painting shows the start under spinnakers of the third and last race in the 1881 America's Cup match between the successful defender Mischief, *foreground, and the Canadian challenger* Atalanta. *The spinnaker in those days was little more than a big jib wung out on a pole; a light jib called a ballooner was carried to leeward. Not until the 1930s were the two sails combined in one called the parachute spinnaker. At the left is James Gordon Bennett Jr., showing "the tired but seductive ennui of a person who has seen too much of the seamier side of life too soon, but is willing to give it one more try." Right, in this Currier & Ives lithograph, a race is started in 1869 off the New York Yacht Club clubhouse on Staten Island. In those days, the boats started from mooring or anchor. From left to right, the first, second, and fifth yachts are the 1866 trans-Atlantic Race veterans* Vesta, Henrietta, *and* Fleetwing.

twenty, appeared with a competitive new schooner, *Henrietta.* She had been designed by Henry Steers, whose uncle George Steers had designed *America,* and who himself, as a teenager, had been a crew member on that great schooner when she beat England's best in Cowes a decade earlier. Despite the club's abhorrence of slave-trading, the Civil War had little effect on the New

THE NEW YORK YACHT CLUB REGATTA.

THE START FROM THE STAKE BOAT IN THE NARROWS,

OFF THE NEW CLUB HOUSE AND GROUNDS, STATEN ISLAND, NEW YORK HARBOR.

York yachting scene; of the fifty-two schooners and sloops in the yacht club's squadron, only *Henrietta* and another vessel enlisted in the Union Navy. Bennett, ever ready for a new experience, prevailed upon his father to find him a naval commission and commanded his new boat on patrol duty for a year or so, after which his superiors tired of his habitual insubordination and sent the young swell and his schooner back to New York, where racing continued on a slightly reduced schedule.

3: The Great Ocean Race

Bennett indelibly made his yachting reputation after the war ended, when he was the only owner to sail in one of the strangest and most tragic events in the history of yachting, the race in December of 1866 from New York to the Isle of Wight, England, for stakes of $60,000.

A contest of such sheer craziness had been approaching for years as the wheeler-dealer tycoons of the New York Yacht Club built ever-bigger schooners to race ever-longer distances up and down the Atlantic coast for ever-grander wagers. The expenses and tragedies of the Civil War interrupted their sport for a few years, but things were back to normal in 1866. That summer, there was a long series of wild, tight, high-stakes match races, the last of which was sailed in a gale on October 9 from New York to Cape May, New Jersey, and return between two one hundred eight-footers, Bennett's *Henrietta* and Pierre Lorillard's new centerboarder *Vesta*. Both boats suffered damage, *Vesta*'s so heavy that she was forced to heave-to for repairs for an hour, which turned out to be *Henrietta*'s winning margin.

However exciting, though inconclusive, those matches were, the 1866 New York racing season was upstaged by news of two transAtlantic voyages by yachts. One was a twenty-six foot lifeboat with the patriotic name *Red, White, and Blue*, which had two men and a dog in crew. The other was a sixty-six foot Massachusetts-based sloop called *Alice*, which made a fast nineteen-day cruise across the Atlantic under the command of Captain Arthur H. Clark, who forty years later would write a distinguished history of early yachting. *Alice*'s crew included Charles A. Longfellow, the son of the poet Henry Wadsworth Longfellow, who, you may recall, had a

special connection with George Crowninshield. There was even a singlehanded attempt in those years; in 1864, Captain John C. Donovan and his dog disappeared after heading east from Boston in a tiny, sixteen-foot brigantine. Obviously, people were beginning to set their sights beyond the breakwater. Perhaps they were inspired by the exploits of the English cruising canoeist John MacGregor, who had spent the summers of 1865 and 1866 cruising in canoes on lakes, rivers, and bays in northern Europe and would soon write his enormously popular book, *The Voyage Alone in the Yawl Rob Roy*.

There was public pressure, too, for sailing out of sight of land. *America* had done it with glory, and there were enough examples of boats that had survived long sea passages to give credibility to such feats. In 1860, Bennett's *Herald* nagged "our smooth water gentry" to "trip anchors and start out on a cruise on blue water." The editorial continued colorfully:

Get off your soundings, trust your sea legs for a while, reciprocate the visits of your English cousins, visit your own coast, go to South America, try Europe, call on the Sultan; or, if you have got the pluck, circumnavigate the world, then come home and write a book. It will perpetuate your memory, reflect lustre on your deeds, and redound to the honor of your country.

So, after a summer in which two yachts had cruised transAtlantic, New York's young sporting bloods had a lot to talk about when they gathered around a bottle in the Union Club on October 26. Before long, Pierre Lorillard of *Vesta* and Franklin Osgood, owner of the fast new one-hundred-six-foot keel schooner *Fleetwing*, were engaged in a half-bragging, half-joking dispute about the relative merits of their vessels that, like most arguments about the boats of the day, focused on the seaworthiness of centerboards. Osgood allowed that Lorillard's wide, shallow *Vesta* might be fast in sheltered water — but could she beat the deep, narrow *Fleetwing* in the open sea? Could *Vesta*, in fact, *survive* the open sea?

The conversation inevitably reached the put-up or shut-up stage. No doubt challenged by *Alice*'s feat, Lorillard and Osgood searched hard and finally found an excuse to sail across the Atlantic: Emperor Napoleon III of France had scheduled a regatta to coincide with the 1867 Paris World's Fair. When the evening finally staggered to its end, each side had agreed on a trans-Atlantic match race to start at New York and finish at the Needles, the stalky chalk rocks on the west tip of the Isle of Wight. With time and lubrication, the stakes slipped up to $30,000 a side, much more than the cost of one of their yachts. They would start seven weeks later on December 11 — December, after all, was a good month for wind. A day or two later, young Jamie Bennett heard about the race, which was right up his alley, and asked and was allowed to join. The stakes rose to $60,000.

The race fascinated all who heard of it, both because the purse was so large and because the intentions of the men involved were unclear. The issue was not whether they could cover their losses; Lorillard dominated the tobacco business; Osgood's father-in-law was Cornelius Vanderbilt; and Bennett's father owned the successful New York *Herald*. What the world was most curious to learn was whether these tycoons would risk their necks as well as their cash out on the ocean. Bennett announced that he definitely would sail on board *Henrietta;* but as autumn chilled to winter the two originators of the project decided, not unreasonably, that racing across the north Atlantic in December was not good for one's health. Lorillard's opting out attracted widespread criticism that he was interested only in free advertising for his snuff; one paper only half-jokingly worried that "the *Vesta* will perhaps carry sails emblazoned with the words *Lorillard Tobacco.*" Probably sensitive about the way that *America* had been unloaded at a profit after only two races, a few people suggested that it would be ungentlemanly if, as was rumored, the owners planned to sell their yachts in Cowes (the excuse of the French regatta having quickly faded from memory).

In sum, the whole thing seemed too outsized and commercial for a gentleman's sport. Commodore William H. McVickar initially refused to have the name of the New York Yacht Club sullied with what promised to be a tasteless combination of overheated stakes and big commerce. However, at a special meeting of the club called to discuss the matter, a member named Leonard Jerome gave a long, funny, and highly convincing speech that brought McVickar and the doubters around. "The question involving the right of gentlemen to bet on the race or to dispose of their boats was mooted,"

noted the minutes, which were of course given a full column in the New York *Herald.*

Of all the characters involved in this outlandish event, Leonard Jerome is in many ways the most appealing. A forty-nine-year-old stock market speculator who had made and lost a couple of fortunes, he was also a part-owner of the New York *Times,* a former American consul to Trieste, Italy, and a well-known man-about-town and sportsman who had recently co-founded the American Jockey Club and built a race track, Jerome Park, in the Bronx. Besides winning the yacht club's endorsement for the race, he succeeded in convincing the doubting Commodore McVickar to serve as the race's official judge. The competitors showed their gratitude and trust in Jerome by naming him the stakes holder, and he convincingly demonstrated his faith in their risky enterprise by sailing in *Henrietta* as a guest of Bennett. Jerome's interest may have been tickled by the fact that he controlled the Atlantic Telegraph Company, whose just-laid trans-Atlantic cable promised to receive excellent publicity by delivering the race results to New York instantly after the finish.

To command their vessels, the owners hired the best captains they could find. Dick Brown, *America*'s skipper when she won the Hundred Guinea Cup, signed aboard *Fleetwing* but proudly quit three days before the start because, for some reason, he was listed below Albert Thomas, the navigator, on the vessel's clearance papers; Thomas took over the command in fact as well as name. On *Vesta,* there was George Dayton, an experienced, cautious squarerigger captain and father of seventeen; and there was twenty-year-old George Lorillard, sent along by his brother to keep an eye on Dayton. The real coup was Bennett's. For a fee of $7500 he brought on the great Samuel Samuels, holder of the trans-Atlantic record under sail in the clipper *Dreadnought.* Dapper and calm on first acquaintance, Samuels had in thirty years at sea honestly earned the nickname, "Bully," and was guaranteed to drive his men, his yacht, and himself to their limits. Each skipper signed up a crew of twenty-two — no easy recruiting task because of the combination of December and competition, either one of which alone might have been tolerable to a professional seaman but both of which together made even strong men think of a warm fire and a family Christmas. Samuels, in fact, may have lived up to his nick-

Sketched by CHARLES PARSONS.   FLEETWING, 212 TONS.   Entered according to Act of Congress, ⦿ 1867 by Currier & Ives, in the Clerks Office of the District Court of the United States for the Southern District of N.Y.   HENRIETTA, 205 TONS.   From the Yacht Club Steamer "RIVER QUEEN."
VESTA, 201 TONS.

THE GREAT OCEAN YACHT RACE.
BETWEEN THE HENRIETTA, FLEETWING & VESTA,
THE "GOOD BYE" TO THE YACHT CLUB STEAMER "RIVER QUEEN." 4 MILES EAST OF SANDY HOOK. LIGHT SHIP DEC.R 11TH 1866.

The HENRIETTA arrived off the Needles, Isle of Wight, England, at 5 45, P.M. Dec.R 25th 1866; winning the Race, and making the run in 13 days 22 hours, mean time.
The FLEETWING arrived 8 hours afterwards, and the VESTA 1½ hours after the Fleetwing.

NEW YORK, PUBLISHED BY CURRIER & IVES, 152 NASSAU STREET.

name too soon, for *Henrietta's* crew walked off the job a few days before the start of the race and, according to one newspaper, "their places had to be supplied by a lot of landlubbers, few of whom could climb a mast." On all three yachts the long tillers were replaced with more manageable worm-gear steering wheels. Samuels and Dayton strengthened the hulls and slightly cut down the towering rigs on *Henrietta* and *Vesta,* and, anticipating heavy seas, built heavy shelters over the cockpits; but, perhaps due to the confusion over her command, *Fleetwing* got little special attention.

Along with the professional seamen sailed the owner or his representative, a few guests, and an observer from each of the other competitors to control cheating. Besides Jerome and Charles Longfellow (making his second trans-Atlantic passage of the year), *Henrietta* took along a reporter from the *Herald,* Stephen Fisk, who was smuggled aboard at the last moment to avoid being served a subpoena to appear at a trial in Manhattan. In his memoirs, Fisk quoted the gruff instructions given him by his crusty boss, old James Gordon Bennett:

This race. Yachts. One of 'em me son's. Cover it. Fall in the sea for all I care but get the news. Properly. Understood?

Since wild twenty-six-year-old Jamie Bennett was little help around the office, perhaps the old man hoped that both men would fall in the sea together, so long as it would make good headlines.

What with the long build-up and an estimated $1 million in bets circulating among the bookies, the start was crowded with spectator boats. One vessel was said to be carrying an English detective searching out an exiled Irish revolutionary named James Stephens who, he believed, was about to be smuggled home in one of the yachts. Even if this were true, nothing could have been done about it in all the confusion. The three yachts slipped their tows, set sail, and finally started to a hail of cannon fire and cheers at 1 p.m., December 11, 1866, rapidly broad-reaching away on the strong westerly that would hold for almost the entire race.

The breeze gradually built to a grim, cold, snowy gale that shook the boats so badly that Leonard Jerome was heaved out of his bunk onto the hot cabin stove. Fortunately, he also knocked over a nearby bucket of water and his wet blanket protected him from burns.

Not at all fazed by this near-miss or by his surroundings ("mournful and depressing," according to Fisk), Jerome entertained himself by sipping champagne while he filled Fisk in on his relations with his mistress and his wife. A hard-bitten police and war correspondent who thought he had seen everything, Fisk was somewhat taken aback by Jerome's frankness. "These seemed curiously intimate revelations to make in the cabin of a tiny yacht tossed about by a brewing gale in the middle of the Atlantic," he recalled in his autobiography.

After a week of hard but controlled two-hundred-plus-mile-days, the yachts were out of sight of each other but running bow to bow when the southwest gale boiled over on December 18. Wave after wave swept *Henrietta,* running at nine knots under forestaysail and double-reefed foresail. She took so much water below through her deadlights that Samuels had the ship's carpenter drill holes in the cabin sole to drain the wash into the bilge. Early that night, a huge breaker dropped on her, stove in a boat, and squeezed so much ocean through her deck seams and ports that the already nervous carpenter went berserk and began babbling that the yacht was breaking up. The icily calm Bennett and Samuels kept panic from spreading among their inexperienced crew. But Samuels, worried that "the little plaything" (as he called the two-hundred-ton schooner) might break up, had the storm trysails brought up from the cabin and bent on, and he hove her to. For thirteen hours she lay "lazily and pleasantly," according to Fisk, until the sea eased. Anything but a bully as he nursed his ship through the storm, Samuels then turned east and commenced living up to his reputation. By nine on the morning of the nineteenth she was scudding along under her huge squaresail.

The brunt of the storm was borne, tragically, by *Fleetwing.* At about nine on the night of the eighteenth, just after the change of watch, a wave knocked her over until her upper shrouds lay in the sea and water covered her main companionway. The two helmsmen and six men huddling in the exposed cockpit were knocked overboard so violently that the helmsmen's tight grips took some wheel spokes with them. Two men saved themselves by grabbing some rigging, but the other six were lost for good. Down below, the sailing master and mate crawled along the side of the knocked-down hull, forward to and up through a small companionway.

They made their way aft, where they were greeted by the grim sight of the empty cockpit and the mangled steering wheel. The survivors hove-to for five hours and searched fruitlessly for their lost shipmates. Finally giving up, they set as much sail as the dying storm would allow them to carry and gloomily resumed racing on a track to the south of their competitors. Not until 1977, one hundred and eleven years later, when a French sloop with seven men aboard would disappear off Marseilles, would so many sailors be lost in a yacht race.

Vesta endured the gale by scudding northeast before it, possibly because Captain Dayton felt that the centerboarder lacked sufficient stability to heave-to safely. During the night she unknowingly crossed *Henrietta*'s wake and soon passed her — a success that, had it been known, might have eased tensions in *Vesta*'s afterguard. George Lorillard had been loudly critical of Dayton's seamanship almost since the start; when not berating him for having too much sail set in the gale, he was hounding him to shake out reefs. On the twentieth, Lorillard ordered the gray-bearded seaman to his cabin, where, as the boy recounted in his journal, "I told him that it was desirous that he should take my advice occasionally about making sail and make his officers hurry the men, as it was much to his benefit." Dayton's passionate response to this no doubt patronizingly offered advice was that as far as he was concerned, the schooner could go to Hell after reaching Cowes. Lorillard might have been less critical had he known that, despite Dayton's caution, *Vesta* was lengthening her slim lead by making two hundred seventy-seven miles while her competitors each logged two hundred sixty.

By now, *Vesta*'s real problem, whether her captain knew it or not, lay not with how hard she was being driven or how fast she was sailing, but with her position. Because she alone had run off before the gale, she was by far the most northerly of the three schooners, about thirty miles above the latitude of the Bishop Rock, the turning mark toward the Channel that lies in the Isles of Scilly. In the westerly that was blowing, she could continue reaching right to the Bishop, so Dayton chose the simple strategy of aiming at the rock and letting *Vesta* fly, which she certainly did. But on *Henrietta*, which came out of the storm about twenty miles south of *Vesta* and ten miles above the Bishop's latitude, savvy Bully Samuels

had different plans. A human pilot book who knew this route blindfolded, Samuels predicted that, as he neared the Scilly Isles, the wind would back into the southeast. He knew that sailing the rhumb-line to the rock would be dangerous; when the wind shifted, he would have to beat slowly to the Bishop. So he trimmed sheets and steered several degrees south of the rhumb-line course, sacrificing a little speed in order to make the southing that, when the wind backed, would later allow him to reach quickly around the Bishop. Some one hundred miles astern and even farther to the south, Captain Thomas of the tragic *Fleetwing* duplicated Samuels' strategy.

On a warm, spring-like December 24 the wind did indeed back. *Vesta*, now caught below the rhumb line, had to come on the wind and beat with painful slowness into the first head sea of the trip. Soon realizing that she could not fetch the Bishop, Dayton came about to port tack, sailed off at almost a right angle to the rhumb line, then tacked back to slog into it some more. At six fifty-five on Christmas Eve, her crew finally saw the lighthouse fine on her lee bow. Dayton, now worried about running aground, continued to squeeze the wind with flat sails. All this reduced George Lorillard to making imprecations that would have been more bitter yet had he known that, although Jamie Bennett had made his landfall on the Bishop fifty minutes after *Vesta*, thanks to Samuels' careful planning he was now flying toward the rock on a thirteen-knot reach. *Henrietta* unknowingly rushed by the pinching, pitching centerboarder in the dark and at ten turned the Bishop and roared toward the Isle of Wight. *Vesta* finally inched around at midnight. She had lost three hours to her competitor in only five hours of sailing. With *Fleetwing* last around at soon before dawn Christmas morning, after almost fourteen days and three thousand miles of sailing, the three boats were separated by less than seven hours.

None of this was known to the competitors, who had not seen each other since soon after the start. Only when a pilot scrambled aboard *Henrietta*, gawking at the cloud of sail she was carrying despite the small gale, did Bennett and Samuels learn they were first. At three forty-five on Christmas afternoon she swept by the Needles, having covered three thousand one hundred six miles (only forty miles more than the great circle distance, so good was Samuels' navigation) in a very good thirteen days, twenty-one hours, fifty-five minutes. Her best day's run was a whopping two hundred eighty miles, and her average day's run of two hundred twenty-three miles gave her a mean speed of nine and three tenths knots. Leonard Jerome promptly returned Jamie Bennett's wager and presented him with a bank draft for $60,000.

And *Vesta*? As Captain Dayton had hoped, she did go to Hell, or at least to the racing sailor's version of those infernal regions. After losing some time taking a pilot aboard in the rough seas, Lorillard learned that *Henrietta* had already come by. This news, he wrote in his journal, "completely crushed us, and with drooping heads and broken hearts we quietly slunk away into our cabin to hold sad converse over our blighted hopes." As if that weren't enough, the pilot — whom Lorillard was convinced was either a drunk or a drug addict — directed Dayton around the wrong side of the Isle of Wight, and she lost enough time while backtracking to finish twelve hours behind *Henrietta* and three behind the fast-closing *Fleetwing*.

The crews celebrated Christmas with varying degrees of promptness and joy in Cowes Roads, but problems with the trans-Atlantic cable kept New York from hearing the results until the thirtieth. Ever since the start on the eleventh, the betting line had swooped and dived depending on whose rumors were believed when. Even old Bennett was dragged into the hoopla. He had the *Herald* run off ten thousand flyers celebrating his son's daring, and spent his evenings with Pierre Lorillard and George Osgood conjecturally sailing backgammon pieces across charts of the North Atlantic and guessing how New York's weather would affect the yachts two or three days later. When the news of the result finally reached America, the response was almost identical to the jingoism that had greeted the triumph of *America* in 1851, with cries of "Young America triumphant" ringing through sermons, editorial pages, and letters to the editor for weeks. Every actual and rumored detail of the race was covered with infinite care; even the yachts' logs were published. The British newspapers, as in 1851, were belatedly taken aback by the Americans' daring. They dealt with its implied smudge on the national character with a mixture of self-criticism ("Our yachtsmen take things comfortably . . .") and damning with faint praise ("We would not for a moment entertain a thought of depreciating this extraordinary Atlantic

match and voyage, but . . .").

At a grand dinner at Cowes' Gloucester Hotel, Jamie Bennett and Samuel Samuels offered gratifyingly humble speeches and Leonard Jerome delivered himself of another witty, rambling monologue meandering toward the satisfying conclusion that the world's salvation depended upon Anglo-American unity. A few years later, Jerome acted on this ideal by marrying off his pretty daughter, Jennie, to the Duke of Marlborough. (After a slow start, their son, Winston Leonard Spencer-Churchill, would show traces of his American grandfather's public speaking skills and serenity under pressure.) Before leaving Cowes, Leonard made two financial contributions, joining the owners and other guests in a subscription for the families of the six dead sailors, and presenting Samuels with the deed for a house. That the house was worth $25,000 and the survivors' fund eventually totaled all of $5,800 suggests how priorities were ordered in those days.

Royalty played two small but significant parts in the celebration. Queen Victoria asked the Americans to sail around in the Solent off Osborne House, her vacation home near Cowes, so she could see them in action, and also formally received Commodore McVickar, expressing her sadness about the tragedy. So far had this and other unforeseen benefits changed McVickar's mind since the race's first announcement that he found it necessary to send a note to the London *Times* bragging, inaccurately it seems, that he and he alone of all the Americans in Cowes had been honored with a royal audience. The sole controversy in the wake of the race surrounded Bennett's impetuous offer of *Henrietta* to Victoria's second son, Prince Alfred, the new Duke of Edinburgh. The gift was politely refused, and with a savage concern for the minutae of court etiquette that perhaps only Americans can claim, the New York papers (other than the *Herald*) lit out after Bennett for not knowing his place.

The event's most lasting contribution was to Anglo-American good will. It had all but disappeared during the Civil War, when the British favored and almost went to the defense of the Confederacy, not so much to defend its views on slavery but to get its cotton. The three American schooners sailed home in 1867; but in 1868 and 1869, another American yacht, *Sappho*, had two good seasons of racing off Cowes, which stimulated Thomas Ashbury to make

Mr. Pottom joins a Yacht Club, and tries on the Uniform.

Having entered for the Regatta, he proceeds to join his Boat.

A little Awkward at first; but then he says that he has not got his Sea Legs on yet.

the first challenge for what was then called the Queen's Cup. In 1870, Bennett sent his new schooner *Dauntless,* commanded by Bully Samuels, to England, and she and Ashbury's *Cambria* enjoyed an exciting match race to New York, which the English yacht won. *Cambria* was soon after overwhelmed by a wave of American schooners in the race for the cup. Of the three yachts that sailed in the amazing great ocean race of 1866, only *Fleetwing* competed in the first America's Cup contest, finishing right behind the challenger in ninth place.

Apparently, the hard race stiffened Jamie Bennett's spine, and he returned to New York ready to go to work at the *Herald.* He soon took over as publisher and became one of the most imaginative circulation promoters of all time, far outdoing the feeble attempts of our contemporaries to milk readership from mindless patriotism, photographs of buxom starlets, and interviews with murderers. Bennett's specialty was the prolonged hunt, whose for-

tunes his writers and editors could follow for months or even years on end. In 1869 he sent his ace reporter Henry Stanley to Africa to find the missionary David Livingstone, and a decade later he financed a fleet to sail to the Arctic to try to reach the North Pole. Stanley succeeded, the fleet failed, the *Herald* profited, and Bennett was elected Vice-Commodore and then, at the tender age of thirty, Commodore of the New York Yacht Club. Apparently deciding that he was over the hill after the grueling December race to England in 1866, he dropped sailing and took up polo and big steam yachts.

4: When Sailors Didn't Know How to Sail

The rise of conspicuous consumption heralded a radical change in styles of masculinity. For many decades wealthy Americans had shared the English landed gentry's ideal of manly competition, but

The young fashionables who took up yachting in the 1870s were easily and frequently satirized. Here, a cartoonist dismembers the pretensions of a certain incompetent Mr. Dolphin, from the day he first tries on his yacht club uniform to the inevitable demise of his ambitions after he discovers some of the frustrations of the sport.

Dolphin's Contribution to Neptune.

The Captain Jibes the Yacht suddenly. Dolphin and Friends assume different Positions. (To jibe a boat is to let the mainsail swing from one side to the other, which it often does with great force.)

The Captain orders all hands to haul aft the Sheet. Dolphin asks if he shall haul one out of the Berth.

For the first time in his Memory, he is Forced to Decline.

Dolphin incautiously sat down directly over the Centre-Board, which just then struck a Sand-Bar, and hoisted him.

The Captain requests him to Let Go the Jib-Sheets. He indignantly replies that he ain't Touching them.

Back to Port again. Thinks he will Ride Home.

Result of Dolphin's Yacht Experience

THE YACHT FEVER.

it lost favor among the American upper classes in the last half of the nineteenth century. This may have been because the growing middle class was beginning to participate in amateur sports, among them sailboat racing, boxing, rowing, golf, tennis, baseball, and football. In order to distinguish themselves in their own social niche, the new American industrial gentry retrenched to an aloofness more reminiscent of the cool, detached eighteenth century than of the hard-fighting nineteenth. Sweat and trim quickness were no longer fashionable. Virility was now proven by bulk in both body and equipment; waistlines, carriages, race horses, and mistresses became ever more massive and heavily decorated.

And so, too, did yachting. For several years in the 1840s, the New York Yacht Club had held an annual Corinthian Regatta — "Corinthian" meaning gentleman athlete — in which the entrants were required to be steered and crewed only by amateur members, although owners could carry professional pilots. However, the race

The Steam Yachts

Some owners did not deign even to sail aboard their schooners. Like owners of race horses, they watched and placed large bets on races from the more familiar comforts of huge steam yachts that served them as luxurious floating mansions. These boats rapidly increased in number and in size, as the following breakdown of the New York Yacht Club's squadron indicates.

YEAR	MEMBER-SHIP	SQUADRON (Sail)	(Power)	LARGEST YACHT (Owner)
1870	503	45	4	145-foot, 275-ton schooner *Sappho* (William Douglas)
1880	324	65	20	146-foot, 465-ton steamer *Jeannette* (James Gordon Bennett)
1890	682	146	71	285-foot, 1,238-ton steamer *Alva* (William K. Vanderbilt)
1900	1,445	195	207	314-foot, 2,682-ton steamer *Lysistrata* (James Gordon Bennett)

The later steamers were extraordinarily comfortable and luxurious vessels whose appeals even to hard-bitten sailors were obvious. We get a hint from a delicious dictum put forth by a woman who was asked if she had found it difficult to make the transition from the hard life of an actress to become the wife of a pleasure-loving tycoon: "A private railroad car is not an acquired taste," she stated. "One takes to it immediately."

The saloon of a decent-sized luxury yacht was expected to be no less comfortable than rooms in the owner's mansion ashore. Right, ''Gilded Age'' is written all over the heavy furniture and rich decorations in the two hundred thirty-nine-foot steamer Wakiva, *which cruised up the Labrador coast in 1909.*

Above, styles were slightly less ponderous when the tycoon and philanthropist Arthur Curtiss James built his two hundred sixteen-foot full-rigged bark Aloha *in 1910. James, who had once cruised to Japan to view an eclipse of the sun, sailed around the world in* Aloha *in the 'twenties.*

PARSONS & ATWATER. DEL.

Entered according to act of Congress in the year 1876 by Currier & Ives, in the Office of the Librarian of Congress, at Washington.

THE YACHT "MOHAWK" OF NEW YORK.

Length over all,   140 ft.
Length on water line,   121 .
Extreme breadth of Beam, 30 6 in.
Depth of Hold,   9 4
Draught of Water,   6
Tonnage, Old measurement, 330 tons.

BUILT 1875.
BY JOSEPH VAN DUSEN
WILLIAMSBURGH L.I.

NEW YORK. PUBLISHED BY CURRIER & IVES, 125 NASSAU ST.

lasted only a few years, perhaps because the amateurs weren't in shape to handle the big, demanding schooners and sloops with the ease of the professional crews. Of the seven starters in the 1847 race, four (including Commodore John Cox Stevens in *Gimcrack*), dropped out in a fresh breeze.

After that, instead of steering and hauling sheets and halyards, many if not most gentlemen yachtsmen sipped tea (or something stronger) while large paid crews did all the hard work. For many, the main point was Being a Yachtsman, not sailing a boat, and James Gordon Bennett's active interest in the handling of *Henrietta* in the 1866 race to England was the exception, not the rule. To be fair, we should acknowledge that to be able to handle the big sailing yachts of the time with competence required skills, physical strength, and leadership ability that the average business tycoon had not had the time to acquire while he worked to make the money that allowed him to buy his yacht in the first place. One indication of this trend is that when an experienced English yachtsman named William Cooper, who used the pen name "Vanderdecken," wrote one of the first "how-to" books about boats, *The Yacht Sailor,* he said almost as much about how to choose, supervise, and outfit a good professional yacht captain and crew as he did about yacht design, navigation, and helmsmanship.

As sailors are usually expected to know how to sail, the trend toward professionally manned sailing yachts did not go without criticism. As early as 1860 Bennett's New York *Herald* observed, "It is a singular fact that half the yachtsmen of the present day do not know how to sail their yachts themselves in a match, and seldom know where to find a good captain for them." Things got so bad that in 1871 some young yachtsmen who enjoyed sailing were forced to create a club where it was socially acceptable for owners to steer their own boats. This was the Seawanhaka Corinthian Yacht Club, named after a tribe of Long Island Indians and located on a beautiful peninsula called Hog (later Centre) Island, near Oyster Bay, New York. The first three objects of the club were that it would encourage members first "in becoming proficient in navigation," second "in the personal management, control, and handling of their yachts," and third "in all other matters pertaining to seamanship." Rule VIII, "Handling," required that each boat in a club race be steered by the owner or some other club member. Most

of the boats in the Seawanhaka fleet were relatively small and usually flew the flag of either of the two major "city" clubs — the New York Yacht Club or the Atlantic Yacht Club of Brooklyn.

Seawanhaka went on to be the foremost club for small-boat racing in the country; in the 1920s, 'thirties, and 'forties its members were winning major international and Olympic championships. Even more significant was the influence of Seawanhaka's activist, amateur ideals, which inspired the founding of hundreds of yacht and sailing clubs, small and large, all over North America.

5: Will Garner and *Mohawk*

Commodore Bennett set the example for rich, socially ambitious men who had got it into their heads that it would be fun to be a Yachtsman. One of these was a textiles manufacturer named William T. Garner.

We can't say exactly what inspired Will Garner to be a Yachtsman, but we may speculate. On a warm Friday in the spring of 1871, he may have been standing on the deck of a Staten Island ferry, heading for a weekend at his country estate, when the cloud of dollar signs in his eyes was broken by a flash of white. Garner might have seen a big schooner yacht charging across New York Bay with a great bone of wave grinding back and forth in the teeth of her sharp bow, and her wide wake shimmering in the low afternoon sun. Squinting, he may have seen a dozen heavily muscled, uniformed men hauling at ropes, and a grizzled man crouching over the long tiller and shouting orders. In the midst of all this action, tension, and power might have been an island of serenity at the forward end of the cockpit. There lounged a small party of ladies and gentlemen, their arms stretched with aristocratic ease over the leather cushions. At a respectful distance crouched a uniformed boy, ready to take their orders from the galley. From time to time, one of the men would casually tilt his head and say a word or two to the instantly attentive helmsman, who would change the schooner's heading while barking another command to the straining seamen.

Through Will Garner's mind — a tightly-packed storage bin of figures and names of cottons and dyes — strayed for perhaps the first time the glimmer of hope that he could enjoy ease and pleasure at last. "After all," he might have whispered to himself, "I can afford it."

He certainly could. Three years before, at the age of twenty-seven, and after fifteen years of apprenticeship to his father, Garner had inherited $15 million and thirteen cotton and print mills located in upstate New York and Pennsylvania. Now, at thirty, he owned one of the country's largest manufacturing concerns, and earned some $2 million annually, tax-free. He had a mansion in Murray Hill, on Manhattan's east side, and an estate on Staten Island. He was a member of the prestigious Union Club. He had married well (his wife was the former Miss Macellite Thorne, of New Orleans). And he enjoyed the paunchy, heavily mustachioed appearance that his peers considered the epitome of manly handsomeness. He was a successful man, and now he wanted something more, which he seems to have seen in the yachting of his day.

And so, thrilled by the prospects of a leisurely life in nature in stylish command of his surroundings, Will Garner decided to become a Yachtsman. He may have raced back to Manhattan on the next Monday and sought counsel among his yachting friends. One of these might have been Jamie Bennett, the raunchy, rakish publisher of the *Herald* and Commodore of the New York Yacht Club. Over oysters at Delmonico's and, later, champagne at the club's station on Staten Island, Bennett would have regaled his friend with anecdotes of the great ocean race, urged him to buy a big racing schooner of his own, and invited Garner to join himself and the other "progressive" millionaire yachtsmen as a member of the New York Yacht Club.

Perhaps the seduction of William Garner happened that way, perhaps not; but something hooked him. We know for a fact that on July 20, 1871, he was elected to membership in America's premier yacht club. A year or so later, he purchased his first yacht, a fifty-two-foot schooner named *Vixen*. Under the captain and crew that he hired, she did sufficiently well in local races to tease his interest. Relatively unscathed by the panic of 1873 (which led to a depression stretching until 1878), Garner next bought a larger yacht, the eighty-four-foot *Magic*. Built as a sloop in 1856, she had been rerigged and rebuilt many times, and passed from wealthy yachtsman to wealthy yachtsman like a prized mistress. In the first race for what was called the *America* or Queen's Cup, in 1870,

Magic had beaten the challenger *Cambria* and thirteen other New York Yacht Club yachts, even though she was the second smallest entry. She won quite a few races under Garner's ownership during the summer of 1874, culminating with a match race in October on which Garner probably won more than $100,000 in wagers. (The newspapers reported that $75,000 changed hands between spectators alone.) Garner was now firmly on the hook and like nearly all racing yachtsmen he could not resist the urge to build a faster, bigger boat. With the expert advice of his new friends and, perhaps, the yachting correspondent of the *Herald*, he took a ferry across the East River to Williamsburgh, Brooklyn, and commissioned John Van Deusen to build him the largest and fastest schooner in the United States.

There were no professional yacht designers in that day. A builder would whittle a block of pine until the hull shape looked right, take some offsets, build molds, calculate displacement using various rules of thumb, and then try to figure out how much sail she would require to sail fast and how much ballast she would need to keep from tipping over. Once built, the yacht would be subjected to the fiddling and adjusting that now takes place on the drawing board. Ballast — all of it internal in the form of iron or lead pigs — would be shifted; sail area would be reduced or increased; the hull might be drastically altered. Once (and if) the vessel balanced and sailed satisfactorily, the builder might base his subsequent products on her shape and rig. Most of these yachts were centerboard schooners, partly because that was the traditional American type (despite *America*'s success) and partly because the racing handicap rule encouraged them. Only a yacht's internal volume was taken into account, in such a way that short-ended beamy boats benefited as predictably as plumb-bowed narrow "plank-on-edge" yachts were born of English tonnage rules. These fat schooners required a lot of sail, and in a day when a yacht's rig was ignored by the measurers ("a tax on sail is a tax on skill," was the saying) they were given a lot of sail — acres of it. Van Deusen had built *Columbia*, a one hundred eight-foot centerboard schooner that was widely considered to be New York's fastest yacht, and she had won two races in the 1871 Queen's Cup match against *Livonia* (and lost one due to damage). Her beam was twenty-five and a half feet, and with her centerboard up she drew only five feet ten inches, five

*T*he typical wealthy man looking to build a yacht was in unfamiliar territory and at the mercy of boatbuilders, consultants, and other self-proclaimed "experts" speaking the strange language of boats and the sea. Here, in one such encounter in a boat yard, a cagey builder seduces a potential customer with a model and a strong opinion. This drawing is from a hilarious cartoon collection about an innocent in the world of yachting, titled Mr. Hardy Lee, His Yacht, published in 1857. The by-line is simply "Chinks," which is thought to have been a pen name for a Boston doctor, Charles Ellery Stedman, although the book has also been ascribed to Winslow Homer.

IV. A Great Man Consulted

Builder: "You don't want her sloop-rigged, more'n you want water in your boots."

inches less than the twenty-four-foot smaller *Magic.* Her draft with board down was twenty-two and a half feet. One of her competitors, *Tidal Wave,* was so beamy that someone said she looked like a snake that had swallowed a toad; but wide beam and a shallow hull under a skyscraper schooner rig typified the yachts built for the wealthy, non-sailor yachtsmen of the 1870s.

Confident that the concept could be scaled up, Van Deusen started work on a one hundred forty-one-footer for Will Garner. She would displace approximately two hundred fifty tons, about one-fourth of which would be lead pigs stowed in her shallow bilge. Though thirty-three feet longer than *Columbia,* the new yacht would draw six feet, just two inches more. A seven-ton centerboard would extend her draft to thirty feet, and a beam of thirty feet would, Van Deusen believed, provide the stability necessary to keep her more or less upright under the press of a sailplan of over thirty-two thousand square feet. From her gold-leafed clipper bow to her wide transom to her maintopmast hounds one hundred sixty-three feet above deck, she would be a great, powerful sail-carrying machine. Everything about her except her hull depth was immense: a forty-two-foot bowsprit, a ninety-foot main boom, a twenty-eight-foot-square main saloon. To the modern eye she looks more like a gigantic dinghy than like an offshore boat, with a turn of bilge that is almost a right angle and a long, flat run aft.

Mohawk she was called, for Garner had mills in the Mohawk valley and her builder was born there. She was launched in a driving rain on June 9, 1875, before a large crowd, including quite a few skeptics who anticipated that she would turn turtle under the weight of her masts, each of which carried a ton of ironwork at the hounds. The mainmast also carried the pennant of the Vice-Commodore of the New York Yacht Club. Less than four years after becoming a member, Will Garner had been elected second-in-command, partly because of *Mohawk,* and also because he had leased the club a long-needed clubhouse at Stapleton, on Staten Island, and his new friends wanted to thank him.

Most newspaper yachting writers were agog with praise for *Mohawk.* Overwhelmed by her size, they filled their columns with her dimensions. There was just enough space left to summarize her amenities, which included steam heat, hot and cold running water, gas lights, and a bell system for summoning stewards. Her huge saloon was crowded with heavy furniture, including a grand piano, and the owner's and guests' cabins were finished off with similar luxury.

These yachting columns were written by people with vaguely maritime interests and irregular nautical knowledge, and appeared under colorful by-lines like "Handy Billy," "Enthusiast," and "Hard-a-Lee." There were a few dissenters, however. "Cutty Hunk" thought her too beamy and shallow, urging, "Take two feet from *Mohawk's* beam and add it to her draft." In issue after issue of the sporting weekly *The Spirit of the Times,* "Devoted Yachtsman" (an insurance man named Edgar E. Holly) nagged her builder for turning out a vessel that was too fat, too shallow, too heavy, and too unfair. A more easily driven and fair hull would need to carry much less sail and be much faster, and the other yachting writers should be ashamed for saying otherwise and telling Garner what he wanted to hear, wrote Devoted Yachtsman. *Mohawk* would, he promised, be both slow and unseaworthy. "I cannot see the first line of natural beauty about her," Devoted Yachtsman declared. "If they ever carry her lee rail under, with all sail set, there will be some danger. It does not answer to get a wide flat boat too far over."

Devoted Yachtsman was quickly proven right about one thing, and that was that *Mohawk* was slow. In all the summer of 1875, she won only one race, and ended the yachting season by losing a match race to Bennett's smaller *Dauntless.* Most of the time, she could not get away from boats thirty or forty feet shorter.

The yachting writers who had praised her were quick to blame her skipper and her sails, but Van Deusen increased her ballast and moved it and her immense anchor chains aft to her long, flat run, stowing them under the saloon floor by dropping the heavy lead pigs through trap doors cut in the sole. The ballast was not secured in the bilge because nobody who built and sailed yachts could think of a reason for going to all that trouble, and the trap doors were dropped back into place and covered with rugs. Apparently, these changes were not effective. *Mohawk's* speed did not improve satisfactorily and the wild yawing that had made it hard to keep her on course did not go away. After she was hauled out in late October, Van Deusen repaired superficial damage caused by a collision with a steamer that had occurred one night earlier in the month. The steamer was almost sunk in the incident, which seems to have been caused by a mutual misreading of the other vessel's intentions as they approached on converging courses. He then went to work on her underbody to deepen her by a few inches and lengthen her keel by seven feet. Van Deusen died before Christmas; but the work continued and she was launched for the Centennial season in June of 1876.

Garner had great plans for that summer, which would match the Bicentennial of 1976 in fanfare; but his fall and winter saw only tragedy, controversy, and disappointment. His great schooner had not fulfilled the promises that all his new friends had made in her name, and then one of his four daughters died. Next, Cornelius Vanderbilt tried to destroy the ferry line that Garner had established between Manhattan and Staten Island. Vanderbilt's line had held a monopoly that was the foundation of his growing fortune. He protected it first with court injunctions, which Garner ignored, and then with a crew of longshoremen sent to tear down Garner's pier. Their three tugs were met by an angry mob armed with stones and fire hoses. Holding the fort were Garner and his employees, some members of the New York Yacht Club, whose base (rented from Garner for a song) stood on the pier, and quite a few local residents delighted with Garner's five-cent fare — half of what Vanderbilt charged. Through a long night of violence in the middle of a stormy nor'easter the defenders held off the attackers. "If a single shot had been fired there is no telling what the consequences would have been," reported the *Herald* after that rough night. Garner obtained a counter injunction, and for perhaps the first time in his life the old "Commodore" quit a fight.

His night playing Horatio at the bridge further encouraged Garner's ambitions. Now a Yachtsman, he was eager to be Commodore. Here he was, one of the richest men in America, owner of the country's largest yacht and the New York Yacht Club's own club house, which he had just saved from destruction. All that, and on the eve of America's great birthday party he was only a Vice-Commodore. His "progressive" friends encouraged him, for (as the *Graphic* put it) he was "young, pushing, wealthy, and generous, and above all the owner of the one yacht in the fleet [from] which they would like to see the Commodore's pennant float on coming occasions when it will be that officer's duty to receive rep-

resentatives of foreign yacht clubs." But there was an obstacle. Commodore George L. Kingsland had, unfortunately, served for but one year, and only one of his seven predecessors had been in office for less than three. Garner would either have to wait his turn or contest what was usually a predetermined election. Kingsland was wealthy, only forty-two, and distinguished (his father had been Mayor of New York City). With a jutting jaw and piercing eyes, he looked like a Commodore, and with his one hundred twenty-one-foot keel schooner *Alarm* he had a suitable flagship. He had done nothing to disgrace either himself or the club in 1875. But Kingsland was of the old guard, the "Seawanhaka faction," and was unfit to head the club in its hour of glory — or so thought the hard-charging young millionaires for whom a huge schooner was just one more glamorous bauble to number among Fifth Avenue mansions, race horses, and well-rounded mistresses. Will Garner allowed his friends to nominate him. On February 4, 1876, the election was held and Kingsland won by one vote. One of Garner's presumed supporters arrived in evening clothes a few minutes late and was not allowed to vote, and this encouraged a few of Garner's friends to accuse Kingsland of "sharp practice" in letters to the newspapers. When the *World* editorialized that the election had been fair, the issue died, leaving Garner with his hurt feelings.

He never raced *Mohawk* again. On the day of the yacht club's Centennial Regatta, she was cruising on Long Island Sound. The darling of the sports pages the year before, she was now ignored in favor of *Amaryllis*, "the nondescript half-Catamaran half-Balsa and wholly life-raft" (as one correspondent called her) that twenty-eight-year-old Nathanael Herreshoff had brought down from Bristol, Rhode Island. *Amaryllis* cleaned up but was disqualified, thereby setting yacht design back almost a hundred years but making a reputation for her talented designer and skipper.

Garner probably was relieved that the pressure on himself and his yacht had eased. He began to use *Mohawk* the way that may have appealed to him when he had first noticed that charging white schooner five years earlier. With his wife, daughters, and friends he went out for short cruises and day sails. No longer a club officer, he may have enjoyed being free of protocol and ceremony. Perhaps he even became interested in sailing. It is not hard to imagine him being tutored in helmsmanship by his sailing master,

Captain Oliver P. Rowland. Yet *Mohawk* still imposed burdens on her owner. Her first sailing master, Captain Comstock, had either resigned or been relieved after the disappointing 1875 season. Apparently all the experienced racing skippers were already hired, for Captain Rowland had no experience in yachts. Man and boy, he had spent all but the first ten of his fifty-three years in coasting schooners, those rough-hewn workhorses of the nineteenth century trade. This may not have been the best training for handling a vessel as refined and cranky as *Mohawk;* but perhaps Garner hired Rowland because they got along well. By mid-July, either the yacht's or her sailing master's eccentricities had led one entire crew to quit and their replacements to grumble so angrily that Mrs. Garner and several of her husband's friends noticed and suggested to Garner that he find another captain. The resentment only deepened after the main gaff broke and tore the mainsail and Rowland punished the crew for carelessness.

On Wednesday, July 19, Garner sent a message to Rowland saying that he wanted to sail on Thursday afternoon. The next day—the fifth anniversary of her owner's election to membership in the New York Yacht Club, Rowland instructed his new first mate, George Osborn, to prepare *Mohawk* for sailing and then went visiting among the other yachts anchored off the Stapleton clubhouse. It was a humid, squally day typical of a New York July, with a light westerly puffing off the shore a quarter mile to windward of the big schooner, which lay bow-to a strong northbound flood current with the wind on her starboard beam. The crew slowly sweated up the immense mainsail and the foresail, then set the two gaff-topsails. It was not standard practice to get under way with topsails hoisted, but the heavy *Mohawk* may have needed the extra sail area to build up steerage way in light air. The sailors, most of whom were Scandinavians, then heaved short on the anchor chain.

At about three in the afternoon, Garner, who had lunched on board, took some visitors ashore in the steam launch, picked up his sailing party, and returned to the yacht. The launch then retrieved Captain Rowland from *Countess of Dufferin,* the Canadian challenger in the upcoming Queen's Cup match. When he was back aboard, Garner told him to get under way. The guests were Mrs. Garner, her brother Frost Thorne, the Misses Adele Hunter and Edith May (whose sister was James Gordon Bennett's fiancée), and Schuyler Crosby, Gardner Howland, and Louis Montant, New York sportsmen and businessmen. They sat in the cockpit or on the afterdeck as the crew hoisted the forestaysail and jib and put their backs to the hand windlass to get the anchor up. The wind must have swung into the south, for Rowland ordered the headsails and foresail backed in order to pull her bow off. Aft, the mainsail was trimmed hard and cleated on two large bollards behind the wheel, at which Rowland stood. The captain may have been frustrated that his orders were followed slowly. One of the quartermasters charged with relaying instructions forward along *Mohawk*'s long deck, Frederick Palm, lay sleeping in the sail bin under the cockpit. In any case, Rowland was distracted and did not notice the black clouds sweeping toward him over Staten Island. Skippers of nearby yachts saw the squall and ordered sails quickly doused, but all except one or two of *Mohawk*'s men continued to heave on the windlass.

It suddenly began to rain heavily. Garner and his guests raced below, where Mrs. Garner and Adele Hunter threw themselves on a sofa on the port side of the large saloon. The men and Edith May remained standing near the fireplace, and Frost Thorne walked forward toward the owner's stateroom on the starboard side of the centerboard trunk, perhaps intending to change out of his wet clothes. Either because he was summoned or because he heard the guests come below and anticipated orders, the young cabin boy, Peter Sullivan, came aft from the galley. Just as he reached the door to the saloon, *Mohawk* was knocked over on her port side.

The anchor was off the bottom and she had just enough way on to steer clear of an anchored brig off her starboard bow. There wasn't much weight in the squall — by all accounts, no more than twenty-five knots. But it caught her at her most vulnerable, square on her beam with all her sails hoisted and either trimmed flat or backed, with very little headway with which to absorb one part of the blow, and with her centerboard two-thirds of the way down so she could not absorb the other part by making leeway. Like a boxer struggling to his feet, *Mohawk* was not yet ready to withstand a right hook, no matter how tamely thrown. As she lay over on her ear, her crew frozen in place by surprise, Will Garner jumped up into the companionway and yelled at Captain Rowland: "She'll come back!" Quartermaster Palm staggered into the cockpit from the sail locker and first mate Osborn clambered aft for orders. The lee rail went under for perhaps the first time in her short career.

The gust passed and *Mohawk* quickly righted herself. But the squall punched once again. Rowland shouted orders to let go the headsail sheets and the foretopsail halyard. Osborn relayed the orders, then slipped on the near-vertical deck and slid down *Mohawk's* broad beam into the water. Somebody followed those orders; other sailors — those who were not clinging in terror to the windward rigging — cut free the maintopsail halyard and the vang that backed the foresail. And she still lay over. Quickly realizing what was about to happen, Quartermaster Thorwald Fergussen smashed through the skylight over the saloon and looked for the guests. He saw Mrs. Garner pinned against the port side by a sofa, and her husband struggling to extricate her.

During the first knockdown, some of the furniture had slid to leeward toward the women, but on the second one sofas, chairs, and the piano fell off the edge of the vertical cabin sole and dropped on Mrs. Garner and Adele Hunter. Edith May hung onto the fireplace. Hearing his wife's screams, Garner swung below from the companionway and clawed at the furniture, which was quickly being covered with pigs of lead pouring out of the bilge after the trap doors fell off. Water washed into the saloon through the skylight, which was now near sea level. Schuyler Crosby caught hold of Edith May and pushed her up the companionway to Howland. Crosby and Montant then pulled a lounge chair off the moaning Mrs. Garner and heaved it, too, up to Howland before returning to help Garner, who was frantically tugging at his wife's right arm. Crosby grabbed Miss Hunter's hand but slipped and fell backwards into the water that now half-filled the saloon. When he regained his feet, she was submerged.

"Schuyler, for God's sake, try and help me pull her out!" Garner cried. Crosby pulled at the left arm as a sailor tried to pull furniture away. *Mohawk* abruptly lurched to leeward, settling deeper on her side, and the water flooded over Mrs. Garner's head. Still Garner would not let go, even when Crosby and the sailor swam for their own lives through the hole in the skylight. They grabbed the keel of an overturned launch, and were soon rescued by a boat from another yacht and taken ashore, where crowds of people stood aghast at the brief tragedy that they had just witnessed.

Mohawk lay swamped on her beam ends with her sails just under the water's surface. Crews from other yachts — *Magic* among them — crawled on her like mountaineers, shouting for survivors. Some cut holes in her deck and house with axes. Soon Captain Rowland, who had fallen under the mainsail, swum out, and been saved by a launch, had *Mohawk* towed to a mud flat in the Kill van Kull. That night she was righted by bringing two schooners alongside and lifting her masts with their halyards, and a diver went down at first light on Friday. Adele Hunter was found under a sofa, Mrs. Garner under a mound of lead pigs. After two hours of work, the diver cleared the pigs away; he cut away Mrs. Garner's dress to clear her from the furniture. Will Garner had floated to the starboard side, but Frost Thorne's body could not be found and was assumed to have floated out through the skylight. Peter Sullivan, the cabin boy, was found standing bolt upright in the door leading forward with his hands tightly gripping the frame.

The two quartermasters swore out a warrant for Captain Rowland's arrest, accusing him of criminal negligence. The coroner's inquest was held on Friday morning. Captain Rowland swore that he had done all he could have. He had put the helm down to bring her into the wind, but *Mohawk* had not responded, and he had cast off the mainsheet, but it had jammed. Thorwald Furgussen loudly contradicted him, and claimed that Rowland had not given sufficient orders. The crowd in the back of the courtroom began to make angry noises and threats directed toward Rowland. He was the expert, and therefore he was at fault. Rowland himself blamed the accident on the shifting of the ballast. The squall was not dangerous, and he had done his job well, but "if the ballast had not shifted she would have righted, I think; the ballast was under the floor of the grand saloon, and the floor is full of trap doors, not fastened at all; this is the way in most yachts . . . After the danger appeared there was no time or opportunity for me to assist Commodore Garner or the ladies."

Responding to the lynch-mob atmosphere, Schuyler Crosby volunteered a defense of Captain Rowland against the charges of his quartermasters. This appeal swept revenge out the door, and the crowd approved the jury's finding of no criminal negligence on Rowland's part. The captain had responded by swearing out war-

Newport, Rhode Island, called "a tolerably dull place of sojournment" by a visiting yachtsman in 1844, soon became one of America's most important yachting centers. When the New York Yacht Club fleet came to Newport on its annual cruise, as here in 1872, the harbor was filled with big schooners manned by dozens of professional sailors, steam yachts carrying the owners (many of whom could not and did not sail), and many small boats running errands to shore and showing the sights to tourists.

rants against Furgussen and Palm, accusing them of libeling him.

When the schooner was pumped out the next day, Frost Thorne's bloated body was discovered in a corner of the saloon. The main boom lay in two pieces as evidence of the force with which *Mohawk* had rolled over. More ominously, the mainsheet was found trimmed tight and cleated and the helm was hard up, which contradicted Captain Rowland's testimony. Amid more threats against his life, he was arrested again and held on $2500 bail. A few hours later, Garner's lawyer — eager to put an end to the entire miserable business — posted bond and Rowland skulked out of New York.

Meanwhile, the boat was cleaned up. The anonymous sailor who had struggled to save Mrs. Garner found a ring that he had pulled off her hand. Souvenir hunters ravaged the saloon and cabins for bits of furniture and the Garners' personal effects, including Mrs. Garner's tattered dress. A gold and bronze clock on the mantel was stopped at seven minutes past four. In muddy disarray around the saloon lay the remnants of Will Garner's dream: broken liquor bottles; his red morocco house slipper; books from the large library and the Springfields from the armory; bits of paintings and mirrors; and a small silver service that was his prize for the only race *Mohawk* won. Hanging in his stateroom closet was his blue-trimmed white yachting suit, which for some reason he had neglected to wear on his last day as a Yachtsman.

The five corpses were buried, the cabin boy after a Roman Catholic service and the owner and his guests after two Protestant Episcopal services, one for Adele Hunter and a joint funeral for the Garners and Thorne. The city's "thrill of horror" (as one of the papers described the reaction to the news of the capsize) gave way to orgies of praise for Garner's heroism, the ladies' beauty and virtue, Thorne's relationship to the hero, and Peter Sullivan's honest loyalty. *Mohawk* got off relatively unscathed, as only Devoted Yachtsman declined to lay all abuse on Captain Rowland's doorstep. Devoted Yachtsman blamed the tragedy on the experts and public opinion. "It strikes me very forcibly," he wrote sarcastically, "that were I a novice in naval architecture, and I owned a yacht on which the entire talent and skill, the entire yacht-building art of this city had been concentrated to build, then I should feel satisfied that I owned about perfection, no matter what any outsider

93

said to the contrary."

Mohawk was patched up, towed to a slip in the Gowanus Canal in Brooklyn, and put up for sale. The United States Coastal Survey eventually bought her in 1878 for $20,000 and renamed her *Eagre*. She was the last big schooner of her type. A few yachtsmen and writers calling themselves "cutter cranks" soon began to preach the merits of narrow beam and deep keels. The rule-of-thumb

skills of John Van Deusen, who had saved himself considerable grief by dying when he did, were soon supplanted by the more scientific methods of A. Cary Smith, Edward Burgess, and Nathanael Herreshoff, the last of whom turned out skimming dishes such as *Reliance* and *Constitution* that rivaled *Mohawk* in dangerous crankiness.

Captain Oliver Rowland appealed for sympathy and support to

the members of the Brooklyn Yacht Club in June of 1877. "I have been unjustly dealt with, shamefully and outrageously abused, maliciously prosecuted, and unjustly imprisoned," he wrote to them, "several times my life actually placed in jeopardy by being exposed to a drunken and infuriated mob on Staten Island." When the letter was read at a meeting, the members sat in stunned silence for several minutes until they burst into shouts and complaints. "A man who gets a boat under way as Captain Rowland did with the *Mohawk* deserves to get his skin wet," one declared. They took no action.

The New York Yacht Club abandoned Garner's Stapleton building after his executors raised the rent. It was towed to Glen Island, on Long Island Sound, where it was used as a bar. A half-model of *Mohawk* hangs on the upper wall of the New York Yacht Club's model room, almost out of sight. In a glass case on an upper floor she sits in full-rigged, miniature glory. Nowhere in the club hangs a portrait of William T. Garner, Yachtsman.

6: The Last Days of Jamie Bennett

Jamie Bennett's career hit snags that he himself threw in its path. Always impulsive, he became erratic, and a scandal finally forced him to leave New York, never to return permanently. While making his rounds of New Year's Day receptions on the first day of 1877, he drunkenly urinated into the fireplace of the home of his fiancée, who was a sister of the young lady who was saved from the *Mohawk* sinking. A few days later, his by now ex-future-brother-in-law, Fred May, got revenge by publicly horsewhipping Bennett in front of the prestigious Union Club. That standoff of insults led the two to a duel in which both fired wildly — May because he intended to, and Bennett (it was said) because he was shaking with fright. Shamed, Bennett moved abroad. Nevertheless, it being the Gilded Age, the New York Yacht Club re-elected him Commodore in 1884. He is the only two-time Commodore in the history of the club.

Portraits of Bennett painted around this time show a lanky, handsomely mustachioed, slightly hungover character peering from under heavy eyelids, with the tired but seductive ennui of a person who has seen too much of the seamier side of life too soon, but is willing to give it one more try. Nautically speaking, his one more try was luxury yachting on a scale that beggars the imagination. In 1883, when he was forty-two, Bennett built a new two-hundred-twenty-six foot steamer, *Namouna*. She was allegedly the first yacht to be called a "floating palace," and she was also described as "a craft of Oriental magnificence." Cluttered with heavy furniture, fantastic decorations, and ingenious design features, she outstretched the second largest yacht then in the New York Yacht Club's fleet, J. Pierpont Morgan's *Corsair*, by a full fifty feet, and cost more than $200,000 — the equivalent of about $3 million today. Contrary to square-rigger tradition, the owner's and guests cabins were located in the bow so they would not be sullied by soot pouring from the smokestacks, and her bathrooms (the traditional term "head" does not quite apply) included full-size retracting tubs.

"Self-willed, authoritarian, suspicious, capricious, socially charming, and vain in almost everything," as one of his employees once described him, Bennett lived aboard *Namouna* for eighteen years, shuttling back and forth across the Atlantic to pay brief visits to his newspapers in New York and Paris, and running up annual operating expenses of close to $150,000. Her fifty-man crew had to conform to Bennett's curious standards of comportment. For example, he would not allow anybody who was bearded to come aboard either as seaman or as guest, and he did not tolerate even the presence of a deck of playing cards, much less gambling.

By 1900 *Namouna* was outclassed by other yachts, so Bennett sold her to South America for use as a gunboat and spent an estimated $600,000 on a three-hundred-fourteen-footer, *Lysistrata*, that came with a crew of one hundred, a Turkish bath, an owner's cabin on each of her three decks (one for each of his mistresses, it was said), and a milk cow in her own stable (a *Herald* foreign correspondent was delegated to walk the cow from a farm in central France to the yacht on the Riviera).

Such profligacy undid the fortune that had once made him the third richest man in America. After spending some $40 million on his fast life, Bennett died nearly broke in 1918, to the end a vivid example to the moralists of his day of those destructive tendencies of inherited wealth of which William Kissam Vanderbilt had so morosely warned.

V

Commodore J.P. Morgan

*"The most interesting thing in this
house is the host."*

Pierpont Morgan's famous advice about pleasure sailing, "If you have to ask how much it costs, you can't afford it," is so familiar that it's trite. There is little doubt that he expressed the sentiment — he was so well-respected (in the business community all but worshipped) that his listeners memorialized his every word — but Morgan's maxim most likely took a slightly different form. One reliable account has been passed on by Bill Robinson in his book, *Legendary Yachts*. One day, Robinson writes, Morgan was asked by a millionaire oilman, Henry Clay Pierce, what it cost to run a yacht.

"You cannot afford to run a yacht," Morgan answered simply.

"Why? I'm pretty warm you know," replied Pierce, using a Gilded-Age euphemism for "wealthy."

And Morgan replied, "You have no right to own a yacht if you have to ask that question."

Either way, what was Morgan trying to say? The common wisdom has been that Morgan was saying, in effect, that the kind of yachting the oilman was hankering after was so expensive as to be beyond reckoning — a truth that owners of even small pleasure boats have ruefully confirmed time and again. I suggest, however, that this interpretation is so simple-mindedly materialistic that Pierpont Morgan would have found it incomprehensible. All during his extraordinary life, he made it his work to measure the values of objects and people not so much by their financial cost (although finance was his business) as by their aesthetic or moral worth. A more satisfying and, in the terms of his life, more consistent interpretation of Morgan's Commandment is that some activities are so important that their rewards far outpace their economic cost. Generally seen as a tycoon's boast, this line may actually reflect a kind of spiritual humility.

To make some sense of Morgan's Commandment, we must make some sense of Morgan, a powerful personality who, perhaps more than any other, is responsible for the style in which yachting, until fairly recently, was carried out in the United States. His is a complicated story, for he was a man of many parts that only occasionally came together. And it is not an easy story to tell with any sure grasp of the man's deepest thoughts and feelings, for late in his life Morgan personally burned most of his papers. What we

On page 96 is the second of J.P. Morgan's three Corsairs, *whose piratical name reflects the style of some of his business exploits. Two hundred forty-one feet long, she was built in 1891 and, seven years later, was requisitioned for Navy duty in the Spanish-American War. Renamed* U.S.S. Gloucester, *she sank an enemy torpedo boat and remained on U.S. Navy duty until 1919, when she was sold and used in commercial service. She was wrecked in Florida during a hurricane. Morgan, showing his sentimental streak, went to great expense and effort to duplicate many of her features in the next* Corsair. *This is Morgan during his school years in Germany. Blazing under his cap is a hint of the intimidating stare, often compared to a locomotive's headlight, that was one of his most reliable tools during a negotiation.*

have been left are a bundle of myths and traditions about him, the memories of his few friends and many acquaintances, the fading clippings from the press that hounded him, and, above all, the record of his fantastically successful and influential business life as a banker, which is difficult to evaluate without making simplistic judgments (the difference between nineteenth and twentieth century attitudes about the role of business in public life being what it is).

Evidence about Morgan's life also exists in the records of his non-profit-making activities in religion, yachting, and art. These are the sorts of things that historians, being powerless and underpaid, tend to take less seriously than politics and economics. That is unfortunate. For some people, volunteer activities often are more important and revealing than paid work; they flesh out a character otherwise only vaguely understood in a sequence of dates and dollars.

So we will look at Morgan from several angles. The biographical sketch of the archetypal yachtsman that follows will, I believe, shed considerable light on the fascinating interplay of insights and traditions, moods and technologies, beauties and actions that make up the golden pastime.

First, know him by his names. In anecdotes and newspaper headlines he was, simply, "Mr. Morgan." To his face, his business partners called him "Commodore"; behind his back they referred to him as "Jupiter" and to his huge cigars — of which he smoked more than twenty a day — as "Hercules' clubs." Indeed, he was a kind of manic choremaster chasing after stables to clean. When called upon in financial panics, he saved entire nations from ruin (a biographer has likened him to a one-man Federal Deposit Insurance Corporation), yet in old age he also almost ruined his family while putting together the largest collection of art ever in private hands. Mr. Morgan revived churches, sponsored archaeological digs, helped found national museums, built the New York Yacht Club, owned gold-plated steam yachts, paid for several America's Cup defenders, terrified tycoons, struggled with presidents, unified the railroads, created the first billion-dollar company, and molded out of the debris of the Civil War a new American aristocracy founded on traditions of Anglican religion, men's clubs, boarding schools, and contradictory but heartfelt male personal demeanor. He was the first great American celebrity — worshipped, feared, and ridiculed often in successive breaths. A man of gargantuan appearance and tastes, he regularly wolfed down eight-course lunches, had affairs with famous actresses, and intimidated anybody brave enough to negotiate with him with a stare likened to the headlight of a thundering steam locomotive. Yet beneath that bulk and apparent ferocity lay the lamblike sentimentality of a romantic who personally chose his daughter's wedding trousseau and who, at the age of sixty, once climbed up a rope ladder suspended over the topsides of a rolling Atlantic steamer in order to embrace his wife, returning from a European trip.

That was Morgan the man, and that was Morgan the myth created during his lifetime and propagated over the seventy years since his death in books with titles such as *Morgan the Magnificent* and *Corsair*. It is difficult to be neutral about him, harder still to write about him without blundering into grandiose clichés. His reputation reached such a level that one recent biography, George Wheeler's *Pierpont Morgan and Friends: The Anatomy of a Myth,* is almost entirely devoted to puncturing his reputation for invincibility, which Morgan himself would have been the first to deny.

Born under the fiery sun of Aries and the airy ascendant of Aquarius, John Pierpont Morgan was a human acetylene torch who cut through and either destroyed or reconstructed much of what was old about his day, which ran at some length from 1837 to 1913. He was born in Hartford, Connecticut, "with one foot in Connecticut trade and the other in a Boston pulpit," as his best recent biographer, Andrew Sinclair, has written. The first American Morgan, named Miles, arrived from Wales — where the name means "sailor" — in 1636, and fought the Indians in King Philip's War. Pierpont's paternal grandfather, Joseph Morgan, was a former farmer grown rich through shrewd investments in insurance, stagecoach, and railroad companies; his maternal grandfather, John Pierpont, was a controversial Unitarian clergyman and poet whose fiery abolitionist views won and lost him several parishes. The Pierpont (originally Pierrepont) name was also distinguished in New England, the earliest Pierponts being important religious figures; a Sarah Pierrepont married Jonathan Edwards, who defined American public theology for two centuries. Through both sides came the heritage of New England Puritanism: a conviction of sinfulness forgiven through divine mercy; a faith in man's (and America's) upward progress toward the kingdom of God; a reliance upon family and its rituals; a respect for money and its safekeeping; and a certainty that the chosen are obligated to reform their surroundings.

His father, Junius Spencer Morgan, was an up-and-coming dry-goods wholesaler. Though comfortably well off, the Morgans could not protect the boy from over-sensitivity and sickness. In fact, afflictions seemed almost his constant companions. He suffered from scarlet fever, frequent headaches, and, most tellingly, a nervous eczema inherited from his moody mother that focused on his nose. When he was in middle age, any sort of tension made his nose so red and swollen that he refused to have his photograph made unless the photographer agreed to retouch it. He was a lonely boy — or at least one who needed more than the usual amount of affectionate parental attention, even a normal amount of which he was not to receive. Discovering the profits of being a middleman between English investors and American producers, his father soon began to spend much of his time away on long business trips to Boston and London. To save his sickly, generally unavailable mother trouble, when Pierpont was thirteen he was placed in a dull boarding school noted mostly for its frequency of temperance lectures. The one Morgan biographer who had access to his diaries, his son-in-law Herbert Satterlee, tells us that the solitary boy found his only pleasure working in the school principal's garden with the hired man, writing long, lonely letters to his family, and reading the Hartford newspapers. Young Morgan must have had a strong sense of order and responsibility, for Satterlee reports that his diaries were "wonderfully neat," and included meticulous accounts of his expenditures, grades, church attendance, and observations.

After the family moved to Boston, Pierpont was left in the boarding school for a while, but then allowed to transfer to a day school in Boston, the famous English High, full of "the old God-fearing, law-abiding, New England spirit" (as Satterlee put it). Boston in the 1850s was an exciting place, booming with new commerce and the spirit of abolitionism and social reform. While the boy seems to have known about it all, at least from dinner-table talk with his father, recurring illnesses frequently kept him out of school. At fifteen he suffered from rheumatic fever, and his parents carried him down to the wharf and shipped him off alone to the Azores to recover in the house of a family friend, Charles Dabney. Two generations earlier, another Dabney had greeted George Crowninshield and *Cleopatra's Barge.* For many years, the family provided consul service for the United States at Fayal in exchange for a small cut on all American goods that were loaded and unloaded there.

On the island, he went on long hikes with a fifty-year-old doctor

who was also recuperating in the Azores (but who soon died); and he haunted shipyards and learned much about naval architecture and rigging, flirted with the girls who were his only peers, and wrote many letters filled with minute observations of Azorean life. He heard rarely from his family; it must have been a lonely time whose only merit may have been that he was forced upon his own resources much earlier than most people. Among his characteristics that surfaced by this time were a passion for playing cards, which he did with such talent and distaste for losing that, later in his life, he found his best opponent in himself; he would play solitaire for hours, meanwhile meditating over business problems.

Though left with a permanent limp, his body recovered, and after a few months he went to London to visit his father who, in 1854, went into partnership with George Peabody, a successful merchant banker and aging bachelor who needed an heir to take over and free him to concentrate his time and fortune (estimated at $20 million) on his philanthropies. Peabody is a case study in the history of American enterprise, and established the mold in which Pierpont Morgan and his generation of businessmen were cast. Born in Massachusetts in 1795, Peabody started out at age eleven as a grocer's apprentice and moved on in the dry-goods business, where he discovered the need for cash by westward-moving, industrializing Americans. On a business trip to London in 1837, he likewise saw the desire for a good return on investments by wealthy Englishmen, so he settled there to play middleman, which often meant acting as an unofficial trade representative and diplomat. (In 1851 he helped finance the American exhibits at Prince Albert's famous Crystal Palace exhibition, which stimulated the construction and visit of the New York schooner yacht *America,* whose triumph in a race around the Isle of Wight led to the America's Cup series of races in which his partner's son would play a major role.) A strong believer in the new country's future, Peabody made his first great success in 1838, when he negotiated an $8 million loan in which the old country bailed the state of Maryland out of bankruptcy caused by the panic of 1837. While Peabody charged no fee for his services, the confidence that he earned on both sides of the Atlantic was the foundation for his later success. More than seventy years later, in 1912, when J.P. Morgan was asked by a hostile American government investigator whether ownership of property was the main qualification for commercial credit, the old man responded, "No sir. The first thing is character."

The boy returned to Boston. With his father absent and his mother's health bad, he was given considerable responsibility at home. School, then, must have been a relief; he did very well after re-entering English High School (without being set back a grade, despite his long absence), was graduated, and was again shipped off to Europe to finish his education. For two years he was at a rigorous, authoritarian Swiss boarding school where he won a reputation for physical daring and mathematical brilliance, but where — judging from his diary and letters home (by his own reckoning, he wrote 130 between June 1855 and June 1856) — he was just as lonely and sickly as ever. From Lake Geneva he went for a year of study to the University of Gottingen, in Germany, where he joined a dueling club, avoided sword fights, and became famous for his ability to make complicated mental calculations. There he ended his formal education. Spurning his professor's recommendation that he become a mathematician, Morgan returned to America to learn his father's trade.

When he reached New York, Pierpont Morgan was an intense Anglified twenty-year-old whose large ears and firm jaw framed closely set, piercing eyes and a thick-lipped, sensitive mouth, which in early photographs formed an uncertain, boyish half-grin, but which later would arch in a patented scowl under a bushy moustache and a nose that was often ravaged by worry into a flesh and blood raspberry ("Old Livernose" he would be called at a safe distance). Having spent a quarter of his life either abroad or in transit, he was remarkably cosmopolitan for an American of any age. It seemed as though he had always been so; as a boy, he had subscribed to the *Illustrated London News* at the then-great cost of $10 a year, and the subject of his graduation declamation at English High School had been not Washington, Jefferson, or the other stock characters of such performances but the Corsican adventurer, Napoleon Bonaparte, his first and perhaps only hero. An adventurer Pierpont Morgan was himself, and so he would remain. His first job was arranged by his father. Beginning as an unsalaried apprentice bookkeeper in a small investment house that did business with the firm that would soon be renamed Junius

S. Morgan & Co., he gradually gained responsibilities, did some traveling, and showed slightly more independence than his superiors wished, although his deals in the coffee and cotton markets were sufficiently profitable to compensate for the surprise they caused. Perhaps most significantly, he saw from close-up the chaos of the panic of 1857, the latest in a long series of wild runs on markets and banks that were instigated by unscrupulous or careless speculators and that threatened the future of whole countries, not to mention firms like his father's.

His bulky enthusiasm and addiction to hard work won him the respect of his colleagues, but they quickly noticed — perhaps more quickly than did he — that when Pierpont drove himself too hard, headaches and skin flare-ups proliferated. One tension almost certainly was the one that arises when a talented son works for a talented father. In 1860, Pierpont formed a firm under his own name; but his primary work was to represent his father, finding American investments for the money that Junius carefully recruited from the immensely wealthy old English families.

Pierpont was Junius's only surviving son as well as his partner. The weekly letters they exchanged reflected their mixed relationship. From London came business news as well as lectures about morality and health. "Do not let the desire of success or of accumulating induce you ever to do a single action which will cause you regret." And, "You are altogether too rapid in disposing of your meals. You can have no health if you go on in this way." Junius was especially worried about his son's refusal to share his heavy work load with a partner. Pierpont explained, "I am never satisfied unless I either do everything myself or personally superintend everything done even to an entry in the books. This I cannot help. My habit since I have been in business has been so, and I cannot learn to do otherwise." Acknowledging some "wear and tear," Pierpont went on, "I have been pretty well the past week and freer from headaches altho' I do not feel very strong." Junius soon stopped asking and began insisting. In 1864 Pierpont went into partnership with Charles Dabney, his host at the Azores, and later, after Dabney's retirement, with Anthony J. Drexel. It seems remarkable from our point of view, but the man whom we know as the most powerful financier in history was not entirely on his own until he was in his fifties, after his father died in 1890, and it was not until 1895 that he formed J.P. Morgan & Company. When independence came he used it decisively.

With the Civil War came the one major blot on J.P. Morgan's career. This was not his hiring a man to take his place in uniform when conscripts were called, which, while it seems shocking from this distance, was not uncommon practice. (All the same, his seventy-six-year-old grandfather John Pierpont volunteered and served as a Union chaplain.) The near-disaster was his involvement in a war-profiteering scandal that has come to be known as the Hall Carbine Affair. In August of 1861, he financed a deal in which a speculator first purchased from the Union Army five thousand surplus Mexican War-vintage carbines of dubious military value at a price of $3.50 each, and then sold them right back for $22 each. Apparently, Morgan delayed delivery until he was paid with interest. ("Good men are losing their lives while the men whom they defend are debating terms," General John Fremont exclaimed at one point.) On a five-week, $20,000 loan, Morgan cleared a profit of $6,300 or more. When the deal and its terms became known, there was a great public outcry that led to a government investigation, which ignored Morgan in favor of some more well-known figures who were involved, so the young financier got off relatively unscathed. Whatever his complicity in this sordid affair, it was the last time that he allowed his private interest to be so blatantly conflicted with the public's.

Around the time of the Hall Affair he made a decision that was as soft-heartedly rebellious, romantic, and impulsive as the gun deal had been hard-nosed and contrived. He became engaged to a beautiful young woman from a good family named Mimi Sturges — a perfect match except that she was dying of tuberculosis. Over the objections of both families, the ceremony took place with the bridegroom physically supporting the weak young bride throughout. For their grim honeymoon, the couple sailed to Europe, and Mimi died in Nice in February of 1862 after only four months of marriage.

His enthusiastic involvement in this tragedy reflects the trait that Morgan confessed in his letter to his father, the need to feel in control of his environment. At its most extreme, as here, it took the form of a passion to play savior to those who came to him in trouble. According to some psychologists, this pattern of attempt-

ed omniscience appears in people who are unable to accept normal human limitations. The term for such an individual is *puer aeternus,* the "eternal boy." As the Jungian analyst Marie-Louise von Franz has written, "The one thing dreaded throughout by such a type of man is to be bound to anything whatever. There is a terrific fear of being pinned down." In *Ego and Archetype,* another Jungian, Edward Edinger, argues that the *puer'*s savior complex may originate in an over-identification either with the all-dominant God or with the all-suffering victim. One is always saving, the other is always being saved — in the terms of William Blake's haunting poem, "The Tiger," one is the "tiger, tiger burning bright" and the other is the lamb. In Morgan's behavior in 1861 there seems to be an element of both deity and victim, tiger and lamb. Within a matter of months he was, first, the powerful arms supplier who, by controlling the flow of weapons to a beleagured army in the field, can actually affect the ebb and flow of war; and second, the gentle nurturer who defies parental authority to ease a dying woman's passage into the grave.

His reading at the time says much about this state of mind. According to Herbert Satterlee, whose sources included Morgan's diaries, around 1861 Morgan repeatedly returned to the same two stories. One was the Book of Jonah in the Old Testament, which tells of a powerful but self-pitying prophet who arrogantly rejects his calling until God hunts him down and humbles him. The other was Nathanael Hawthorne's "The Birthmark," in which a brilliant scientist devises a potion that removes the single blemish on the skin of his beautiful wife, but that kills her in the process. The last words of Hawthorne's tale echo von Franz's description of the *puer:* "He failed to look beyond the shadowy scope of time, and, living once for all in eternity, to find the perfect future in the present." These are stories about people caught indecisively between present and future, on the one hand in total control of their lives, on the other hand absolutely without control. Unlike most of us, they are not just teetering on the tightrope of life, two steps forward and one step back. Rather they sway wildly from one side to the other, all the while trying to stay suspended in mid-air. To fall is to invite mental illness; to keep up the performance is to invite creative genius.

While we should not forget that Morgan's salvationistic urges had enormous and often helpful social consequences, and while it can be all too easy to be deterministic about someone's youth once his or her adult life is familiar, we can't help speculating about the origins of this particular trait. Even the least psychologically-oriented reader must have picked up a thread or two in this account. Morgan's painful swings of health and mood become understandable when we think of his long periods of solitude in strange surroundings, his sickly, withdrawing mother, his demanding and distant father. His illnesses and prolonged absences from school and family might well have left young Morgan with a powerful mixture of loneliness, rejection, and responsibility — just the right chemistry for becoming an over-achiever. At least he survived to achieve. His younger brother Junius was so persistently ill that the family called him "the Doctor"; he died at the age of twenty-two, in 1858.

This sad childhood will seem uncannily familiar to somebody who has read David McCullough's sensitive biography of the young Theodore Roosevelt, *Mornings on Horseback*. Both Morgan and Roosevelt were sickly, depressive, regularly apart from their fathers, and emotionally distant from their mothers. Both had siblings who died young and tragically, and both lost their first wives early to debilitating illnesses (Roosevelt's wife and mother died on the same night in the same house). Both found an outlet in competition, travel, hyper-masculinity, and codes of exaggerated moral purity. Both lived deadly serious existences broken unexpectedly by impulsive, child-like playfulness. And both perpetually sought out responsibility, Roosevelt noisily at the head of a charge toward a confrontation and Morgan, the classic fixer-up, quietly in the background shadows. Morgan the fixer was forever plugging his power and influence into holes in dikes in order to rescue people, businesses, even countries on the edge of disaster, and, more often than not, succeeding far better than he did with poor Mimi Sturges, whom only God could have saved. They would have had much to talk about had Roosevelt as President not been so belligerently critical of Morgan in the early years of the progressive era — but perhaps that wish demands too much of history.

Not until two months after Mimi's death did the broken Morgan return to New York. He spent most of his free time with her family, only gradually returning to business, which included a controversial and, in the end, unprofitable bout of gold speculation that, once again, seemed unpatriotic everywhere but in the New York and London banking communities. By 1864, when he was twenty-seven, he was earning about $50,000 annually in commissions from fairly easy, safe work — securities sales, currency transfers between the two financial centers, and his firm's own investments. A year later, he married again, this time with family approval, to a pretty home-loving woman, Frances Tracy, whom he had met at St. George's Church. Soon they were settled in a large brownstone house off Fifth Avenue and spending holidays in a rambling house up the Hudson at Cragston, near West Point.

Though he was yet to be in total control of his own business and financial life, after the war Pierpont Morgan began to establish the myth that was later woven by his extravagant accomplishments. As he looked around him, he saw nothing but the same kind of chaotic, untrammeled, acquisitive greed that had produced the panic of 1857. Everywhere the gravy spread, it poured from the pitcher of the railroads. In 1837, Morgan's birth year, there had been fifteen hundred miles of operated track; in 1875 seventy-four thousand miles of iron rails crisscrossed the country. While there was plenty of track, much of it was badly managed and needlessly duplicated. Pierpont knew that; back in 1854, at his father's request, he had toured rail lines in upstate New York and New England. The competition between lines was harsh and ruinous, and although passengers and farmers might benefit from low fares today, the odds were equally good that tomorrow all the lines would go into collusion and double their rates. The effects extended far beyond the rails. When a Cornelius Vanderbilt or an E.H. Harriman decided to build a new line — whether to expand an empire or merely to flex some muscle — the venture would be financed with stock watered down almost to the point of worthlessness, and any hint of trouble would incite investors to panic. When investors panicked there were runs on banks, which would fall, which would lead to yet another recession or depression. The potential profits were enormous, and so were the potential losses. Almost none of this was regulated by the government, and the only industry self-regulation took the form of price-fixing.

It is hard for us to appreciate how chaotic the United States was in the late nineteenth century. We have a suggestion of it today in the confusing effects of airline and telephone deregulation; but now there is a sense that we are a united people and not just a jumble of regions. One single fact tells how far we have come in a century: before 1883 there was no such thing as Standard Time; every town and city kept its own solar time — Boston a few minutes ahead of Hartford, Hartford a few minutes ahead of New York, New York a few minutes ahead of Philadelphia, and so on. It didn't seem to matter. You could live your whole life in Hartford and never care what time it was in Boston. But when the railroads began regularly scheduled intercity traffic, Standard Time and time zones became necessary so that printed schedules would make some sense.

So it was that the railroads changed our perception of time. Simultaneously, under the leadership of Pierpont Morgan, they altered our understanding of organizations. For with the railroads, Morgan developed the idea of the large corporation.

Through the seventies and eighties he gradually came to exert influence and control over the system — not the control of ownership but the power of financial leverage. Morgan was a railroad builder, but not in the track-laying way that Jay Cooke, Jay Gould, the Vanderbilts, E.H. Harriman, and other promoters were. His creativity was fiscal. Railroading had become too expensive for a line's founder to manage without financial assistance; Morgan was the faucet for the cash required to lay all that expensive track. With the access to capital acquired over the years by himself, his father, and George Peabody, he assembled syndicates of American and British financiers to build new railroads, to shore up undercapitalized lines weakened by overcompetition, or to buy sound ones.

For his labors, he received a cash fee or commission and, perhaps more important, blocks of dividend-paying stock and appointments to the boards of directors, which he invariably chaired. Complained one flustered president who had lost control of his company this way, "Wherever Morgan sits on a board is the head of the table, even if he has but a single share." For example, in 1879, after the death of "Commodore" Cornelius Vanderbilt, he organized a syndicate to buy $18 million of the old tycoon's New York Central stock to place through his father's firm in England. The deal netted Drexel, Morgan more than $2 million in profits

and placed Morgan on the Central's board of directors, where he sat until his death in 1913. (His successor, interestingly, was the Commodore's twenty-nine-year-old great-grandson Harold Vanderbilt, a three-time defender of the America's Cup in the 1930s and, like Morgan, a Commodore of the New York Yacht Club. As the inventor of contract bridge, Vanderbilt was also a cardplayer of some note.)

Soon the interlocking directorships were so thickly laid on that, it was said, Morgan could control policy on most of the country's lines, and those lines that. he did not control he could often bludgeon into compliance with his policies by threats of takeovers. Those policies differed strikingly from the ideas of the entrepreneurs. "Consolidation" was the governing word. Morgan closed some lines, sold more, merged many — always with the goal of ending wasteful competition and establishing orderly control. "Morganization" the strategy was called, but "trust" became the most widely used name. Potential conflict of interest ran rife; but at a time when government looked the other way, it was widely accepted as a price worth paying in exchange for minimizing the risk of economic chaos.

Years later, the reforming lawyer (and later Supreme Court justice) Louis Brandeis would criticize Morgan as serving both as an undertaker and as a midwife: every time Morgan & Co. closed down some lines, it created a new one — which, of course, it controlled. The two men were worlds apart in their points of view. Writing in the progressive era of the early twentieth century, Brandeis assumed that there was such a thing as a general public interest that must be served by business and government. Morgan would have found that assumption incomprehensible: the world that he knew was composed not of abstractions like "public interest 'but of constructive individuals of good character who, by pursuing their own specific interests in an honorable way, led the nation to its best interest. He would have applauded the corporate lawyer in Louis Auchincloss's novel *The Rector of Justin* who declares, "It is the moral tone of the business community that sets the moral tone of the nation." It was a perspective that many called arrogant, and arrogant it could be, but it was also lonely and anachronistic.

Just how anachronistic was made apparent in 1901. It had been an exceptionally busy and creative year for J.P. Morgan. He had put together a syndicate to buy out his friend Andrew Carnegie's steel holdings for almost half a billion dollars and create the gigantic United States Steel Corporation (Carnegie had taken his part of the deal, which he estimated at $213 million, and begun to sprinkle the country with public libraries and educational institutions). He had moved toward purchasing two trans-Atlantic steamship lines (whose fortunes never rose and finally sank with their queen, the *Titanic*). And he had barely fought off a raid on the stock of the controlled Northern Pacific Railroad by E.H. Harriman (father of the statesman Averell Harriman). The line was controlled by Morgan and James J. Hill, and Harriman was backed by John D. Rockefeller. With such huge egos and fortunes behind it, the railroad battle got out of hand and started a stock-market panic in which the price of shares of Northern Pacific and other Morgan properties, sold to find cash, swung madly. The crisis ended when Morgan and Harriman compromised on the composition of the Northern Pacific's board of directors. To guarantee stability, Morgan and James J. Hill created an immense trust, the Northern Securities Corporation, which was capitalized at $400 million and which created an immense monopoly of all rail traffic between Minneapolis and the Pacific Northwest states.

Also in 1901, Theodore Roosevelt had become President of the United States following the assassination of William McKinley. Like Morgan in many ways, as we have seen, Roosevelt also shared the older man's conviction that power was a tool of morality. His appearance, exuberance, and reputation to the contrary, Theodore Roosevelt was hardly a radical. If anything, his family, old New York Dutch gentry, had more at stake than Morgan's when it came to the social order. His father and Morgan were rough contemporaries and had traveled in the same circles (they were co-founders of the American Museum of Natural History). But accountable to different communities — Roosevelt to politicians and voters, Morgan to financiers and stockholders — they had inevitably grown apart. Recognizing this division, when he became Vice-President in 1900 at the age of forty-one, Roosevelt hosted a dinner in honor of the sixty-three-year-old banker. After succeeding to the Presidency, Roosevelt assured his banker brother-in-law, "I intend to be most conservative, but in the interests of

the corporations themselves and above all in the interests of the country . . ."

Nevertheless, Morgan's behavior in the Northern Pacific near-catastrophe could not be ignored. Things had come full cycle. Years before, Morgan himself had set out to tame a greedy, rampant Wall Street with the whip of financial leverage and, to a considerable extent, he had succeeded, to his own considerable advantage. Now the lion tamer had become a lion. Lacking any other force, the government would have to enter the cage. In February of 1902 Roosevelt decided to punish Morgan and his colleagues by breaking up Northern Securities under the provisions of the long-ignored Sherman Antitrust Act. The first Morgan heard about it was in the Attorney General's announcement. He rushed to Washington and suggested the kind of simple, private accommodation that had always worked in business. To the President of the United States he proposed, "send your man [the U.S. Attorney General] to my man [a Morgan lawyer] and they can fix it up." Roosevelt demurred. Morgan then asked if the government would go after his other trusts. Roosevelt responded with a Morgan-like moralism: "Certainly not, unless we find out that in any case they have done something that we regard as wrong." Two years later the Supreme Court ordered the dissolution of Northern Securities. The rules had changed.

While railroad reorganization was the foundation of his activity, Morgan's energies were not devoted solely to profiting from a national rail system. For example, he was delighted by and invested in Thomas Edison's phonograph and electric lights, which illuminated his house long before they were in common use in New York. That was, however, small potatoes compared with his international activities: the firm underwrote two wars, making $5 million on a loan to the French during the Franco-Prussian War of 1870 and thirty years later providing Britain twenty percent of the money needed to fight the Boers in South Africa; helped finance the Panama Canal (thereby aiding Roosevelt); played a key figure in the development of Alaska; refinanced the national debt of Argentina; offered to finance the London transit system; and on, and on. Given the number of Morgan's activities, mistakes were inevitable. They often occurred when he strayed from the path of his expertise: the shipping lines he bought made no money and, after he purchased the near-bankrupt publishing house of Harper & Brothers, his accountants discovered that the book business had its own inscrutable rules well beyond their experience and comprehension. But sometimes he was too cautious: he turned down Henry Ford's request for a loan because the automobile quite obviously had no future.

He was at his best during crises. In 1877 he cashed $2.5 worth of U.S. Army pay vouchers at minimal charge while enabling legislation was held up in Congress. It was in financial panics that he thrived. In 1890 and 1893 he leveraged his immense commercial credit and well-regarded reputation to convince other financiers to join him in large syndicates to shore up failing banks. The 1907 crisis he could not stop — it was too great — but he was able to mitigate its terrible effects by backing failing trusts and banks. Finally, he told the presidents of several trusts and banks to gather in his library to work out something and sat himself down in another room to play solitaire. "I don't know what to do myself," he confessed to an assistant, "but sometime, someone will come in with a plan that I know *will* work. And then I will tell them what to do." They came to him with ideas, he did mental calculations and judged, and eventually something was worked out at a loss of only eight failed banks in Manhattan and Brooklyn. A few days later, the City of New York asked for $30 million to meet its payroll and pay its bills. Morgan reflected for two days, negotiated with city officials for a quarter of an hour, and personally drew up a contract. When the panic finally cleared, unlike most of Wall Street he was no poorer, and possibly much richer, than he had been when it began.

His success depended on several characteristics, foremost of which was hard work. Through long, exhausting hours of research that drove some of his well-paid junior partners to the brink, he and his colleagues gained intimate knowledge of the people and firms they were dealing with. Still, the bottom line for him was not a businessman's balance sheet but his character; Morgan was reported to loan tens of thousands of dollars to people with whom he had exchanged little more than a handshake, on the sole basis that he thought them "good men." Finally, his intense personality, which combined the domineering and the mysterious, was a valuable trump card in any negotiation. Wrote a contemporary, "He

has the driving force of a locomotive. He cares nothing for show; he is a plain man of action. He strikes hard blows; he is naturally aggressive. In speech he is candid to the verge of bluntness; in action he is short, sharp, and decisive." When he needed to, he would call upon his sheer physical presence to get men whose wealth was equal to his own to do his bidding. Here is how Herbert Satterlee vividly described his seventy-year-old father-in-law making his rounds in the financial district to put out brushfires of panic in 1907: "He did not dodge, or walk in and out, or halt or slacken his pace. He simply barged along, as if he had been the only man going down the Nassau Street past the Sub-Treasury. He was the embodiment of power and purpose."

Finally, he was lucky to have lived when he did. To paraphrase a political figure of the day, he saw his opportunities and he took them. Many men less talented than he made fortunes in Gilded Age America simply by being in the right place at the right time. In such an unsettled, booming period, most of the barriers against an individual's success are let down. A white male Protestant American with a little seed money, some courage, and a special skill could find opportunities. Of course, Morgan had some special advantages (European connections among them), and as the heir of Junius Morgan and George Peabody he was by no means a new kid on the block. But he went with the flow of commerce, doing what he did best and trusting in his country. Like Peabody, who had made his reputation by successfully backing the state of Maryland in the 1837 panic, Pierpont was bullish on America, and while resisting advice to export his cash in the middle of the depression of 1895 he was heard to mutter, "The man who is a bear on the future of the United States will always go broke."

Not that he seemed to care, but his public reputation changed through all of this from that of a greedy young war profiteer to a heroic battler against uncouth scavengers to a titan equal in power and presence to the kings with whom he was friendly. His wealth and power were so ubiquitous that he became the subject of cautious jokes. By the turn of the century one could purchase, for a penny, a "license to live, signed by J. Pierpont Morgan." The dialect humorist Finley Peter Dunne had his "Mr. Dooley," a cunning observer of American life who disguised his wisdom behind an Irish accent, say this about Morgan:

Pierpont Morgan calls in wan iv his office boys, th' president iv a naytional bank, an' says he, "James," he says, "take some change out iv the damper an' r-run out an' buy Europe f'r me," he says. "I intind to re-organize it an' put it on a paying basis," he says. "Call up the Czar an' th' Pope an th' Sultan an' th' Impror Willum, an' tell thim we won't need their sarvices afther nex' week."

Within a decade this joviality had turned sharper under the grinding wheel of the progressive movement; investigative journalists, Congressional committees, and government agencies were examining Morgan's tactics and goals with the same regulatory fervor with which the great financier had gone after the warring railroad builders in the 1870s and 1880s. Short of opening his books, he did his best to explain his *modus operandi* to them, but his language — guarded, elliptical, moralistic, and overflowing with individualism — was like Chinese to reformers who thought in terms of social groups, public benefits, and concrete, measurable reality, and who could not understand how making a killing on the stock market was a matter of "character." He was an old man; they were young men.

What drew them to him was, of course, that he was a wealthy man who cared not to hide it. By the mid-1870s he probably was earning half a million dollars a year as a partner of Drexel, Morgan. Half of it he reinvested in the firm; the rest he spent on himself (the government got very little of it, as during his lifetime income taxes were collected only during the Civil War and for a few years after 1894, before the Supreme Court declared the tax unconstitutional). By 1880, when he was forty-three, his net worth was estimated at $25 million, and his peak earning years lay ahead of him. Therefore, after his death in 1913, there was some surprise that his estate was valued at only $77.5 million. Though large for a banker, it seemed small for a Morgan. It seemed smaller yet when compared with the estates of the great manufacturers and producers like Andrew Carnegie, who had $100 million even before he was bought out in 1901, and John D. Rockefeller, who *gave away* perhaps $500 million in his long life and who, on hearing of Morgan's leavings, was moved to comment, "And to think that he wasn't even a rich man."

Where did all the money go? Unlike Rockefeller and other classically American millionaires, who seemed to enjoy money only for its own sake, Morgan liked to spend it. In that way he was very much like the wealthy Englishmen and Europeans whom he used to visit on his long trips abroad. To quote Andrew Sinclair, "He spent it like a patriarch who was dominated by another patriarch who was influenced by the ultimate matriarch of them all" — Queen Victoria. She, Junius, and Pierpont did not want anybody to forget that they had both good taste and the funds to expend tastefully. Though Junius was a bit cautious, the younger Morgan, like the great Queen herself, poured money into yachts, religion, art, and travel.

Not until the 1870s, as he was approaching middle age, did Morgan begin to use his money royally. While he had not been parsimonious — there were city and country homes, clubs, trips abroad — he had not allowed himself the time to spend it well. What brought the change was his old enemy, physical breakdown. Frequent eruptions of the ghastly eczema, chronic headaches, and fainting fits began to pile one upon the other and led him to take increasing time off from work. Eventually he would learn how to pace himself and take a regular long annual vacation. "I can do twelve months work in nine months," he once said, "but not in twelve months." Fortunately his ability to spot and hire good partners and assistants enabled him to ease his burden at no financial sacrifice. But in 1871 and later in 1876, when the pressures and his body's protests against them became unbearable, he took a year off to tour Europe, taking the waters at fashionable German spas, climbing Swiss mountains, and running up the Nile in steamers to gawk at ancient ruins (like the one at Khargeh where he would fund a dig), before stopping for a while in London to do business with his father. Later, after his fascination with antiquities and religious art inevitably drew him to Rome, someone inquired after his favorite places. With usual succinctness, Morgan answered, "New York, because it is my home; London, because it is my second home; Rome and Khargeh."

Of the interests, collecting would take up the most time and money. Perhaps as an outgrowth of his passion to control everything, he was by nature a collector. As a boy in Europe, he would crawl around the walls of old churches picking up pieces of broken stained glass, and nag bishops for their autographs. Much later, he would bring back small antiquities from his Egyptian trips and a few paintings by minor French artists; but it probably was more out of civic duty than any special interest that he agreed to be a trustee of the new Metropolitan Museum of Art in 1888. Sometime around then, he spent $90 on his first manuscript, the work of William Makepeace Thackeray. His father's death two years later, besides increasing his resources, seemed to liberate him to follow his impulses, and in the twenty-three years before his death he amassed what has been estimated as the largest art collection ever in private hands in the west. He devoted perhaps half his wealth (and, some think, all his income from his firm), to this accumulation of manuscripts, paintings, and sculpture; in 1912 he estimated its value at $50 million. His vacations abroad became extravagant shopping sprees, with art dealers crowding his hotel lobby. On one of these trips, in 1906, he paid $750,000 for art in only two months. Sometimes he was burned by forgeries or excessive prices — but not often, for he quickly developed a sensitivity to both. When the dealer Joseph Duveen offered a group sale of twenty-four so-so miniatures alongside six extremely rare ones, Morgan saw the trap, dismissed the mediocrities, and bought the valuable pieces at a relative bargain. His uncle Henry Duveen, also a dealer, gloated, "You're only a boy, Joe. It takes a man to deal with Morgan."

So great was his expenditure that, contrary to popular expectation, he did not bequeath the collection to the Metropolitan. This was only partly because, as Calvin Tompkins describes it in his delightful history of the museum, *Merchants and Masterpieces,* their relationship was a stormy one. The main reason was simply that he was art-rich and cash poor. So much of his estate was tied up in the collection that he feared that, were his heirs unable to sell part or all of it, they would not have enough cash to pay the inheritance taxes. Eventually, after selling some art, his son donated about forty percent of the original collection to the Met and placed the remainder in the Pierpont Morgan Library. Located at Madison Avenue and Thirty-sixth Street, and an expansion of his father's personal office-library (which still is there as Pierpont used it), the Morgan Library is one of the most pleasant public places in Manhattan. It holds ongoing exhibits of illuminated

manuscripts, drawings, and fine books. In all it can be said that Pierpont Morgan almost singlehandedly introduced European art to the United States.

This Continental side of Morgan fascinated people who tended to associate the words "American millionaire" with crude provincialism, and it fit into his daily life as snugly as a hand in a glove. Rather than merely accumulating art, he acquired a taste for what he liked and surrounded himself with it. "I doubt if any private citizen lived in as comfortable splendor as did Mr. Morgan," his friend Bishop William Lawrence wrote. "Some may have had more comfort, others more splendor, but his was splendor with comfort . . . I never knew a man to whom in expenditure the question of dollars was of less interest, nor one who so naturally surrounded himself with all that was richest, most convenient, and artistic." Lawrence was thinking especially of Morgan's London house (now the United States Embassy), but his New York accommodations had the same quality. His personal office in the Morgan Library is a small museum in itself; his desk is surrounded with exquisite crucifixes, triptychs, and religious paintings.

Comparisons with Renaissance potentates were inevitable; in the 1950s, a director of the Metropolitan, Francis Henry Taylor, would say of Morgan and Lorenzo de' Medici, "both men looked upon money as a source of maximum power and infallibility — never as an end in itself." On that note, it is fascinating that Morgan, about whom everything else was giant-sized, specialized in acquiring tiny items: Chinese porcelains, Holbein miniatures, religious icons, illuminations — and (most interesting) children's books, which now fill the shelves of the Library's East Wing only a few steps from the room where their purchaser wielded such power. Some might see in his fascination with small objects a passion to dominate, but there may be something else in it. In Egypt, Bishop Lawrence once watched Morgan pick up a tiny Coptic box with "a delight [that] was that of a child who has happened upon an unexpected toy." Morgan would not be separated from the object for the rest of the trip, Lawrence observed in his autobiography, *Memories of a Happy Life.*

While such behavior may hint at Charles Foster Kane's neurotic longing for a sled named "Rosebud," in Orson Welles's film *Citizen Kane,* there is something more playful and elemental about it, as though this man whose business it was to help others buy and make things had discovered his own corner of creativity. Perhaps the same interpretation can be made about his passion for original drafts of creative writing like Lord Byron's manuscripts, which a relative of the poet's had in Greece. "Libraries in England were after them. I wanted them," Bishop Lawrence quoted Morgan as saying. "I therefore, through the advice of an expert, engaged a man, gave him a letter of credit, and told him to go to Greece and live until he had gotten those manuscripts. Every once in a while, during several years, a volume would come which the relative had been willing to sell, until the whole was complete." What mattered, besides the originality of the object, was "the whole"; Morgan usually preferred to purchase entire collections and sets rather than individual items.

Like Lorenzo the Magnificent, Morgan was attracted most to religious objects. Mrs. Morgan once remarked that if her husband knew that Mary Magdalene's finger still existed somewhere, he would search the world for it. The man who heard that comment regarded it as a joke; but if it was it may also have been one of those slips of the tongue that Freud found so serious. Some people cannot look at a rich man's religious life without cynicism; but by all accounts Morgan's was honest and deep. Despite his claims to the contrary, he modified the old-fashioned, hymn-singing piety in which he had been raised with an element of mysticism seen at various moments in his life. For example, in 1881, he joined his father for a Mediterranean cruise on a chartered yacht. They cruised to the Holy Land, where he went ashore and toured Biblical sites, eventually arriving at the Church of the Holy Sepulchre, allegedly built over Christ's tomb. In a letter to his wife, quoted in Stanley Jackson's biography, he vividly described his pilgrimage to the church:

A death-like stillness pervades, the distant sounds of an organ in a distant part of the Church are heard, awestruck and impressed you stand almost breathless upon what must have been the most sacred spot on earth. I cannot attempt to describe my feelings, words fail me entirely. I could only say to myself, it is good to be here. While we stood there pilgrims came in one after the other, in rapid succession and thus, I suppose, it has been for centuries

... Through a door about four feet high into a vestibule you pass through another door and you are in the Sepulchre of our Lord. There is the slab on which He was laid. Impelled by an impulse impossible to resist you fall on your knees before that shrine.

On returning to New York, Morgan made two of his most impressive decisions: he bought *Corsair* for use primarily as a ferry boat to run him up to his house at Cragston (ever the romantic, he retained her old piratical name); and he hired a radical preacher, the Rev. William Stephen Rainsford, to be his priest at St. George's Church, on Stuyvesant Square on East Sixteenth Street in Manhattan. Morgan, like many people of his background, had been recently confirmed in the Episcopal Church. The American gentry were becoming increasingly Anglified after the Civil War — Morgan himself was in all respects but bloodline an Anglo-American — and there are few American institutions more Anglified than the Episcopal Church. St. George's had been left behind by the move uptown by the upper classes, and Morgan typically decided to save it.

When Morgan allied himself with an institution, he supported it. Not only did he cover much of St. George's expenses, but he was a regular and generous attendant at the Episcopal Church's triennial general conventions, often transporting flocks of bishops and priests on his private train. At the request of Bishop Lawrence, he made the first big donation to the church's pension fund. His aesthetic sensibilities and desire to import European art led him to support the construction of the enormous Cathedral of St. John the Divine, on New York's Morningside Heights, as well as Fifth Avenue's St. Thomas's Church.

Yet, like most people, while he was at ease with the institution he was inarticulate about the spirit it represents. In his memoirs, *The Story of a Varied Life,* Rainsford described him as defensive, rigid, suspicious of ritual and liturgy — a man showing few doubts whose religion "has become a water-tight compartment in life's ship, separated quite from the miscellaneous cargo which it carried. Perhaps," Rainsford allowed, "it may keep the ship from sinking. If so, that is all that can be said for it." Yet we know that while Morgan delighted in Sunday-evening family hymn sings, he would sometimes spend an evening sitting alone in the darkened nave as the organist played. His mysticism extended beyond the bounds of organized religion. A well-known astrologer named Evangeline Adams regularly read his horoscope, and his interest in Egyptology probably extended to some dabbling with theories of reincarnation — though maybe not to the extent described in the brilliant fanciful-historical novel *Ragtime*, where E.L. Doctorow portrays the aged Morgan spending a night alone in the Great Pyramid impatiently awaiting an announcement concerning the future of his soul.

Perhaps because he had traveled with Morgan and seen him with his art collection, Bishop Lawrence sensed his complexity better than Rainsford. Overhearing a woman praise Morgan's collection, he declared to her, "The most interesting thing in this house is the host." The bishop elaborated in his memoirs:

He was in some ways as simple as a child, most emotional, most bashful, masterful, courageous: a genius in his instinct for things beautiful; with a brain that drove him ceaselessly in his search for beauty and his desire to acquire the best. His dominant characteristic was his search for truth: his eye and mind seemed to pierce and consume shams and lies.

Rainsford once caught Morgan himself in one of these shams. Morgan's redeeming feature, Rainsford wrote, was "his constant habit of trusting men who did things. He was always looking for men fit to lead. He believed more in men than in measure . . . He was ever in support of anyone who could do things that *had* to be done." A social reformer whom Morgan traced down and hired from a Canadian parish, Rainsford made it clear that he would not drop his radicalism just because he preached in Pierpont Morgan's church. He asked for and got Morgan's promise of continuing support. So that newcomers of all incomes would feel welcome, he insisted that the church drop the old system of pew rents. Morgan went along. Then he created what today is called a street ministry, taking in the poor and expanding the congregation to callous-handed workers. Morgan also went along, at least in public.

Finally, Rainsford went too far for Morgan. In 1902 he asked the vestry to take among them a working man who had run the Sunday school with great success. Morgan would not have it. "I want at times to have these vestry meetings held in my study," Rainsford quoted him as responding. "This vestry should be composed, in my judgment, of men whom I can invite to my study, and who can help me carry the heavy financial burden of the church . . . I do not want the vestry democratized. I want it to remain a body of gentlemen whom I can ask to meet me in my study." The remainder of the vestry, which included the Mayor of New York City and a man in deep debt to Morgan, voted with Rainsford against Morgan, who the next day sent Rainsford a letter of resignation.

The story continues toward a strange and moving ending. The two men had become extremely close over the years, at least partly because they both suffered from overwork and occasional physical breakdown, and they were used to sharing a weekly breakfast at Morgan's Madison Avenue home. Despite the vestry blow-up Rainsford went as scheduled the next week, and when Morgan grouchily asked if he had submitted the resignation, he answered that he would not because to do so would allow Morgan to renege on the pledge of support he had made when Rainsford was hired. "I told you I was a radical," the clergyman reminded him. "I told you I would do all I could to democratize the church. I am only keeping my word. I shall certainly not now, nor at any time, do anything to help you break yours."

The subject never came up again, and a few weeks later Rainsford went down to the dock to see Morgan off to Europe. "As I went up the gangplank, I saw Mr. Morgan standing at some distance surrounded by his friends. At the same instant he saw me, and coming out of the group, signed me to follow him. We made for his cabin, entered quickly, without saying a word, and shut and bolted the door behind us." Morgan threw himself on his knees and despairingly asked Rainsford to pray for him. After that, Rainsford wrote, "We never had another falling out."

Perhaps this was one of the few occasions, Rainsford mentions, with a confessor's tact, that Morgan cracked. He was "more reserved than any man I ever knew. When under life's stress that reserve broke down, then the profound emotionalism of his nature had its way with him. The great deeps were broken up, and he called aloud for help." In all the thirty years that Rainsford knew Pierpont Morgan, and he probably knew him in strength and weakness as well as any man, such release came only three times.

Here is Morgan in his yachting uniform during his tenure as Commodore of the New York Yacht Club between 1897 and 1899. He was then in his early sixties and at the peak of his powers and independence as a banker, art collector, and yachtsman. The key to his success and influence was that he saw moral and spiritual value in what he did. Morgan ''looked on money as a source of maximum power and infallibility — never as an end in itself,'' a director of the Metropolitan Museum of Art has written.

Those moments of deep emotion came rarely in public. All who knew Morgan agreed with Rainsford that the great man was also an intensely private man forever playing the cards of life close to his vest. It wasn't that he was afraid of people. He had no compunction against taking the elevated railroad to his office and to church, and in his office at 23 Wall Street he worked in plain view in a small glass-walled cubicle in the middle of an open floor crammed with his partners and their functionaries. In fact, access to others was one key to his success, for his way of doing business depended on quick communication and decision-making, and the fishbowl office allowed him both (not surprisingly, when the telephone came along he immediately subscribed). But Morgan, who had none of the traits of the natural extrovert, must have suffered for that accessibility. Even before he became a celebrity, the kind of lonely privacy that he endured and often enjoyed as a child had become habitual, and as he aged he found it more and more frequently on his yachts.

Nothing is known of his interest in yachting before 1881, when he decided to buy his first yacht. Yachting had become the rage of the New York gentry, and Morgan placed an option to buy a one-hundred eighty-five foot black-hulled steamer called *Corsair* from a member of the New York Yacht Club, then went off to cruise to Palestine with his father, presumably with some idea of seeing if he might enjoy the pastime. He made good on the option on his return, and the next year he quite naturally became a member of the club of which he, his son, and two of his grandsons would eventually be Commodore.

Corsair was the second largest vessel in the club's squadron. By the end of the decade she was dwarfed by other steamers, so Morgan built a new two hundred forty-one footer to the design of an Irish émigré named J. Beavor-Webb who, having drawn the lines of Britain's 1885 and 1886 America's Cup challengers, had settled in the United States to make a good living creating fashionable steam yachts. Morgan took little interest in her, merely giving a business associate a book of blank checks and instructions to come back with the best possible vessel.

The second *Corsair* was one of those yachts that truly deserve the clichés "sleek," "powerful," and "piratical." Morgan used her well and hard until 1898, when the government requested that he hand her over for naval duty in the war against Spain. A man who rarely failed to control his surroundings, he was helpless in this situation; there was no decent way that he alone among the twenty-one grand yachtsmen who had been approached could disobey this implied command, even though he needed *Corsair* as his flagship during his tour as the yacht club's Commodore. Not placated by her distinguished war record — as the U.S.S. *Gloucester,* she sank a Spanish torpedo boat in a battle off Cuba — Morgan impatiently ordered a new, three hundred four-foot *Corsair.* He had grown to enjoy yachting, and this time he took more interest in his yacht's design and construction. Like a sentimental man attempting to remake a woman in the form of a previous love, he insisted that she be a replica of the old vessel, right down to the rug pattern (since the mill had gone out of business, the carpets had to be custom-woven). With the same gleaming black topsides, sweeping sheerline, and gilt clipper bow, the replacement flagship was finished in time to join Sir Thomas Lipton's big *Erin* at the head of the triumphal parade honoring the Spanish-American war hero, Admiral George Dewey, just before the 1899 America's Cup match between Morgan's *Columbia* and Lipton's *Shamrock.* Although there is a mention or two of Morgan's going aboard a racing sailboat, like almost all owners of big yachts in his day he was a spectator when the racing got serious.

Morgan's summer routine was to spend weekends with his family on his estate up the Hudson River, and on Sunday night steam down the river in *Corsair.* Early on Monday morning he went ashore and spent the week at his office, in his town house, or aboard the yacht entertaining friends and clients on evening cruises. On Friday afternoon, *Corsair* would steam back up the Hudson. Although he was once quoted as saying, "You can do business with anyone but you can only sail with a gentleman," Morgan may not have been as snobbish on board *Corsair* as he was among the vestry of St. George's Church. Although his relationship with Mrs. Morgan seems to have been initially warm, as his children grew and he began to travel the family spent less and less time together. The yachts became the site for gatherings with card-playing men friends who made up a group called "The Corsair Club" — and for parties that included more than a few actresses and singers. One of these, the glamorous Maxine Elliott, later

Islands of Privacy

As Queen Victoria, Kaiser Wilhelm, and countless other monarchs had discovered, a yacht also provided secrecy. On the *Corsairs,* Morgan could conduct the most sensitive meetings out of the spotlight of an increasingly inquisitive press. For example, to arrange a settlement between two competing railroads fighting a ruinous tariff war that was lowering profits for Morgan and other investors, he invited the presidents out for a sail on the Hudson. Ordering the captain to keep steaming up and down the river, he refused to let his prisoners go ashore until they agreed to his terms. Later, when he offered to loan the U.S. Treasury a substantial sum of money and a public meeting between him and Grover Cleveland would have been politically fatal to the President, he had *Corsair* steam to Shelter Island, where she quietly dropped anchor one evening near another steamer, *Oneida,* on board which Cleveland was cruising. Morgan went over in a launch and the two men negotiated the loan in the privacy of the warm evening. (Cleveland benefited from a yacht's privacy in another way. At a time when a report of serious illness would have intensified the economic distress of the Panic of 1893, he was secretly and successfully operated on for cancer on board *Oneida.*) And the third *Corsair* was the safe house for a conference in 1900 between Morgan and presidential candidate William McKinley's right-hand man, Mark Hanna, in which the financier was assured of McKinley's conservatism.

This 1883 painting by Frederic S. Cozzens catches one of the turning points in maritime history. The old era is represented by the big cargo-carrying sloop drifting down the Hudson River under the cliffs of the Palisades. The new era is represented by the big steamers Stranger, *left, and* Atalanta.

claimed that she convinced Morgan to redesign the third *Corsair*. A story told about Morgan and one of his partners, Charles A. Schwab, suggests the importance of the yachts in this capacity. After Schwab's indiscretions on the Riviera got him into the gossip columns, Morgan bawled him out. Schwab protested that he was only doing in public what Morgan had been doing behind closed doors. "That," snapped Morgan, "is what doors are for!" And perhaps yachts, too.

Corsair was not a mere business tool, however, a floating version of today's corporate jets. When aboard, owners like Morgan took great pride in their vessels, pampered them with money and gilt, and perpetually struggled to make an accommodation between their love of luxury and the harsh marine environment. A famous and perhaps even true anecdote concerns Morgan's partner Anthony J. Drexel, whose affection for roses was so great that he installed a garden on the deck of his steamer *Sayonara*. It might have worked with wild roses, but the cultured ones he planted only wilted and died in the salt air. Stubbornly ordering some painted rubber roses, Drexel was again disappointed when their pigment bled and stained the teak deck, which forced him to lay a special carpeting that cost $15 a square yard.

Morgan cared about his yachts, certainly, but he also showed concern about the health and image of his social class. At one time he was a member of nineteen different New York men's clubs. While they all must have been important to him for some reason or another — at the least, as a place to do a little business over a quiet lunch — the New York Yacht Club got a great deal of his attention. It can be honestly said that he was the godfather of the modern New York Yacht Club and, therefore, of modern elite yachting. In the index to the two-volume club history, written by John Parkinson Jr., no other member — not even the N.Y.Y.C.'s founder, John Cox Stevens — enjoys as long a listing as Morgan. He joined in 1882 and fifteen years later was elected Commodore without having gone through the usual initiation of first serving as Rear or Vice-Commodore. Being Morgan, he took special interest in that larger-than-life event, the America's Cup, and, as we will see in the next chapter, played an important role in dealing with the Earl of Dunraven's claims that the American yachtsmen who defended the Cup in 1895 cheated.

Besides helping to fend off the attack from the old world, Morgan's most memorable service to his club was to buy the plots of land on which the new clubhouse was built. In the Morgan fashion, he imposed two stipulations: it must be a big building (the street frontage would be exactly seventy-five feet); and the increased cost of management must be covered by doubling the annual dues from $25 to $50. Using his typical strategy of a surprise attack, he made this announcement with no warning at the 1898 annual meeting, leaving the unprepared members no alternative but to go along. The eclectic William Warren-designed building was opened in 1901. Besides having all the normal luxuries — an oyster bar, a big dining room, a quiet library — it was an unmatched temple to boats with its ship-like exterior and magnificent model room, whose ceiling included acres of Tiffany glass. There businessmen would gather to talk about boats and, more frequently than sometimes, about business and politics, too.

Here in his club and yachts, as much as in his churches, we see Pierpont Morgan in all of his grand contrariness: a self-advertised conservative out to tame and radically reshape the chaotic world around him. Unlike the wild-eyed James Gordon Bennett Jr. and other Gilded Age tycoons who enjoyed luxury yachting with an abandon that seems wonderfully Mediterranean and loose, the more somber and northern Morgan took his greatest satisfaction — "pleasure" isn't quite the word — not in yachting competition but by using the arena of competition as a place for creating an ethical standard for the class of American businessmen whose moral as well as financial leadership he was quick to assume. Puritan in both tone and daring, this project was a disciplined synthesis of many old values to fit a new people in a new land. The taking-off point was the apparently disintegrating morality of the English aristocracy, yet the means was the appropriation and reformation of that same aristocracy's institutions and symbols — among them yachts and men's clubs and Anglican churches. This mix of Anglophilia and Anglophobia saturated the Gilded Age, and remains a major force in certain parts of our society. Anybody seeking prestige and power inevitably is drawn to it and its trappings. And for that we have Morgan to at least partially thank (or to blame).

After some modernization, the N.Y.Y.C. clubhouse is still much

the same as it ever was, and with a membership of about twenty-five hundred men and women (gender distinctions were finally erased from the club's by-laws in 1984) is both the closest there is to America's national yacht club and, packed to the walls with leather chairs and oak tables, the best approximation of what a nineteenth-century tycoon's townhouse and club were like. For many years before it went to Australia in 1983, the America's Cup was on display in a small trophy room off the main bar. In its place now is a magnificent model of a Tudor warship that Morgan donated. Morgan's imprint is everywhere. His official Commodore's portrait glowers from a stairwell wall. In the model room, scale models of the second *Corsair* as yacht and as warship vie with tiny versions of the great Cup defenders that he paid for. If the Pierpont Morgan Library is one of New York's loveliest buildings accessible to the public, Morgan's other gift remains one of the most pleasant private buildings. Perhaps not coincidentally, at the first corner on the way from the yacht club to the library there is a branch of the Morgan Guaranty Trust Company, which people still call "the Morgan bank."

Morgan was sixty-three when the new clubhouse opened, seventy when he helped put out the contagion of the 1907 Panic. That he had lived so long so actively despite his history of bad health speaks of the strength of the "water-tight compartment" of simple faith of which Reverend Rainsford was so critical. Yet his continuing passion for art testifies also to an extraordinary inner vitality. Mostly retired from work, he spent more time abroad extending his collection with typical extravagant abandon. In the winter of 1912 he sailed up the Nile on his new one-hundred thirty-foot luxury barge. Bishop Lawrence, who was aboard, found it a tiring sprint. "Our movement was fast," he wrote in his memoirs, "really too fast to observe the beauties of the tranquil atmosphere of Egypt. In less than a month we had run up and down the Nile, two thousand miles, besides making many stops and excursions at various points." Somewhere along the way Morgan pointed out the exact spot where Moses was found in the bulrushes, declaring with the certitude of an old man grasping for hope, "Critics may say there were never any bulrushes or any Moses; but I know that there was a Moses and that he was hidden in the bulrushes, for there is a spot. It must be so."

A charming liveliness was still there in his relationship with women. With considerable circumspection, he enjoyed the company of Maxine Elliott and, later, Lady Victoria Sackville, the somewhat notorious half-Spanish illegitimate daughter of an English nobleman. Morgan had helped Lady Victoria financially, and she returned the favor by flattering and flirting with him and opening her ear to his complaints and opinions. "He told me many of the bothers of being rich," she wrote in her diary in 1911, "but the great thing was to have personality, which he has to an infinite degree." She called on him at his London house in May of 1912:

He was arranging a loan with ten men, for China, but he gave me half an hour all the same. He came in like a whirlwind and crushed me, saying he had longed for this moment, that he had told nobody of his return, but wanted to see me at once . . . I can think of nothing else. That man has such marvelous personality and attraction for me.

That was his last flirtation. He returned to America to endure the spotlight of the Pujo Committee investigations into what was called "the Money Trust," which led to banking reform laws that undid some of Morgan's practices, among them interlocking directorships of banks. Morgan was undone by the hearings, partly because of his shyness but mainly because he was told that his behavior and policies, which he and others had long regarded as grand public service, were little more than petty acts of greed. Even Theodore Roosevelt had approved of Morgan's maneuverings in 1907; now, President Woodrow Wilson declined to meet with him.

Feeling rejected in the new world, he retraced his steps to the old, but Egypt no longer satisfied. Tormented by nervousness, indigestion, and the nagging of the ubiquitous journalists and art dealers, he fled to Rome. It was Easter, but he felt no joy. Satterlee, called from New York, found him deeply depressed and refusing to eat. Taking to his bed in his suite in the Grand Hotel, Morgan maundered on about his boyhood and his old Hartford acquaintances until, early in the morning of March 31, 1913, he gestured toward the ceiling and mumbled, "I've got to go up the hill."

Moments later, the torch was extinguished.

VI

The Bottom Line: The America's Cup, 1870-1913

"I pledge you, sirs, the Cup!
May we never give it up!
A bumper, sirs: the Club! Hurrah!
The Cup! The Cup! The Cup!

ohn Cox Stevens and his partners in the *America* adventure brought the Hundred Guinea Cup back to New York in the late summer of 1851, and there it stayed for one hundred thirty-two years until, on a September evening in 1983, a Brink's armored truck carried it off to Newport to be presented to another group of high-stakes sportsmen. One indication of the significance of the victory of *Australia II* is the following table of results of America's Cup matches between 1870 and 1980:

	NEW YORK YACHT CLUB	CHALLENGERS
Matches won	24	0
Races won	81	8

In a phrase, the New York Yacht Club dominated this event in a way that no other group has ever done in any sport. How did this happen? One reason is that the club was always represented by skilled yacht designers, sailmakers, equipment manufacturers, and sailors. But that is only part of the answer; challengers were often equally talented at "hardware" skills and at making sailboats go fast, and sometimes were clearly superior in these departments. No, the main reason for this long winning streak is the "soft" skill of good management.

In expense, technical challenges, and personnel problems, a Cup campaign is an industrial corporation writ small, and it was Americans who invented and refined the modern corporation. Like J.P. Morgan's financial trust, a well-managed Cup syndicate tamed the natural human impulse toward individualism and wasteful competition, and obsessively and cold-heartedly focused resources toward a single bottom-line goal: to win the Cup. Cup defense managers, many of them trained as bankers and corporate officers, knew how to set goals, find talented people, and delegate responsibility, always acting from a position safely in the background. Perhaps most important, they never became complacent. Because it was never lost — because only three times between 1870 and 1980 was there even any serious risk that it *might* be lost — the America's Cup should have seemed as secure in its glass case as, say, the Statue of Liberty was in the harbor where Cup races once were sailed. Nevertheless, with each foreign challenge, the yacht club's members pursued a successful defense with the fervor of the

directors of a successful company grasping at more profits. Once a campaign's budget was toted, the only tolerable bottom line was the largest possible winning margin over the English, Canadian, Irish, or Australian challenger.

A price is paid for this tight management. Just as the machine-like trust was a world far removed from the wild, loose frontier entrepreneurship of the Gilded Age, the successful America's Cup campaign organization is foreign to the joy of old-fashioned sailing. Organization men did well in this arena; individualists either did not or stayed away from it. J.P. Morgan helped finance several Cup yachts, but James Gordon Bennett, that prince of spontaneity, never did get deeply involved with Cup defenses. The free-wheeling individualists who challenged for the Cup — aristocrats and entrepreneurs, on the whole — were out of their league. As a rule, any America's Cup campaign that is better known for impulsiveness and charm rather than for cold competence is, in terms of the bottom line, a failed campaign. This means that the most appealing people in Cup history usually have been losers. Here we will see how this rule is illustrated in the America's Cup matches through 1903; in a later chapter we will show how the bottom line has dominated since 1920.

The members of *America*'s syndicate did not know what to do with the ugly ewer once they stopped showing it off at sumptuous welcoming dinners. For a while, they considered melting it down to make medallions for their children and grandchildren; but sometime in 1852 they decided to give it to the New York Yacht Club. In a short letter serving as a deed of gift, they established it as "perpetually a Challenge Cup for friendly competition between foreign countries," and called for "matches" to be held between yacht clubs, and not individuals. Taking possession of the trophy after the death of John Cox Stevens in 1857, the yacht club invited challenges for it from eighteen British yacht clubs and others in Canada, Belgium, the Netherlands, and Russia, promising "a liberal, hearty welcome, and strictest fair play."

Before we proceed, let us make sure that we understand one important truth about the trophy: it was owned by the New York Yacht Club. It was first known by its original name, the Hundred Guinea Cup, or sometimes as the Queen's Cup because Stevens had enthusiastically, but inaccurately, claimed that Queen Victo-

On page 116, James Gordon Bennett's Dauntless *crosses the bow of James Ashbury's* Livonia *in a private race sailed after the controversial 1871 Cup match, when the New York Yacht Club picked its defender daily from a fleet of four yachts. Ashbury protested so vehemently that the club returned the trophies that he had presented.* Livonia, *named after a Russian province where Ashbury's railroad enterprises thrived, still won a race when the defender of the day broke down. A New York newspaper ironically explained, "It had been supposed that the New York Yacht Club had made their preparations so carefully as to leave Mr. Ashbury no chance whatsoever of winning a race. Accidents, however, can annul the most careful preparations." Painted by James E. Buttersworth, one of the foremost marine artists of the period, the picture throbs with the power of the sea and these large vessels. Opposite, in one of the races held in England in 1868 that soothed diplomatic tensions after the Civil War and led Ashbury to challenge for the Cup, Ashbury's* Cambria, *right, passes the visiting American schooner* Sappho, *which later won two races in the 1871 match.*

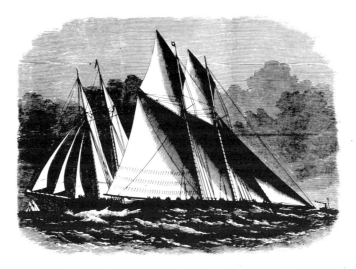

later, Ashbury demanded more even treatment; "match," he argued, clearly implied a one-on-one race. He was supported by George L. Schuyler, the surviving member of the *America* syndicate, who said that a race like the one in 1870 "renders the *America*'s trophy useless as a challenge cup." The club complied, but with a hitch: each morning it would choose its representative from among four yachts. Not surprisingly, each of the four was especially fast in a specific wind condition. Ironically, the club's clever strategy backfired due to poor preparation. The only boat available to sail in the third race was the beamy *Columbia*, a prototype of *Mohawk*. Not in good condition and sailed by a volunteer crew, she went out of control in a strong wind, broke down, and eventually finished nineteen minutes behind Ashbury's *Livonia*. That win was the first by a Cup challenger; it was also the last one until 1920, the thirteenth match.

The next two challenges were from a determined Canadian named Alexander Cuthbert. In the entire history of the America's Cup, nobody has been more out of place than this romantic boatbuilder who, almost singlehanded, paid for, constructed, and captained his own challengers. Only the Florida boatbuilder Charley Morgan, who sailed *Heritage* in the 1970 defense trials, made such a personal commitment. Many Cup historians have made fun of Cuthbert because his boats were crude and slow and he tended toward quixotic optimism. But, to quote Winfield S. Thompson's praise of him in *The Lawson History of the America's Cup:*

> *Captain Cuthbert handled the straight-edge and the adze, and he was the only man who ever challenged for the Cup who could and did himself create with brain and hand a vessel to sail under his challenge. His efforts and motives should be rated accordingly.*

His first vessel was *Countess of Dufferin,* best known as the first Cup boat named for a living human being, the wife of the Governor-General of Canada, who was one of the first cruising yachtsmen and who twenty years later would help talk Sir Thomas Lipton into challenging. Two defenders were named, but only one sailed in what turned out to be a walkover. That *Countess* was badly beaten only seemed to encourage Cuthbert, who came down

ria had donated it to the Royal Yacht Squadron. By the mid-1870s, it came to be called "the *America* Cup" in honor of the yacht that won it. Later, that was transformed to "*America*'s Cup" and, eventually, "the America's Cup". Although the italics are missing in the most recent and popular name, no one should make the mistake of believing that this Cup belonged in any way to the nation. If anybody owned the Cup, it was the New York Yacht Club. Acknowledging this fact would have saved a few people a quantity of money and many more people hours of sentimental weeping over lost ideals of fairness.

The first of those tears were shed in 1870 and 1871, when the initial two challenges for the Cup came from James Ashbury, whose father had made a fortune off railway carriages, and whose aim was publicity to help him win an election to Parliament. (With some exceptions, Cup defenders and challengers through the sixteenth match, in 1937, were financed by fortunes made in transportation, while later ones tended to be backed by communications and real estate tycoons.) In 1870, the yacht club's way to define "strictest fair play" and "match" was to duplicate the 1851 race by sending its fleet of schooners out to race against the sole visitor on the tricky, narrow club course in New York Bay. Ashbury's *Cambria* was badly beaten and the race was won by the much shorter *Magic,* which William Garner soon bought. A year once again five years later. By then, Schuyler and others had succeeded in convincing the club to modify its curious definition of "match," and only one defender was named. From then on it was a true one-on-one match, best out of three races (later five and seven) to take the Cup.

By this fourth match, in 1881, the club had worked up enough pride in the Cup for some of its flag officers to commission the first yacht to be built expressly for the trial races that would be held to determine the defender. Named *Pocahontas*, this boat disappointed everybody by being very slow. The fastest boat in the area was unavailable because she was owned by a non-member (remember that by the terms of the deed of gift the match is between clubs, not individuals). This left two boats of roughly equal speed, *Mischief* and *Gracie*, to fight it out in the final defense trials. A Cup selection committee was authorized to choose any boat it pleased, and after winning two races to *Gracie*'s one, *Mischief* was selected. *Gracie*'s supporters let out a great howl; she had won her race by four minutes and had been beaten by only fourteen seconds in the last one. But the selection committee stayed firm — as its successors would. For many years thereafter, the best racing of the summer was held in the defense trials, the Cup match itself serving as a bit of a letdown when the challenger turned out to be not quite the flyer that the romantic "experts" writing yachting columns in the press had promised.

The 1881 match was a disaster for Cuthbert and his *Atalanta*. With the last mostly-amateur crew in Cup competition for many years, she was badly beaten in a series whose main historical distinctions were, first, that *Mischief* was one of the very first metal, scientifically designed yachts in America; and, second, that the spinnaker was introduced to America's Cup competition. Alexander Cuthbert's announcement that he would return sent the yacht club scurrying to find a way to keep him away; these Canadian challenges were becoming embarrassing. At the club's request, George Schuyler rewrote the deed of gift, doubling it in length, couching it in language that was considerably more legalistic than the original, and finding a way to fend off Cuthbert (and other lake sailors) by insisting that participating clubs conduct their races on "an arm of the sea."

In the same year as the second match against Cuthbert there

appeared an indication that perhaps the Cup was vulnerable. This was a forty-six foot cutter named *Madge*, designed by the English naval architect George L. Watson and built on the banks of the Clyde estuary, near Glasgow in Scotland. A classic English "plank on edge" cutter, she was narrow and she was deep; her beam was seven feet nine inches, her draft eight feet three inches. A New York sloop of comparable length was twice as wide and half as deep. She was a sensation not only because of her unusual appearance ("as wet as a half-tide ledge in a sea way," Winfield Thompson wrote of her) but also because she was fast. *Madge* won six out of seven races and inspired people who called themselves "cutter cranks" because they made sure everybody knew why cutters were superior to beamy centerboarders like the late *Mohawk*, which had capsized and sunk in 1876.

In 1884 came not one but two British challenges, one for 1885 and the other for 1886. The boats would be designed by the well-regarded J. Beavor-Webb. Not seeing much hope in its current fleet, the New York Yacht Club sent circulars to several U.S. yacht clubs inviting entries in the defense trials, ". . . the Committee reserving to themselves the right of forming their own judgment as to fitness for the purpose in view, irrespective of the actual result of the races." Interestingly, considering a controversy that would be churned up in 1901, nothing was said about a requirement that owners of defense candidates must be members of the club (though that condition may have been assumed). The appeal found a response in Boston, which for almost half a century had been competing with New York as the yachting capital of the New World. Some members of the Eastern Yacht Club of Marblehead met to discuss the possibility of building a boat. Leading the discussion was J. Malcolm Forbes, a well-rounded sportsman of the old school. (Of his father, Ralph Waldo Emerson once wrote, "It is of course that he should ride well, shoot well, sail well, keep horse well, administer affairs well, but he was the best talker, also, in the company . . ." The same could have been said of the son.) Also present was Charles J. Paine, a Union general in the Civil War and, like Forbes, a wealthy railroad and shipping investor. Forbes agreed to pay most of the bills, Paine agreed to manage her, but who, they asked, should design her? They asked the club's secretary, Edward Burgess, for his advice, and Burgess nominated himself. Trained

A Stern Chase and a Long One" is the title of this Frederic S. Cozzens watercolor of the second race in the 1876 match. The defender, Madeleine, *leads the Canadian* Countess of Dufferin *as the twenty-five-year-old* America, *an unofficial entrant, trails. Though* America *started the race four and one-half minutes late, she later caught* Countess *and beat her by almost twenty minutes. As the painting suggests, the Canadian boat was very similar in design to the U.S. vessels. The pipe-smoking lobsterman in the spritsail-rigged dory is no artistic invention; in the early Cup races, the yachts had to elbow commercial craft for room in New York Harbor. Using a cooler, less dramatic style than Buttersworth, Cozzens produced many popular watercolors, drawings, and lithographs of marine subjects.*

as an entomologist, he had only recently taken up yacht design. He had spent the summer of 1883 on the Isle of Wight, studying English yachts.

The result was *Puritan,* a "compromise" sloop that, while still a centerboarder, was moderately narrow and deep. To many, she seemed awfully foreign-looking. Burgess' patriotism was questioned, as was his design ability, but she was fast. She won a close set of trials, then went on to beat the challenger *Genesta* in an even closer series of races. The most exciting event in the match was a collision between the two yachts, *Puritan* being at fault as she was on the port tack. The race committee immediately disqualified her and asked Sir Richard Sutton, *Genesta*'s owner, to sail around the course and win the race. Quite extraordinarily, he refused, saying, "We want a race, we don't want a walk-over." He even turned down Paine's offer to pay for repairs. His sportsmanship was acclaimed. A third-generation member of the Royal Yacht Squadron, Sutton was highly accomplished. He won two important races during his visit and, in 1887, won the first race around Britain — at fifteen hundred miles a long and challenging course.

These yachts were the first racing yachts to be managed seriously. Beavor-Webb spent days refining *Genesta*'s sails. General Paine was a strong leader as well as a brilliant sailor with a well-developed intuition for making a boat go fast. All this meant that he was plenty competent to handle the yacht's budget, work with Burgess on technical details, and deal with the professional skipper and his twenty-man crew. The Paine-Burgess team came back in 1886 and 1887 to easily defend the Cup again in *Mayflower* and *Volunteer.*

One indication of the new seriousness with which racing and the America's Cup were being taken was the controversy over the challenger *Thistle* in 1887. A Watson design, she represented Scotland's Royal Clyde Yacht Club, which had become one of the major racing clubs in Britain, where yachts made an annual summer circuit between regattas on the Solent, in the West of England, and up to Scotland for Clyde Week, near where many of the top boats were built. *Thistle* was constructed under unprecedented secrecy; what was known was that she was eighty-five feet on the waterline — a dimension that, according to the deed of gift, had to be transmitted with the official challenge so that the New York Yacht Club

would build a boat of around the same size. The Scots launched her with a great canvas shroud around her keel (a tactic that has become an honorable tradition in the America's Cup). This bit of showmanship titillated everybody; so, too, did Watson's planting the plans of other boats he had designed with gullible journalists whom he assured were receiving the actual plans of *Thistle.* Rumors about this boat's fantastic speed and radical design flew across the Atlantic.

After *Thistle* finally appeared in New York to the flurry of bagpipes from her supporters' steam yacht, the Americans were first surprised, later scandalized, and finally triumphant. First off, anybody could see that her hull was extremely unusual for a cutter. A change in the British handicapping rules allowed greater beam, and the new boat was all of five feet wider than *Galatea* and only three feet more narrow than the new defender, *Volunteer.* Of course, *Thistle* lacked a centerboard; but for the first time it could be said that an American defender and a British challenger had come from the same school of yacht design, albeit not from the same classroom. The challenger had an unusual cutaway keel. After much research, Watson had designed her to reduce wetted surface and so speed the boat up in light air.

The scandal was that *Thistle* was nowhere near the size that her people had claimed. Instead of eight-five feet, her waterline length was eighty-six feet six inches. Although the time allowance tables would compensate for the difference (and the handicap was only five seconds, anyway), the yacht club was offended at what was perceived as duplicity on the part of the Britons. If the boat had been built more openly, perhaps the outrage would have been tempered, but she wasn't and it wasn't. The issue quickly rose above measurements to honor and trustworthiness — old-fashioned English aristocratic values that Americans had been told about for years and into which they were now delighted to rub their visitors' noses. Something else in the air seemed to sharpen the defenders' wrath. Reflecting the insecurity of the American Gilded Age, the yacht club feared that it was losing control of its own trophy. After all, this was the cup won by its founder's yacht and given to the club by that founder. If the *Thistle* "waterlinegate" controversy had any lasting message, it was that the New York Yacht Club was not about to let anybody forget who owned the America's Cup.

After making grumbling noises about punishing the Scots by canceling the match, the yacht club agreed to drop the measurement mess in the lap of George Schuyler, who had made something of a career of interpreting the deed of gift. After taking testimony from all the parties, he scolded Watson for providing "remarkably inaccurate information" but went on to clear him of charges of acting in bad faith. That judgment by one of its members affirmed the club's control over the Cup. The air now cleared, the races were held and *Thistle* was beaten by eleven minutes in one and nineteen in another. The keel was too small and she made excessive leeway. However, the concept of a cutaway keel was proved to be at least feasible; Watson and other designers would soon develop it to the ultimate in the huge Cup boats that culminated in *Reliance* in 1903.

At a club dinner in 1887 the members of the New York Yacht Club sang "The Song of the Cup," written by a former commodore:

The Cup! The Cup! Fill up! Fill up!;
　O sirs, the night is young;
And faint the heart would care to part
　before the song is sung!

'Tis Neptune strikes the string,
　till the grand traditions ring
Oh, never yet have yachtsmen met
　a nobler theme to sing!

Then pipe the watch and pop the cork —
　let landsmen go below —
Upon my word, they always do
　when'er the breezes blow.

I pledge you, sirs, the Cup!
　May we never give it up!
A bumper, sirs: The Club! Hurrah!
　The Cup! The Cup! The Cup!

There were those who thought that the club's next reaction to the *Thistle* controversy was an outrageous violation of just those "grand traditions" that "The Song of the Cup" celebrated. A month or so after the last race, the club rejected a challenge by a Scot named Sweet because he had not satisfied the conditions of a *new* deed of gift. When it finally surfaced, this document was a shocker. While its two predecessors had been relatively informal letters of transmittal, this was an official (some thought officious) legal document five times the length of the original 1852 deed and overflowing with contractual language. Apparently written by a club committee and presented to the aging George Schuyler for approval, it reflected the opinion that the Cup matches had become too important to be conducted in a less than businesslike manner.

The deed presented several uncontroversial reforms — and one highly unpopular one. Nobody argued with the new rule that matches would no longer be held in the tricky confines of New York Bay, where local knowledge often made all the difference; henceforth, the boats would race out in the ocean. In addition, there was little opposition to the rule that protected the American type by declaring that centerboarders would always be eligible to sail; to nail this down, the deed specified that the race course be at least twenty-two feet deep (with her board down, *Volunteer* drew twenty-one feet). An additional clause allowed some provisions to be waived by mutual consent between defender and challenger.

However, there was real issue taken with a new stipulation about how and when the club would be told about the challenging yacht. Before, all it wanted to know was the waterline length six months before the match. Now it wanted ten months notice and some extremely telling information that, some thought, would all but draw the challenger's lines on the club's wall. In those ten months, the club could build any number of boats that improved on the challenger, and then, while the challenger waited, run a long series of trial races to tune up the best one. This seemed patently unfair. To the yacht club's surprise, the new dimensions clause was greeted by howls of protest that the club was more concerned with its own self-interest than with fairness. There was some truth in that; as Winfield Thompson gently put it, "It appears the committee, while always having in mind the interests of the New York Yacht Club as defender of the Cup, never lost sight of the club's welfare should it ever find itself in the position of the challenger for the Cup." John Cox Stevens' love of risk had lost its appeal.

Probably most objectionable to the British was the implicit

In the second Cup race in 1885, the Burgess-designed compromise sloop Puritan *inches away from the narrow cutter* Genesta *after passing her on the beat to the finish from the turning mark set more than twenty-five miles out into the Atlantic. In one of the most exciting races yet, the lead changed hands three times and the defender won by the narrow margin of one minute thirty-eight seconds. Trailing the racing yachts are three spectator steamers, while a pilot schooner sails by to windward. Prints like this one by Currier & Ives were widely distributed and reflected national interest in the Cup matches.*

claim of absolute ownership that the New York Yacht Club was making. After all, only two generations earlier the Cup had been just another trophy offered by the Royal Yacht Squadron for a sporting event in English waters. This assumption of unquestioned jurisdiction seemed like yet another act of American imperialism at a time when the United States was fiercely challenging Great Britain's interests on issues such as Canadian fishing rights and Latin American boundaries. What especially galled the British was that the Americans couched this apparent theft in the stiff, legal language of that most American of institutions, a written document. The new deed was "altogether too complicated a document to govern a matter of sport such as yacht racing," complained the Earl of Dunraven, a Squadron member and a potential challenger. Ignoring the new deed and the club's assumption of ownership, he proposed a classic English solution: three Americans and three Englishmen should meet "in New York or London, or in some other convenient place — Paris might be suitable" and simply "sit down and discuss the matter thoroughly and draw up definite rules" before drawing lots to determine the site of the match. Now it was the yacht club's turn to be astounded. Having lived through seven Cup matches, many of which involved one wrangle or another about the rules, its officers saw no alternative to drawing up legal parameters. The event had become too complex and prestigious to do otherwise. And since there was absolutely no question in their minds as to where the Cup's ownership rested — it did, after all, sit in the trophy case of their yacht club — they claimed the responsibility alone to write the rules as clearly and, they believed, as fairly as possible. Obviously, two languages were being spoken here.

Too, the yacht club was offended by Dunraven's swipes at business. Despite the common perception that, as in England, American sportsmen in the late nineteenth century were not commercial people, the yacht club's hierarchy was peopled by go-getters. Of the seventeen commodores between 1844 and 1900, only three appear to have been men of leisure relaxing in inherited wealth. Four were bankers or stockbrokers; one was a fruit auctioneer; two were active in shipping and railroads; one was a corporate lawyer; another (James Gordon Bennett Jr.) published a sensationalistic newspaper; one was an inventor; and the remainder were salesmen

or company officers. Some, like J.P. Morgan and Bennett, built on foundations that they had inherited. But at least one, James Dickinson Smith, who as Commodore in 1882 and 1883 and chairman of the Cup Committee from 1886 through 1895 played a key role in producing the new deed of gift, was a self-made man straight out of an Horatio Alger story. Starting out poor, as a clerk in a country store, Smith had his own investment firm when he was forty-four and was president of the New York Stock Exchange in his fifties.

This was the age of action, of ambition, of accomplishment — preferably, money-making accomplishment. "I will be perfectly satisfied with you," one tycoon is reported to have told his son, "if you will only always go to bed at night worth more than when you got up in the morning." But any sort of accomplishment might do. Urged the Gilded Age's premier clergyman, the Boston Episcopalian Phillips Brooks:

The man whom the world delights to feel is the man who has evidently conceived some strong and distinct purpose for himself, from which he will allow nothing to turn his feet aside, who means to be something with all his soul; and yet who finds, in his own earnest effort to fill out his own career, the interpretation of the careers of other men; and also finds, in sympathy with other men, the transfiguration and sustainment of his own appointed struggle.

More crudely, a Tammany Hall politician named George Washington Plunkitt summarized his philosophy in the words, "I sees my opportunities and I takes them." There is no better epigram for the Gilded Age.

Eventually, the yacht club quite sensibly waived its new rules about disclosing measurements and accepted two challenges by Dunraven, one for 1893 and the other for 1895. Against his two yachts named *Valkyrie* the N.Y.Y.C. sent sophisticated sloops designed by the rising star in yacht design, Nathanael Greene Herreshoff, whose appetite for speed and experimentation was voracious. Fast but inherently unseaworthy, the Herreshoff boats that defended between 1893 and 1903 were the ultimate "out-and-outers." Winfield Thompson called the first Herreshoff defender, *Vigilant*, "the prototype of a vicious kind of yacht, whose existence

The Yachtsman Who Hunted With Buffalo Bill

The most fascinating character in America's Cup history was the man who almost ended it in scandal. Windham Thomas Wyndham-Quin, fourth Earl of Dunraven and second Baron Kenry of the United Kingdom, was born in County Limerick, Ireland, in 1841. Descended from the Hy-Ifearnean clan, he was heir to one of the few Irish titles of Celtic origin. He had a childhood almost guaranteed to produce a feisty adulthood. Forbidden by his father, a Catholic convert, to live with his Protestant mother, he was packed off to a school in Rome, where he soon began to display the "obstinate resistance" (as a biographer put it) that reverberated throughout his life. After attending Oxford, he served in the Life Guards and, despite being small and frail, became an enthusiastic steeplechase rider. He settled down to a rigorous life as an adventurer-writer and reported on the 1867 military expedition to Abyssinia and the 1870 Franco-Prussian War.

In 1871, Dunraven traveled to Nebraska to hunt elk with Buffalo Bill Cody. Fascinated by the American west, he returned many times to hunt and eventually bought sixty thousand acres of land in Colorado for a game preserve. He wrote books both about his hunting adventures and about spiritualism (a curious combination). Taking an interest in politics, Dunraven took his seat in the House of Lords and was twice appointed Under-Secretary for the Colonies (resigning over a matter of principle). He later chaired a committee working for the reform of sweatshops, those hellholes where women and children were forced to labor for up to fifteen hours a day for minuscule wages. His political career might have advanced further had he been less independent of his party, the Liberals; he himself spoke of his "cross-bench mind." In the 'nineties, he committed himself to land reform in Ireland. He was convinced that the solution to civil disturbances was simple: civil war

would be avoided if the big landholders like himself sold out to their tenants. At the age of fifty-eight, he raised and commanded his own unit in the Boer War and won two medals. It was said that he was a brilliant violinist.

With typical contrariness, Dunraven began sailing big yachts around the time that he was working against the sweatshops. He quickly learned enough about sailing to steer his own yachts and even to design his own small, radical, and highly successful racer. In the mid-'nineties, he earned master's and extra-master's certificates, which qualified him to command just about any kind of vessel; he also wrote an instructional manual about navigation. At the age of seventy-three, he commanded a hospital ship during World War I. When Dunraven died in 1926 at eighty-five, he was planning a new yacht.

In his life and portraits, Dunraven comes down to us as somebody more interested in abstractions than in flesh and blood people — a cool, detached, and brilliant technician who would have been more at home in the eighteenth or late twentieth centuries than in the passionate nineteenth. His eyes are unfocused, his mind seems distracted with some scheme that a more worldly person would find implausible, like aborting Irish nationalism by selling off a few acres of land or settling disputes over the America's Cup by getting a few people to "discuss the matter thoroughly." He was unable to make much sense, but what sense he did make was brilliant.

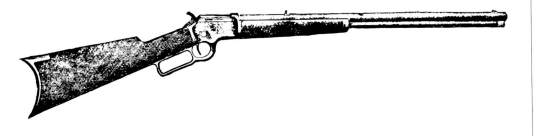

has been more a curse than a blessing to the sport of yacht racing." Costing more than $100,000 to build and race — perhaps three times the cost of *Volunteer* — she needed a crew of seventy not so much because her rig required them but because the sailors' combined weight of five tons added to her stability and sank her lower in the water, thereby increasing her sailing length and her speed. So wild was she that only Herreshoff could steer her, though he was sometimes forced to leave her wheel in order to supervise repairs to her complicated rig and fragile hull. She was managed by C. Oliver Iselin, a wealthy, intense banker-yachtsman who had earned a reputation for cunning and toughness in small boats called sandbaggers (because bags full of sand were shifted around to keep them upright). "There was no sentiment in the game of sandbag racing," the yachting historian W.P. Stephens wrote. "The first thing was to win, the second was to get the prize after you had won it." *Vigilant* won in three straight races, the last of which was close enough to encourage Dunraven to come back with *Valkyrie III* to sail an America's Cup series in 1895 against the Herreshoff-Iselin *Defender*.

Defender won the first race rather easily — too easily, Dunraven thought. He insisted that she be remeasured. He had seen the American crew working late on the Herreshoff boat, and he knew they were adding ballast because a drain hole that had been clear of the water was now submerged. The remeasurement showed that *Defender* was no lower and no longer on the waterline. At the start of the second race, an excursion steamer blundered away from the vast spectator fleet and across the line, forcing the two boats together. The end of *Valkyrie III*'s long boom snapped one of *Defender*'s shrouds, and the topmast almost broke. Herreshoff nursed the boat around the course (losing by only forty-seven seconds), and the yacht club's race committee quite properly disqualified the challenger. Dunraven, who could not be convinced that his yacht was in the wrong, refused Iselin's offer to resail the race, as to do so would be an admission of guilt. He also warned the race committee that unless the spectator boats were kept under better control, he would not compete in the next race. Apparently unswayed by the yacht club's efforts, he had *Valkyrie III* start the race under cruising canvas, and then immediately drop out to bring the match to an extremely unsatisfying conclusion.

*A*t the turning mark of the
third race in the 1893 match, sailed in
a strong east wind, Dunraven's
Valkyrie II *led* Vigilant *by two
minutes, but* Nat Herreshoff,
commanding the seventy-man crew of
the defender, sent a crewmember aloft to
cut the reef points on the mainsail and
had the spinnaker, balloon jib, and big
topsail set. The more seamanlike crew
of Valkyrie *eventually followed suit
but watched two of their spinnakers
blow into shreds.* Vigilant *averaged
eleven and one-half knots on the fifteen-
mile run to the finish and won by only
forty seconds. These yachts were the
first of the "big class," the
complicated, fast, fragile, and expensive
"out and outers" that were the
superstars of international yacht racing
until the eve of World War II. Black
smoke pours from the stacks of spectator
boats; more than fifty thousand people
watched the 1893 races from the water.*

128

That was bad enough; but when Dunraven returned to England he revived the first controversy and publicly accused Iselin of cheating by adding ballast after measurement. In the first race, Dunraven claimed, *Defender* was at least one foot longer on the waterline than her original measurement had indicated. Both in substance and in openness it was a startling claim. While some Americans who had sailed against Iselin believed him capable of shaving the rules, they could not publicly come to Dunraven's defense since the issue had, apparently, already been settled by *Defender's* remeasurement after the first race.

The New York Yacht Club could have responded indirectly as it had after James Ashbury had accused it of various kinds of foul play back in 1871. Then, it had simply returned the trophies that Ashbury had donated and written letters of explanation to other yacht clubs. Or it could have asked a distinguished older member to hold an informal investigation, as George Schuyler had done during the *Thistle* difficulties of 1887. But Schuyler was dead and subtlety was not the style of the times, especially when the club's very image seemed to be at stake. So the club appointed a court of honor to render judgment. The names of the members of this panel indicate the seriousness of its mission: J. Pierpont Morgan, chairman; Captain Alfred T. Mahan, the famous naval strategist; Edward J. Phelps, a former Ambassador to Great Britain; George L. Rives, a former Assistant Secretary of State; and William Whitney, a former Secretary of the Navy. They were all club members; but each enjoyed a reputation for trustworthiness that was above public dispute, and each had strong connections with England.

If the only issue they confronted was whether an apparently addled peer had or had not seen *Defender's* port-side bilge pump discharge pipe below the level of the water — and that was Dunraven's sole evidence — this remarkable jury would have been an example of administrative overkill along the lines of, say, having David Rockefeller, Henry Kissinger, and the Archbishop of Canterbury settle a contractual dispute between a professional athletic team and its star player. But this obviously was not the issue; anybody with a reputation for fairness could have presided over the Dunraven hearings and the testimony about weights and buoyancy by Herreshoff and other technicians. Rather, the controversy was over whether the Old World's aristocracy of ancient lineage could sit in judgment over the morality of the New World's aristocracy of recent accomplishment. Dunraven was not criticizing the personal honor of C. Oliver Iselin. He was attacking the whole system. In his autobiography he wrote of sports in terms that would be repeated in the 1970s and 1980s:

I am not sure that I like international contests. In such matters as yacht racing, polo, golf, and so on, I think they tend to demoralize sport by turning it into a serious business in which national prestige is at stake, and to convert amateurs, playing a game for the game's sake, into professional specialists struggling for their country's sake.

That is what he had seen in New York. Angered in 1893 by the way that Herreshoff and Iselin had artificially increased *Vigilant's* speed by crowding on more sailors, he had been made even more alert to the possibilities of cheating by his work in yacht design. His new boat, which he knew was very fast, had been badly beaten. Why? Some American friends hinted that Iselin might be up to the old tricks he had learned in the anything-goes school of sandbagger racing. That the New York Yacht Club was countenancing such behavior — perhaps even encouraging it — had to be pointed out. Hence his accusations. Dunraven's radical critique of the American way was obvious not only to the yacht club's hierarchy. When he arrived in New York for the hearings, Dunraven's ship was met by crowds of angry protestors. He was secreted to a midtown hotel and protected by guards.

The hearing was quick and conclusive. Herreshoff, *Defender's* crew, and consulting engineers testified, first, that the purpose of the night-time activity had been to permanently store ballast that was already on board; second, that to lengthen her waterline another foot would have required an enormous amount of new ballast — as much as thirteen tons; and, third, that the telltale discharge pipe could be submerged simply by shifting the boat's enormous boom from the centerline to the port side. Perhaps a less intransigent man than Dunraven might have won a compromise ruling; the defenders' behavior did seem mysterious, to say the least, and the yacht club's handling of his original complaint had been somewhat officious. But he had boxed the club into a corner

129

from which the only response was counterattack. The panel ruled in every way against him. Dunraven refused to apologize; the yacht club expelled him as an honorary member; and, to save what face remained, he resigned.

The Dunraven affair almost killed off America's Cup competition at the very time when the New York Yacht Club's members were most ambitious to prove themselves in the international arena. The Royal Victoria Yacht Club sent a challenge but, facing English criticism that it was collaborating with the enemy, quickly withdrew it. American attempts to recruit a substantial challenge (even, by one account, to finance one) met no apparent success until April of 1897, when rumors of a challenge from northern Ireland's Royal Ulster Yacht Club began to appear. For more than a year, the Marquis of Dufferin's name was closely linked to this problematical effort. Finally, in August of 1898, it became clear that this experienced diplomat (and New York Yacht Club honorary member) had been nothing more than a noble ambassador between the club and Sir Thomas Lipton.

Before Lipton sailed to America for the 1899 match, he was begged by the Colonial Secretary, Joseph Chamberlain, to avoid straining international relations with another debacle. However, the last person on earth who needed that advice was the ever amicable Sir Thomas. He was everything that Dunraven was not: a self-made man, genial, extravagant, a publicity hound, and as an America's Cup challenger a good as well as a consistent loser. If he was the answer to the yacht club's prayers, the yacht club was the answer to his. Between tea, grocery stores, and stockyards, he had enormous retail business interests in America as well as in Britain and needed all the advertising he could get. Between 1899 and 1930, his *Shamrocks* raced for the Cup five times, winning only two races out of eighteen, and Lipton became an American celebrity.

The year of Lipton's second challenge, 1901, was one of the most interesting in the Cup's history, not so much because of the final match, which *Shamrock II* lost in three close races, but because of the maneuvering on and off the water among the Americans. That year, a wealthy Bostonian named Thomas W. Lawson challenged the New York Yacht Club's hegemony over the Cup in a campaign that at best can be called quixotic. Not a member of the club and determined never to join, Lawson still had a few things in common

with its members. He had made and lost a couple of fortunes and was a betting man; but he was also the kind of stock-market speculator that J.P. Morgan despised and the Securities and Exchange Commission was eventually formed to control. It was said that he once made a million dollars in a single day. His enemies in these escapades frequently included Morgan and others who were attempting to squash his kind of independent and frequently disruptive activity. Lawson struck out at this new order in several ways that seemed to accomplish little more than to shoot his own interests squarely in the foot. For example, he wrote muckraking articles about business that were eventually collected in a book with the suggestive title *Frenzied Finance*. Not surprisingly, this bout of criticism lost him a lot of business and he died a relatively poor former tycoon.

Another of Lawson's outbursts was his curious campaign with a Cup contender designed by George Crowininshield's great-grandnephew, Bowdoin Crowninshield. The most sensible thing about her was her name, *Independence*. She was an extremely radical boat. Inspired by the flat-bottom small keel racers and inland lakes scows that were being developed for racing on flat water, Crowninshield had given her a long light hull, a tiny keel, and a mountain of sail. Potentially very fast, she rarely lived up to that potential in the few races that she sailed because she was extremely difficult to handle and leaked so badly that her pumps were going all the way around the course. Charles Francis Adams, New England's top racing helmsman, claimed that she steered like an ice wagon.

His yacht's crankiness was one problem; but Lawson's biggest challenge was simply getting her on the race course. He never bothered to notify the yacht club's America's Cup Committee (which included Morgan) of his plans. After newspaper clippings made his intentions clear, he was informed by the committee chairman, Lewis Cass Ledyard, a Wall Street lawyer, that if *Independence* were to race, she would have to fly the yacht club's burgee. This meant chartering her to a club member, although Lawson and his crew could remain on board and sail her. In his response, Lawson studiously misrepresented Ledyard's message to mean that he would have to separate himself entirely from the boat. In the exchange that followed, letter after letter from Led-

*O*ne hundred forty-four feet long on deck, Reliance *seems to stretch right into her opponent's jibs during a tune-up race early in the summer of 1903. She was so extreme that even Nat Herreshoff, her designer, thought her unhealthy; he developed the Universal Rule, which controlled*

yard made clear to any reader except Lawson that the only requirement was that the yacht fly the club's burgee, however Lawson could arrange it. And letter after letter from Lawson stated his conviction that, as he put it, "No American other than a member of the New York Yacht Club has a right to take part in the defense of an international cup, rightly named America's and belonging to all Americans." He finally agreed to charter the boat — but to the committee itself. This led the exasperated Ledyard to write back: "Your last letter . . . indicated a settled purpose on your part to misunderstand the position of the committee, which has been again and again stated to you in terms too plain to any but willful misconstruction." The committee cut off negotiations.

You will not be surprised to learn that Lawson carefully kept the press informed of his self-imposed plight, and that there was widespread sympathy for his position. Finley Peter Dunne's humorous character "Mr. Dooley," a wry Irishman who commented on the events of the day, summarized Lawson's message:

"Yachtin' is a gintlemans' spoort," he says, "an' in daling with gintlemen," he says, "ye can't be too careful," he says.

The real problem, Lawson said, was that the New York Yacht Club was not represented by gentlemen at all. Morgan and the others were not members of the great "American democracy of wealth." No, they composed a new social class that he called the "mushroom aristocracy" because that was the way their wealth grew. They were men who "knew no law but might, who admit no God but self, whose standard is cunning and whose code is 'get there.' " They controlled politics, the courts, the banks, industry. Now they wanted to take over international yachting using "methods that required of gentlemen a mental activity which, while perhaps allowable in trade, was rather too wearing for healthy sport." This was exactly the point that the Earl of Dunraven had so unsuccessfully attempted to make in the 1890s. The analysis is correct, of course, although its phrasing no doubt reflected Lawson's personal pique at being turned down. Even one who is sympathetic with Lawson's passion to run his own life must wonder why he chose so odd an arena as yachting in which to express his individualism — indeed, his eccentricity.

shape, rig, and construction techniques, to make sure that she would not be duplicated. Many of her sophisticated winches, designed and built by Herreshoff, were still being used on Cup defenders in the 'thirties.

Right is the genial Sir Thomas Lipton, whose five challenges between 1899 and 1930 made everybody forget the time of the Dunraven troubles.

So *Independence* was not allowed to race in the club's trials. She would have done poorly, as her performance in a handful of other races indicates. In the long run, Lawson's greatest imprint on the America's Cup was neither his boat, which was broken up by a wrecker before the summer was over, nor his crusade, which did not change any minds. It was *The Lawson History of the America's Cup,* a beautifully illustrated and handsomely printed book that he published in a limited edition of three thousand copies. The first two hundred seventy-three pages, written by Winfield Thompson, make up a lucid and authoritative history of the Cup matches through 1899 and a somewhat biased account of the 1901 trials and match. In the remaining ninety-five pages, Lawson made an ingenious defense of his actions in the *Independence* campaign. To support his case, he appended a collection of documents that he claimed was complete but that did not include the final letter from an exasperated Ledyard.

Despite Lawson's shenanigans, there were America's Cup trials in 1901 and they were fascinating. Nat Herreshoff had launched a new boat named *Constitution*. Like the 1899 defender, *Columbia*, she was ninety feet on the waterline, the maximum size permitted by the deed of gift. *Columbia* was back. J.P. Morgan and his distant cousin Edwin D. Morgan had bought her for $20,000, less than one-tenth the cost of a new boat. A former Commodore and ambitious yachtsman, Edwin D. was described by W.P. Stephens as a man who "thought no more of buying a yacht than the average man does of picking up a paper as he passes a newsstand." At first, the idea was that *Columbia* would be the new boat's trial horse to tune her up for the final match. But her skipper, Charlie Barr, kept the old boat competitive all summer, sailing almost equally with *Constitution* in speed and often beating her with aggressive if not rough-house tactics that seemed to intimidate his opponent, Captain Uriah Rhodes. *Constitution* also had a habit of breaking down that did not endear her to the America's Cup Committee, which had final choice and which wanted its defenders to finish the races they started. J.P. Morgan became so excited about the trials that when the Herreshoff sail loft said it would make sails only for *Constitution,* he set up the English firm of Ratsey and Lapthorn in business on City Island in the Bronx.

The old boat won the first of the final trial races, and was leading the second when the wind died. Barr sailed all over and fouled Rhodes at the start of the third race, which *Columbia* went on to win. This left Ledyard's Cup Committee to make a pair of decisions that says much about the New York Yacht Club's whole attitude about the America's Cup: they both disqualified *Columbia* from the race *and* selected her to defend against *Shamrock II,* which she beat not because she was inherently faster but because Barr was the more aggressive skipper.

There were no controversies in the 1903 Cup match. Drawing some inspiration from Crowninshield's *Independence,* Herreshoff designed and built one of the most remarkable yachts ever launched — the monster *Reliance.* From tip of bowsprit to end of

132

Although the enormous Cup spectator fleet was patrolled in 1899 for the first time by vessels like the U.S. Navy torpedo boat, left, and a New York Yacht Club member's launch, near the white Fall River line steamer, right, the yachts still were squeezed into a narrow patch of open water. The commander of the Navy's patrol fleet, a hero of the Spanish-American War named Robley Evans, would sometimes warn a boat away by firing a shot across her bow. Here Columbia, *leading, and* Shamrock *wend their way down a narrow smoke-clogged channel. The black steamer is J. P. Morgan's third* Corsair; *behind her, the white steamer with the yellow stack is Lipton's* Erin. *This painting was produced in 1906 by Chevalier Eduardo de Martino, marine painter in ordinary to King Edward VII. It may well be the most magnificent piece of art ever done of an America's Cup scene.*

133

Charlie Barr

Nat Herreshoff's son L. Francis described the one-hundred-thirty-foot, one-hundred-ton skimming dishes that sailed for the Cup in these days as having "one head or brain (the captain), several mouthpieces (the mates), and twenty or thirty bunches of sinew, muscle, and leather, which acted instantly at each order." The captain commanding this crew had immense responsibility, and when an amateur like Charles Francis Adams steered a big racing boat around a course, it was headline news in the papers. The best racing skipper of the day was tiny Charlie Barr. Born in Scotland in 1864, he had sailed across in a British racing yacht in 1884 to join his half-brother John, himself a fine captain, in the profession of sailing yachts. He quickly earned a solid reputation as a helmsman of racing yachts and (perhaps more important, considering the demands of these boats) as a recruiter and commander of the tough Scandinavian, British, and Maine seamen who manned them.

In 1895, in command of *Vigilant,* he was bullied all over the starting line and race course by Captain Hank Haff, on *Defender.* Haff won the trials and Barr learned his lesson. Six years later, it was Barr who dominated. Wrote W.P. Stephens, who was there: "Handling *Columbia* as a man would a bicycle, turning her as on a pivot, he took chances that would have been dangerous in the extreme for an average good skipper." Before starts, Barr hounded Uriah Rhodes so tightly from astern that *Columbia's* long bowsprit sometimes waved over *Constitution's* after deck. "Barr simply made a monkey of the other man," wrote Thomas Fleming Day, editor of *The Rudder.* "He forced him to do whatever he wished and shoved and jostled *Constitution,* the latter's skipper giving way in the most complaisant manner." Unquestionably, *Columbia,* the slower boat, was selected to defend because she was

commanded by the better skipper. This faith in men, not machines, was typical of the tycoons who ruled both the yacht club and the economy. "I believe J.P. Morgan had a kindly glint in his burning, diamond eyes for those who did things well," wrote L. Francis Herreshoff, thinking both of his father and of Charlie Barr. Barr himself knew many rich and powerful men; the one he most respected, he said, was Morgan.

Barr's later career was equally distinguished. He was captain of *Reliance* in 1903 and of the three-masted schooner yacht *Atlantic* when she won the 1905 trans-Atlantic race, setting a speed record of twelve days, nine hours that was not broken until the 1980s. What were his rewards? He might be paid $3,500 — the price of a new mainsail — for a Cup campaign. Deckhands would earn $45 a month, plus $5 a race. Sailors with dangerous jobs, like the topmasthands working eighty feet above deck, got bonuses. The work was long and it was hard. A five-minute jib change was something to brag about. Simply drying the acres of cotton sails required more time than the four- or five-hour races, of which there were only fifteen or twenty in a Cup season for fear that something might break.

boom she stretched over two hundred feet. At more than sixteen thousand square feet, her sail area was about equal to the combined areas of the 1885 and 1886 defenders, *Puritan* and *Mayflower*. Her topsail alone was larger than the total sail area of a modern America's Cup Twelve-Meter, a large boat today. The greatest accomplishment of her team, which included Barr as skipper and Iselin as manager, was that despite her brute size and light construction, she stayed in one piece throughout her short, happy, one-summer lifetime. In the match, she whipped *Shamrock III* in two races, and then Lipton's challenger got lost in the fog and did not finish the third. A year or so later, she suffered the fate of all Cup boats of her day and was broken up.

Quite understandably, Lipton was disappointed. He had lost three matches in five years; but, more significantly, he and his yachting advisors were appalled by the extremes to which big-boat design had gone. Even Nat Herreshoff agreed that *Reliance* was too big, too expensive, and too unseaworthy. In 1907, Lipton challenged again on the condition that the next match be held in smaller boats designed to Herreshoff's Universal Rule. These would be J-Class yachts about seventy-five feet in waterline length and one-hundred ten feet long overall, forty feet shorter than *Reliance*. The New York Yacht Club promptly turned him down. Yachts of such "insignificant power and size" would lower the America's Cup to second-rate status, claimed Ledyard, who was now Commodore; "the fastest and most powerful vessels that can be produced" must race for the Cup, argued J.P. Morgan.

Lipton held off until 1913, then challenged with a boat that, he said again, would be only seventy-five feet on the waterline. In another of those exchanges of carefully-worded letters, the club kept insisting that the boats must, as before, be ninety feet long. Seeing that he wasn't getting anywhere, Lipton gave in and challenged unconditionally, wherewith the yacht club declared that the match would be held in seventy-five footers. The issue had not been the size of the boat at all. It was the New York Yacht Club's authority as owner of the America's Cup. If that was not the bottom line, it certainly was a major part of the calculation. As we will see in Chapter Nine, the issues of Cup ownership and defender management that became so lively in the first forty years of Cup competition would, if anything, be more keen in later years.

VII

The Yacht Designers

"The yacht designer could not have existed prior to the time when yacht owners had been educated to appreciate his services."

hile many of the characters who have owned yachts have been more fascinating than the boats themselves, we must resist the great temptation to devote this history of the golden pastime solely to the tycoons who spent the money and took much of the glory. John Cox Stevens, J.P. Morgan, Lord Dunraven, and the other enthusiasts that Alfred F. Loomis called "fire-breathing, wallet-slapping sportsmen" relied on technical geniuses like George Steers, Nathanael Herreshoff, and George Watson to design and build their boats. These men were themselves adventurers — quieter and more intellectual, but explorers all the same in the strange and tantalizing pastime of seafaring for pleasure.

In sailing as in only a few other activities — mountaineering, flying, and fly-fishing spring to mind — there is a marriage of romance and technology. The mystery of the latter may actually enhance the allure of the former. To quote the Biblical author of the Book of Proverbs:

There be three things which are too wonderful for me, yea, four which I know not: The way of an eagle in the air; the way of a serpent upon a rock; the way of a ship in the midst of the sea; and the way of a man with a maid.

From time to time, the mystery of "the way of a ship" is probed by a gifted man or woman who has been drawn to the pastime by its romance. The list of technically-oriented sailors who found an outlet for both their passion and their engineering aptitude in designing and building boats and boating gear is a long and distinguished one. In this chapter, we will look at how yacht design progressed from an arm of shipbuilding to a hobby for amateur sailors to a full-blown profession during the century of peace between Napoleon and World War I. As we will see, a key feature in this development was the arrival of a theory of yacht design that, even though it was eventually disproven, challenged designers to come up with something better. Yacht design's first hundred years brought keen competition and intellectual excitement to the golden pastime.

As you may have already concluded, the problem of yacht design can be summarized simply as the choice between shallow, wide boats that sail *over* the water and deep, narrow boats that sail *through* water. This choice applies to the naval architecture of both sail and power. Depending on the boat's purpose, the sailing conditions, racing measurement rules, and other factors, one type of boat may be appropriate and the other inappropriate, but neither is universally wrong. "Wide," "narrow," "deep," and "shallow" are relative terms. The challenge is dual: how does the designer decide how far to go? How are his or her conclusions applied? As is true of most technologies, yesterday's innovation is today's tradition, and tomorrow's "invention" is often a restatement of a long-forgotten idea. In the history of yacht design, every ten or twenty years some refinement of old principles appears to challenge prevailing ideas and settled stereotypes. The agenda was established long before yacht design developed as a profession in the 1870s. However, the terms of the debate were fixed during that decade when a few prominent architects and builders developed an objective, scientific approach to producing yachts.

Before about 1875, there were not enough yachts to make it worthwhile for a naval architect to specialize in pleasure-boat design. Even if the demand had been there, yachts were so similar to contemporary commercial vessels in general shape, proportions, and rig that hiring a specialist to customize a design for pleasure use was usually not necessary. If the owner had strong opinions, he would impose them on the builder. In those early days, most vessels were designed by "rule of thumb," or, for the more experimental, "cut and try." An in-house designer at a boatyard would produce the new boat's hull shape by whittling a small half-model from a block of wood. When the model "looked right" — which usually meant that it didn't look too different from other boats — the three-dimensional shape of the model was taken off with templates and put on paper as a simple set of drawn lines from which construction molds and frames were taken. The more advanced shipbuilders could develop a full set of hull lines that represented cross-sections from different perspectives: waterlines were horizontal slices of the underbody, the hull below the water; buttocks were vertical sections taken fore and aft; midship cross-sections were vertical slices taken from rail to rail; and diagonals were sections taken at an angle to show what the water "felt" when the boat heeled. Using these lines and mechanical devices that

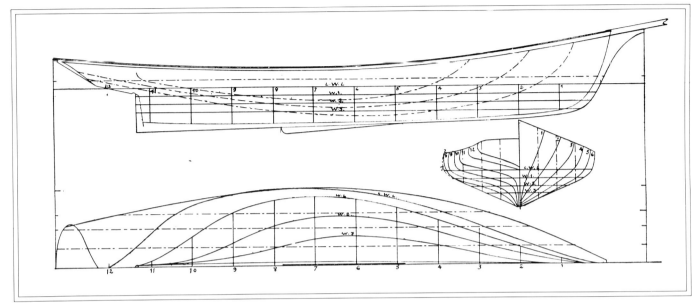

The day of the big centerboarders gradually came to a close as their inherent instability led to some spectacular capsizes. As we saw in Chapter IV, Mohawk went down with four people. The Cozzens painting on page 136 shows Grayling's capsize on her first outing, soon after her launching in 1883. Charles P. Kunhardt and other cutter cranks called these boats "death traps." On the right is a typical centerboarder, the much-altered Gracie. When these lines were taken off in 1882, her overall length was eighty-two feet six inches and her beam was twenty-one feet six inches, for a length-to-beam ratio of about four to one. The cutter cranks favored ratios as high as seven to one.

measured areas, the builder could compare boats with some mathematical precision, but the model was the foundation of the whole design and construction process.

In a sketch of the sail plan, the designer would crowd on as much sail as he thought solid wooden masts and stretchy rope standing rigging could support. He would also try to predict the weights of the hull, rig, and furnishings and the ballast needed to keep her upright when she sailed. If he was right, she would float on her lines at rest and safely carry her sail when underway. But it was usually the case that he was wrong about some things. Some (and often many) alterations would be made after the yacht's trial runs: the bow or stern might be rebuilt; the masts might be lengthened, shortened, or moved; and tons of lead and iron ballast, all of which was carried loose in the bilge before the late 1870s, would be shifted around.

"Looking right" was, of course, a relative consideration, and designers, builders, and owners held rather firm principles based on their experience. Men who were raised on shallow, flat-water bays like New York Harbor were used to big, beamy, shoal-draft centerboarders, and scorned anybody who would fool around with deep keels. Men from Boston and the south of England, where the water was rougher and deeper, would have little to do with centerboards. People who lived between areas where such prejudices held sway could pick and choose without violating a local chauvinism. (Perhaps it was no accident that the greatest designers. Nathanael and J.B. Herreshoff, came from Rhode Island's Narragansett Bay, between Boston and New York.) Any benefits that were identified in the design and construction of one boat were hopefully ascribed to boats of similar shape but different size. Therefore, builders readily scaled boats up and down in size from a particularly successful model.

Other than Archimedes' principle of buoyancy, there was very little general theory. It was known that big boats sailed faster than small ones, and that wide, shallow hulls ("skimming dishes") sailed faster than narrow deep ones in smooth water but were slower in rough water. The closest thing to a theory of design was the idea, arrived at through simple observation and analogy, that a boat should look like a fish, with a bluff front and a long, tapered tail. This theory, such as it was, was summarized in the picturesque phrase, "cod's head and mackerel tail." This lack of a general theory of hull shape bothered some designers. Back in 1775, in his *Treatise on Shipbuilding*, the Swede Fredrik af Chapman (who is often called the first naval architect) pessimistically evaluated his trade as follows:

> *It thus appears that the construction of a ship with more or less good qualities is a matter of chance and not of previous design, and it hence follows that as long as we are without a good theory on shipbuilding, and have nothing to trust to beyond bare experiments and trials, this art cannot be expected to acquire any greater perfection than it possesses at present.*

In the production of yachts, that observation held true for a hundred years, during which many "rule of thumb" boatbuilders made it quite clear that "trial and error" or "cut and try" were more accurate descriptions of how they worked. Mistake after mistake was launched. As we have seen, *Mohawk* was one. In 1883, a brand-new New York Yacht Club centerboard schooner named *Grayling* capsized and sank on her trial run with no fatalities. Other big skimming dishes disappeared at sea with their crews. Some boats were rebuilt time and again. *Gracie* was drastically altered three times in her seventeen-year racing career, starting out as a sixty-foot schooner with a beam of eighteen feet eight inches, and ending up as an eighty-footer with a beam of twenty-two and one-half feet.

In the hands of a genius, the rule of thumb method could produce memorable successes. The most notable of these was *America*, the first of two clear watersheds in modern yacht design. Her model was whittled by her builder's house designer, George Steers, who had cultivated his considerable talent in the loam of one of the great testing grounds of naval architecture in the history of sailing — the great days of New York commercial sail. Under the hard press of mercantile competition, owners, builders, and designers struggled for quarter-knot increases in boat speed with the fervor of a modern-day computer manufacturer sweating out a microsecond improvement in calculation velocity.

For more than one hundred thirty years, *America* has been praised to the skies as a radical breakthrough in the history of naval architecture. On the other hand, when looked at in its con-

text, Steers's accomplishment was the fruit of long development. As everywhere else in the history of creativity, we should be wary of words like "innovation" and "breakthrough" when they are used to describe successful boat designs. On close analysis, the most original innovations in hull shape and rig often turn out to be ingenious amalgams of and improvements on old ideas, some of them failures. While *America* may have been an unusual-looking yacht, as a New York schooner she offered little that was surprising. For several years before 1851, Steers had been borrowing ideas from various traditions to gradually develop a type of fast, weatherly, and seaworthy schooner for carrying pilots out to ships waiting to enter New York Harbor. Ironically, the one idea that Steers did not borrow for some of his pilot-boats and for *America* was the centerboard, that most American of small-vessel devices.

Although he was only thirty-two when he designed *America*, George Steers was no flash in the pan. The son of a naval architect, he started messing around with boats early. Beginning in 1837, when he was only eighteen, he turned out many successful pilot schooners and yachts, among them John Cox Stevens' cod's-head *Gimcrack*, in whose cabin the New York Yacht Club was founded in 1844. Stevens' backing was extremely valuable, for a well-financed and well-sailed yacht is a designer's best advertisement, no matter how well or poorly she may be built. Steers succeeded in ship design as well. Two years after *America's* triumph, he designed a clipper ship that he promised would make good twenty knots. She was never built, but people who had a peek at her plans saw much of *America's* easy-flowing lines in her. Well on his way to becoming New York's premier naval architect, Steers was killed in a carriage accident in 1856. He was but thirty-six.

If Steers had a theory about naval architecture, he never verbalized it other than in the charming claim that the lines of the clipper ship were inspired by the gradual taper of "the well-formed leg of a woman." He was most articulate through his vessels themselves.

The feature that was generally regarded as the magical element in *America's* design was the fine shape of her bow. The stem was cut away, the waterline sections were hollow, and her widest beam was far back, slightly more than half-way abaft her stem. While sharp and even hollow bows were nothing new in America — clipper-ship and pilot-boat design had begun to move in that direction

*I*n this bow-on photograph of the replica of America, *built in 1967 to George Steers's design, the hollowness in her forward sections and the far-aft location of her maximum beam are obvious. She established the shape of yachts from the 1850s into the 1890s, when Nat Herreshoff introduced the spoon bow.*

in the 1840s — not many British pleasure sailors had seen boats like this. To them, a bow was not a knife but a blunt head of a codfish. The widest beam should be on the boat's shoulders, about one-third of the way aft from the stem, and from there to the narrow stern should be a long tweezers. No wonder that, after seeing *America* perform, the Earl of Anglesey commented that he had spent his lifetime sailing backwards.

Violating as she did "the old, established ideas of naval architecture," the cod's head and mackerel tail idea, as a British observer noted in 1851, *America* seemed to confirm another, more complex theory. This was called the Wave Line Theory, which John Scott Russell had developed in 1835 after testing models and conducting mathematical analysis. Russell was a Scottish marine engineer and shipbuilder who built many steamers according to his principles (one was the enormous liner *Great Eastern,* which he codesigned with I.K. Brunel). The issue, he declared, was to minimize the wave-making resistance of the hull. His model-testing convinced Russell that there was an optimum hull shape for each and every vessel and that this shape had nothing whatsoever to do with fish. First, he announced, the widest beam should be way back, two thirds of the vessel's length abaft the stem. Second, the underwater waterline sections either side of that point could be predicted mathematically: the forebody should have the shape of a versed sine curve (a long, graceful convex curve ending in a smooth concavity); and the short afterbody should have the fuller shape of a trochoid curve. The exact dimensions varied from boat to boat depending on size, but the shape was a constant.

Despite Russell's vigorous propagandizing in its favor, for many years the Wave Line Theory was not taken very seriously by English yachtsmen. Before 1851 only three yachts were built to it. They were not failures. *Mosquito* won many races; *Volante* led the fleet in the race for the Hundred Guinea Cup for the first hour and a half and pressed *America* hard until her bowsprit was broken in a collision; and *Titania* (which Russell himself designed) inspired so much confidence in her owner that he challenged Stevens to a match race *(Titania,* which was very tender, was badly beaten in a gale of wind). That the Wave Line Theory eventually caught on had little to do with these three boats. Rather, it owed its success to the fact that *America*'s lines all but fit the theory exactly.

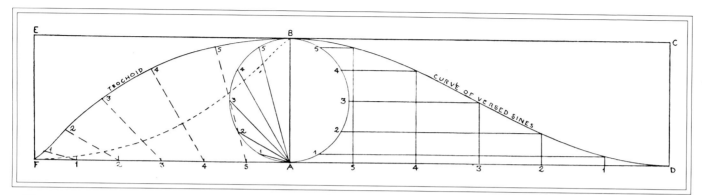

This similarity between Russell's theory and Steers's practice may have been accidental or synchronistic. On the other hand, there may have been a direct trans-Atlantic link. In the 1925 book on *America* that he co-authored, the very knowledgeable yachting writer W.P. Stephens suggested that Steers may have learned about the theory through John Cox Stevens, who had many English connections. (Given the ferocious nationalism that often leeched onto the nineteenth-century America's Cup matches, there can be little wonder why Stephens waited until 1925 to suggest that *America* was inspired by an Englishman.) Whatever its

ancestry, *America*'s sharp bow turned English yacht building on its head. English yachtsmen who had ignored Russell for almost twenty years suddenly could not get enough of the Wave Line Theory. While some keen-eyed observers noted *America*'s less radical advantages — for example, her flatter sails — the new dogma of the hollow bow quickly buried the old cod's head maxim, and Solent boatbuilders struck it rich in lengthening and hollowing out bows in the *America* style.

Thanks mainly to *America*, the Wave Line Theory was the first scientific explanation of how boats moved through the water to

In the top drawing is John Scott Russell's ideal waterline shape (as seen from above) according to the Wave Line Theory. The stern is to the left, the bow to the right. Below is the iron schooner Titania, *which Russell designed in 1851.* America, *which might also have been designed to the theory, beat her in a match race. The Wave Line Theory stimulated much research and experimentation in yacht design, bringing science to the pleasure-vessel branch of naval architecture for the first time.*

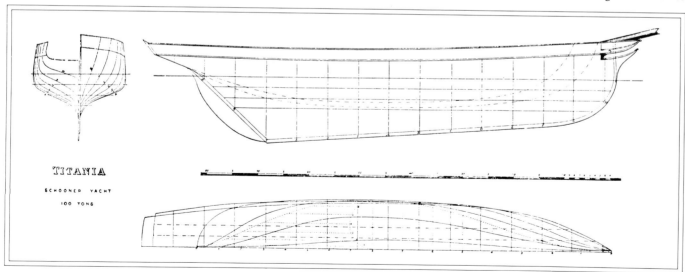

TITANIA

SCHOONER YACHT

100 TONS

gain a wide following among yachtsmen. Although it was eventually shown to be wrong, it influenced many sailors to think analytically about how boats functioned. It worked like a fishing lure: although it was not the real thing, it caught the fish all the same. Thanks to *America*'s fine demonstration of a theory that her designer may not have known anything about, a scientific approach to yachts became popular in both Britain and North America. Out of the ranks of the passionate, technically-oriented sailors who came of age between about 1860 and 1875 appeared the most important writers and designers of the pre-World War I period. They in turn influenced the designers and writers who have influenced us. The most important feature of every branch of the family tree has been its willingness to approach yachting as a serious technical endeavor. A generation after *America*'s visit to Cowes, and thanks partly to it, sailors were thinking and talking in a whole new way about boats. Where once only a Russell or the odd amateur — a Thomas Assheton-Smith, a Robert Stevens — would mess around with yachting theory and technology, by the 1890s there was a well-established profession for people who wanted to study and design and build pleasure boats. The dawn of the day of the yacht designer came in 1851. Of all the accomplishments of Stevens, this one (entirely unintended) was the most valuable.

The word was spread locally in conversations and seminars at yacht clubs and internationally and nationally by print — mounds of it. I know of no pastime in which there has been as much technical writing as pleasure sailing. John Scott Russell himself helped the cause in 1865 by producing an enormous fifty-pound tome called *The Modern System of Naval Architecture,* which spread his ideas and stimulated debate in America and Europe. Around the same time there even appeared a book, William Bland's *Ships and Boats,* that explained how to conduct model experiments. This field of research had two attractions for professional and amateur engineers alike: first, as the dispute was mostly about theory and involved many variables, much of what was debated could be neither proved or disproved with absolute conclusiveness; second, the calculations, theory, and research involved were accessible to the average technically-trained person who cared enough about boats to take the time to master them.

And so, stimulated by Russell, people conducted model testing in various parts of the world. Yet what they found seemed to contradict their master. A Norwegian boatbuilder named Colin Archer and a New York ventilating engineer named John Hyslop independently concluded that, although Russell had asked the right questions and come up with some accurate waterline sections, he had missed the whole picture. The Wave Line Theory was devised for steam vessels that do not heel. Sailboats, on the other hand, *do* heel; and when they heel the effective waterlines are not the waterline sections shown on the lines plan but rather those shown on the diagonals. Agreeing with them, W.P. Stephens compared Russell with a person "who, by long search, discovers a fine house but is unable to locate the entrance." Coming across each other's writings in magazines — Hyslop's in the American magazine *The Country* and Archer's in the English sporting journal *The Field* — Archer and Hyslop corresponded at great length about what they called the Wave Form Theory. Separately, they turned out some interesting yachts, Hyslop as an amateur and Archer as a professional. Archer's name will forever be attached to the hefty double-enders that he originally designed for pilot-boat and rescue-vessel duty, but that later were converted to yachts (the best known among them are the Westsail 32 and the "Tahiti Ketch" designed by John Hanna.)

The most important figure in the movement toward professional yacht design was Archer's editor at *The Field,* Dixon Kemp, who, in his administrative work, his designs, and especially his own writings became the major spokesman for technical sailing. Born on the Isle of Wight in 1839, Kemp may well have been the first person in recorded history to have been sidetracked by sailing on his way to a respectable career. His father intended for him to be an architect, and he actually designed houses for a moment or two when he was able to get away from boats. He reported on yachting for a local newspaper, then for *The Field* after 1863. Like many English boating writers over the next century, Kemp also dabbled in yacht design; he was the first person to describe himself as a yacht designer.

His books were Kemp's greatest contribution. The first, published in 1876, was *Yacht Designing.* Its subtitle neatly summarizes his approach: "A Treatise on the Practical Application of the Scientific Principles upon Which is Based the Art of Designing

Yachts." While not the first manual about the design of yachts, Kemp's had the distinction of being the first to stress both scientific values and artistic ones such as proportion. In it, he described the application to yacht design of the theories of Russell and other researchers, such as William Froude, who worked on the importance of skin friction at low speeds. Later, in the nine editions of his *Manual of Yacht and Boat Sailing,* which was first published in 1878, Kemp told his readers how to buy and sail scientifically designed boats. Kemp rarely held back; the ninth edition of the *Manual* is more than four inches thick.

Dixon Kemp once observed that "the yacht designer could not have existed prior to the time when yacht owners had been educated to appreciate his services." That time came with the increased complication of yacht design, construction, and handling — in theory and in practice — reflected by his books. By the late 1870s, most pleasure boats were very different from commercial sailing vessels. Several features stood out, but one made all the difference: the yacht's ballasted keel.

There had always been ballast to provide stability, but until then it was located either deep in the bilge or on deck, where it was shifted to the windward side whenever the boat changed tacks. Since lead was extremely expensive, most yachts (including *America)* used iron ballast, which, because it was less dense than lead, took up more room. Compactness was not important, however, since the common wisdom was that ballast should be left somewhat loose. To pin it down too securely was no good for the boat, which was perceived as needing flexibility. "The more metal we cram into a yacht's intestines," cautioned "Vanderdecken" in his 1853 manual *Yachts and Yachting,* "the more we destroy her elasticity and buoyancy in a seaway." A few years earlier, in his *Yacht Architecture* (probably the first book on yacht design), Lord Robert Montague proposed that ballast be made "live" by hanging it in hammocks or placing it on straw.

Once shifting ballast was prohibited for racing in Britain in 1856, attitudes about "dead ballast" had to change. As the traditionally narrow English cutter had little or none of the designed-in form stability of the beamy American sloop, the only way to make the boat stiff enough to carry her sail was to lower the center of gravity, even if this meant pinning the lead in the keel. Through-

out the 1860s and 1870s, builders and designers cautiously increased the amount of iron or lead in keels, all the time worrying (with good reason) that the added concentrated weight would strain hulls. A yacht that was built in 1873 with three and one-half tons of outside ballast was soon carrying another four and one-half tons. Later, fifteen more tons were added to the keel. One solution to the construction problem was to use metal for the hull; but this demanded new, specialized skills; old-time boatbuilders knew wood, not iron hulls and reinforcements. In less than a generation, yacht work went from rule of thumb and wood to the mathematics of the Wave Line Theory and the complex composite construction of ballast-keel boats. Specialists were now in demand. And so the profession of yacht designer was born.

One of the best of the new breed of designers nursed on the Wave Line Theory was George Lennox Watson, a Scot from Glasgow who entered the boat business as a naval architect's draftsman when he was sixteen years of age, in 1867. Like many successful innovators, he was lucky to come along when he did. Not only were the shipyards of his native Clyde estuary beginning to turn out the best-built iron boats in the world, but with the development of the ballasted keel he stood on the frontier of the new school of yacht design unfettered by old habits and outdated prejudices.

Watson and his peers faced three overlapping technical problems. First, the Thames Tonnage Rule that the English used to handicap yachts of different size encouraged narrow beam. Second, as we have just seen, narrow beam required deep, heavy keels. And third, as the model tests of William Froude had recently shown, a large keel slowed a boat in light winds by increasing the resistance to the water. In one way or another, every designer of sailing vessels has had to deal with the problem of designing a stable boat that has low resistance. But the designer of racing yachts has an additional problem: the boat also must have a low rating, or measured size according to a rule. In Watson's time, and for five hundred years before, the measured size of British vessels was expressed in "tonnage," which had nothing to do with displacement and weight. Tonnage was a measure of a boat's bulk or volume (the term was probably derived from "tun," a standard-sized barrel for wine, beer, and other spirits) and was determined by multiplying her length by her beam by her depth. Shipping duties,

A cutter crank's ideal, this is a six-beam cutter, thirty-six feet on the waterline and with six feet of beam, that C.P. Kunhardt designed in the 1880s for his book Small Yachts. *Obviously, roominess was not one of the appeals of these floating toothpicks. W.P. Stephens called the disputes over yacht design in the 1880s ''the battle of the types.'' By the end of the decade, the winner was neither the cutter nor the beamy sloop; rather it was a healthy compromise between the two.*

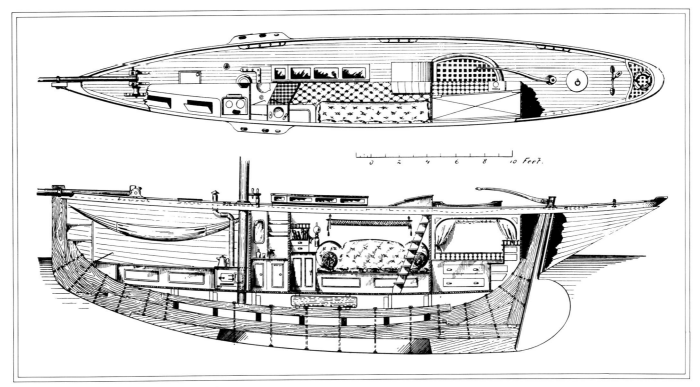

taxes, and — in racing boats — handicaps all were determined by tonnage, which in turn was directly affected by the boat's dimensions. The higher the tonnage, the greater the cost. Later, when different formulas were used (some more simple, some more complex) and ratings came to be expressed in feet, designers were no less concerned to find the lowest rating by massaging the dimensions of boats on their drawing boards. In modern yachting history, rating rules and racing have had more influence over the shape of all boats, cruisers as well as racers, than probably any other factor. As Watson himself put it, "Throughout the modern story of yachting the tonnage question has been the all-absorbing one."

Watson's first boat was launched in 1871 — a failure. Undiscouraged, he proceeded to try to fit the pieces of the puzzle together in a series of highly original boats that grew ever-narrower, ever more heavily ballasted, and ever more cut away under the

water. Sometimes he overdid it and learned from his mistakes. Between 1871 and 1886, when the rating system was changed to a simple balance between length and sail area, Watson, John Beavor-Webb (an architect), William Fife Jr. (a third-generation Scottish boatbuilder), and other young British designers produced a whole new type of racing boat best known by the evocative names "plank-on-edge cutters" and "lead mines." Models of these thin, long-legged boats seem to be perpetually teetering on their supports. At their most extreme, the cutters had a waterline length that was five, six, or even seven times their beam (as against three or four beams in the traditional American sloop), and they carried sixty or seventy percent of their displacement in ballast, all or most of it in their keels. In all conditions, they were wet, fast, and virtually uncapsizeable.

To get an idea of the difference between the types, compare the dimensions of *Madge,* the five-beam Watson-designed cutter that won seven of eight races in the United States in 1881, with those of the 1871 Herreshoff-designed compromise centerboarder *Shadow,* the only boat to beat the English invader:

	MADGE	SHADOW
Overall length:	46′	37′ 2″
Waterline length:	39′ 9″	34′ 2″
Extreme beam:	7′ 9″	14′ 4 ″
Draft:	7′ 8″	5′ 4″ (centerboard raised)
		12′ (centerboard lowered)
Displacement:	36,960 lb.	31,360 lb.
Ballast:	22,400 lb.	10,976 lb.
	(keel)	(bilge)

Though *Shadow's* waterline length and displacement were about eighty-five percent those of *Madge,* the American was twice as beamy and thirty percent shallower, and carried half *Madge's* ballast. And *Shadow* was by no means an extreme example of the skimming dish.

When *Madge* and other English cutters reached the United States, they created a sensation. In the "cutter craze," the English lead mines were praised, purchased, and copied by sailors who hated the shallow, broad skimming dishes that, though dry on deck and quick in smooth water, were uncomfortable, slow, and hard to handle whenever the sea picked up. As the *Mohawk* story made very clear, if the centerboarders were not handled carefully, they could capsize in relatively easy conditions. The clincher for Americans was that the cutters were usually faster than the skimming dishes. More often than not — to make our point again — racing performance has been (and remains) the decisive issue when people are forced to choose between boats, even if they never intend to race.

Like the yachts, the sailors and yachting writers of the 1880s were divided into two schools, one angrily defending the traditional American type of boat, and the other bitterly attacking it. Members of the latter group were called "cutter cranks," and were known individually by the extremity of their passion as "four-beam," "five-beam," and "six-beam" cranks. (In vituperation, the arguments over the cutter craze challenge the debates of exactly a century later, when beamy, shallow, and often unseaworthy skimming dishes were produced for ocean racing under the International Offshore Rule for another generation of wallet-slapping owners.) Of course, when words like "evil" and "death-trap" are thrown around publicly, facts are forced to the side. W.P. Stephens enjoyed telling a story on M. Roosevelt Schuyler, one of the seven-beam cutter cranks. Schuyler, whose nickname was "Robo," had gone out for a trial sail in a cutter.

On the return Mr. Schuyler made his way up the pier and was hailed by a friend: "How did she go, Robo?" The reply was: "Dry as a bone, not a drop of water on deck," while at each step rivulets of water flowed down the legs of his trousers and squirted out of his shoes.

One of the crankiest cutter cranks in America was Charles P. Kunhardt, a part-time designer and yachting columnist for an outdoors magazine called *Forest & Stream.* Kunhardt's savage "weekly assaults" (as Stephens put it) on the skimming dishes were extremely influential, as was his book of yacht plans, *Small Yachts: Their Design and Construction* (the third edition was handsomely reprinted in 1985 by *WoodenBoat* magazine). Kunhardt's affection for thin boats was such that in *Small Yachts* he even paid a backhanded compliment to the Thames Tonnage Rule, which he otherwise called "illogical and unfair," for giving accidental birth to the cutter. Kunhardt, who seems not to have been very stable, periodically disappeared from the cutter fray to try to make his fortune in the gold and silver rushes in Nicaragua and Colorado. Having failed in that department, he took the winter of 1885-86 off to cruise alone to North Carolina and back in a traditional American catboat, which, of course, was just the kind of vessel that he had spent his career lambasting. In March of 1889, he died in the wreck of a gunboat that he had fitted out and was taking to fight in a revolution in the Dominican Republic. Without oddballs like C.P. Kunhardt, even a pastime as hearty as yachting would sometimes seem anemic.

Amid the chaos of the cutter craze, the profession of yacht designer was developing in the United States. The first American to make a living designing pleasure boats was a Bostonian named Louis Winde, who worked in the 1840s; but otherwise, until about 1880, most yachts were designed by their owners or were spinoffs of the shipbuilding business. A reasonable explanation for this is that the ballast keel, with all its complexities of design and construction, did not become popular in America until around then.

The first American yacht designer worth the title was Archibald Cary Smith, a Manhattan preacher's son who was born in 1837. His early career followed the usual pattern, with a hot passion for sailing displacing any thoughts of earning a respectable living. Soon after his father took him to see *America* on the stocks in William Brown's yard, he was sailing model boats in puddles on Manhattan streets. Facing facts, his father in 1855 apprenticed him to a well-known New Jersey boatbuilder named Captain Bob Fish, who taught the boy how to make and sail catboats on the Hudson. His ambitions quickly grew beyond the rule of thumb, and he paid a shipbuilder $25 to teach him how to draw a boat's lines. There was little business in the 'sixties, so he soon set those technical skills aside and became a successful marine painter.

In 1870, a wealthy man named Robert Center asked Archie Smith to help him design a sixty-three foot cutter, *Vindex*. Center was one of those colorful all-round gentleman sportsmen in the Stevens mold, with equal and legendary enthusiasm for horses, hunting hounds, single-scull rowing shells, and sailboats. A story had it that one day he both raced a yacht and rode in a steeplechase. He personally maintained his boats, and was known as "watch-tackle Bob" because of his enthusiasm for taking up the slack in his yachts' rope stays with a block and tackle (after wire rigging and turnbuckles for adjusting it were introduced in the 'eighties and 'nineties, this was no longer necessary). In 1867, while touring Europe after racing across the Atlantic on board the ill-fated *Fleetwing,* Center bought both a new-fangled Michaux velocipede and a copy of one of the early English books on yacht construction. He brought both back to New York where he created a sensation with the first and, with Archie Smith, used the second as a guide to design and build *Vindex.*

She was America's first true cutter (with impeccable Wave Line Theory waterlines) and one of the first iron yachts built anywhere. Perhaps more important, she was the first yacht designed in the United States with a complete set of drawn plans. *Vindex* launched Smith on a long, successful career as a designer of yachts and steam passenger boats. To distinguish himself from another Smith in the boat business, he used the name A. Cary Smith professionally. As for his partner, Bob Center was a moderate four-beam crank during the cutter craze of the 'eighties. In 1895, while riding one of the new low-wheeled bicycles on Central Park West, he was run down and killed by a coal wagon.

The cutter-sloop controversy would inevitably have been resolved in some sort of compromise. It came in the work of the designer Edward Burgess, who, as we saw in the last chapter, designed the three Boston defenders of the America's Cup between 1885 and 1887, and in the development of another kind of measurement rule.

Born in 1848, Edward Burgess lived in Boston and grew up sailing with his five brothers on Massachusetts Bay. His inquiring mind led him into science, and he studied entomology at Harvard and taught the subject for almost fifteen years. However, when his father, a sugar importer, lost all his money in the late 1870s, he had to find more remunerative work. He turned to the only other area that he knew anything about and set up shop as a yacht broker, representing A. Cary Smith and commissioning and setting up boats for clients. Inevitably, he became interested in yacht design. He had some limitations, the greatest of which was that, unlike Smith and Nat Herreshoff, he knew almost nothing about yacht construction. But he had a feel for boats, was a good draftsman, and read the literature assiduously ("I have greatly enjoyed your books," he wrote Dixon Kemp in 1880, "and have used them until the binding is about gone"). His scientific training had made him a keen observer. Instead of bugs, he now studied yachts, and he knew where to go to see the best of them. In 1883, he and his family spent the summer on the Isle of Wight so he could observe the top English cutters. He came back a cutter crank, but soon regained his respect for the American type. His first design, in 1884, was a thirty-six foot yawl, *Rondina*, that showed both English and American traits, with a heavy ballasted keel but a length-to-beam ratio of only four to one. The word that best described her was "compromise."

Burgess, therefore, was prepared when, in their meeting to orga-

W.P. Stephens

I n the early 1870s a Philadelphia-born civil engineer named William P. Stephens read John MacGregor's account of cruising in a canoe, *The Voyage Alone in the Yawl Rob Roy*, and quickly became another casualty to the pastime. After doing some sailing, he felt sufficiently knowledgeable and confident to design a canoe of his own, and one day in 1877 he set out into the far reaches of West Tenth Street in Manhattan to show the plans to the day's great yacht designer, A. Cary Smith. This is how Stephens remembered the conversation, complete with Smith's stutter:

> *Though but one of the many strangers who intruded on similar missions, my reception was most gracious; he examined my plans and took down the new quarto,* Yacht Designing, *by Dixon Kemp, and showed me designs of canoes. When I ventured to say that I would like to be a yacht designer he replied: "My-y-y b-b-boy, you had b-b-better g-g-get a j-j-job on a peanut stand; it will p-p-pay you b-b-better in the end."*

Many years later, a prominent yacht designer gave me the same advice in somewhat different words: "Anybody who wishes to be a yacht designer," he said, "should have a good long talk with his investment banker." W.P. Stephens did not become a peanut vender, and as far as I know was not born with a trust fund. He didn't become a full-time yacht designer, either. Yachting historians are the beneficiaries. His calling was as a boating writer. Stephens did design some small cruising boats, the first defender of the Seawanhaka Cup (one of the earliest American boats with the triangular Bermudian rig), and many canoes, which he built in his boatyard on Staten Island; but that was a hobby. In 1883, he succeeded Charles Kunhardt as

Ethelwynn, *left, was the first boat to carry the Bermudian (also called jib-headed and Marconi) rig in an international race. Designed by W.P. Stephens, shown above in cheerful old age, she was the U.S. defender in the first match for the Seawanhaka Cup, in 1895.*

canoeing and yachting editor at *Forest & Stream,* where he fought the cutter-sloop battles with gusto (he termed himself a seven-beam crank) and followed the America's Cup matches and yachting politics with care. In 1903, he became the first editor of *Lloyd's Register of American Yachts.* Until his death at the age of ninety-two in 1946, he one way or another stayed in touch with almost every important figure and development in yacht racing and design.

Thanks to a phenomenal memory, he was able to write it all down in a series of eighty-three essays called "Traditions and Memories of American Yachting," which were originally published in *Motor Boating* magazine between 1939 and 1946. Most were later collected in a book of the same title and, in 1983, a complete collection was published by Roger Taylor at International Marine Publishing Company, in Camden, Maine.

Taking in the years from John Cox Stevens' boyhood to the 1920s, and including the plans of several hundred boats, *Traditions and Memories* is an invaluable source for the yachting historian. In these extraordinarily detailed yet engagingly written chapters, the reader can feel what it was like to be on the frontier of the pastime in the 1870s and 1880s. Stephens (who was unrelated to the designers Olin and Rod Stephens) covered some of the same ground when he wrote a privately published history of the Seawanhaka Corinthian Yacht Club for the years 1871-1896.

Betraying his romantic side, Stephens was otherwise best known for his elegant handlebar moustache and passion for opera. In 1943, the Metropolitan Opera Company honored him as its oldest living subscriber, sixty years after he first attended.

nize an America's Cup syndicate in 1885, General Charles J. Paine and J. Malcolm Forbes agreed that neither the extreme American centerboarder nor the six-beam cutter seemed the best direction to go with a new boat. During the remainder of his meteoric, seven-year career, Burgess designed both wide centerboarders and deep-keel boats; but he was best known for the compromise yachts — three of them America's Cup defenders — that dominated races almost everywhere on the east coast and restored Boston to prominence in yachting. His work was amply rewarded. In 1887 and 1888, he was the recipient of three cash gifts of more than $10,000 each, raised by public appeal. His fame was by no means local; the St. Petersburg Yacht Club, in Florida, gave him a cup valued at $700. Besides the Cup defenders *Puritan, Mayflower,* and *Volunteer,* his best known boat was *Papoose,* for young Charles Francis Adams III and his brother George, which inspired the first successful restricted-design racing class in America, "the Forties." The class was dominated not by a Burgess design but by a boat drawn by the Scot, William Fife. In 1886 Burgess redesigned *America* for General Ben Butler, giving her a thirty-ton lead keel and a new rig. The next year, the government hired him to help select designs for new ships that would be part of the Great White Fleet. Designing during the day and trying to educate himself in mathematics and ship design at night, he wore himself down to the point where he was unable to resist typhoid fever, and he died in 1891 at the young age of forty-three, leaving two sons, William Starling and Charles Paine Burgess. Starling became a poet, a yacht designer (like his father, he designed three Cup defenders), and an aviation pioneer. In 1910 he built the first airplane to fly in New England. Later he opened the first aircraft manufacturing company in the United States. Charles, named for General Paine, was an aeronautical engineer; his brother recruited him to design a sophisticated mast for *Enterprise* in 1930.

While valuable, Edward Burgess' contribution did not long outlast him. Between 1891 and 1900 the design of sailing yachts went through a transition that would deserve that much-overused adjective "revolutionary" if it were not a logical development of the previous generation of boats. The watershed yacht — the second after *America* — was the sloop *Gloriana,* designed by Nathanael Herreshoff. She was different in profile from just about every boat that came before, with a sharply cut-away forefoot that made her look positively chinless compared to one of the old plumb-stem boats. And she was different in hull shape, with a rounded forebody replacing the hollow waterlines that had been obligatory for forty years, ever since *America.*

As brilliant as *Gloriana* and her designer were, neither appeared out of a vacuum. The yacht herself was designed to meet the demands of a racing measurement rule, called the Seawanhaka Rule because it was sponsored by the Seawanhaka Corinthian Yacht Club. The rule had been written to address a truth made clear by the success of the long, narrow cutters: boats with long waterlines were faster than boats with short ones. The old measurement rules that in various ways tried to calculate volume did not accurately take that fact into account. In the words of Edward Burgess, "length on the load waterline is the fairest standard for racing measurement." In 1883, a committee that included Bob Center and John Hyslop recommended that racing yachts be rated by a simple formula that balanced the two speed-producing factors, length and sail area, against each other. The formula was:

$$\text{Rating in feet} = \frac{\text{Waterline Length x } \sqrt{\text{Sail Area}}}{2}$$

To calculate the handicap, the rating was entered into time allowance tables that had been devised in 1866 by Nathanael Herreshoff for the Boston Yacht Club (these tables are still in use in the 1980s). Five years later, Dixon Kemp proposed a similar rule that was adapted for English racing.

Some critics were worried that the new rule would encourage designers to produce boats with short waterlines and long, dangerous forward overhangs that would plunge into seas. And designers did pare away at the forebody; the first may have been George Watson, whose *Thistle* had a slightly cutaway bow that produced a relatively short waterline for measurement but a longer one when she heeled and the forward overhang inclined into the water. And before his death, Edward Burgess had whittled away some more. But *Gloriana* was quite different, for far from simply shortening the underbody, Herreshoff both shortened the waterline and lengthened the bow. This decreased the rating, which was pulled

back up by increasing her sail area. And, to counter the outsized sail area, he put on an especially deep ballasted keel. To keep the long bow from submarining, Herreshoff gave it the round, full sections of a spoon instead of the traditional knife-like shape that everybody was familiar with since *America.* Although this bow looked awkwardly bulbous on the level, its diagonal sections were extremely efficient, and when *Gloriana* heeled — which she did quickly enough under her large rig — she presented a powerful and effective waterline that was much longer than her measured waterline. In the summer of 1891, she quickly won eight straight races before her owner, E.D. Morgan, withdrew her from competition. That's when the real race started. Just as happened forty years before in England, boatyards were busy rebuilding bows, only this time hollows were sliced out in favor of the convex sections of the "spoon bow."

The "Wizard of Bristol," as Nat Herreshoff came to be called in the summer of *Gloriana,* was by no means unknown to American and even British yachtsmen. Unlike his friend Edward Burgess, Herreshoff had been designing boats for many years. Perhaps even more important, he had been building them, too, and yachts from the Herreshoff Manufacturing Company were noteworthy as much for their exquisite lightweight engineering as for the fast shapes of their hulls.

Born, like Burgess, in 1848, Nat had been brought up sailing in small boats on Narragansett Bay, near his father's farm near Bristol, Rhode Island. His was an extraordinary family, descended on the Herreshoff side from a favorite guard of Frederick the Great of Prussia and the distinguished Providence merchant family, the Browns, and on his mother's side from New England sea captains. Of the nine boys and girls in Nat's generation, several were prominent as engineers, musicians, or chemists — but due to an hereditary illness, four became blind. The star was Nat's older brother John Brown Herreshoff, known as J.B., whose commercial and creative instincts quickly matured despite the loss of sight in one eye due to a cataract. At the age of twelve he had his own ropewalk, where he made rope to sell to manufacturers of hoops for skirts. A year later, he put together a machine shop where, in 1855, he started work on a little twelve-foot sloop called *Meteor.* But when the boat was partially finished, he lost the other eye while roughhous-

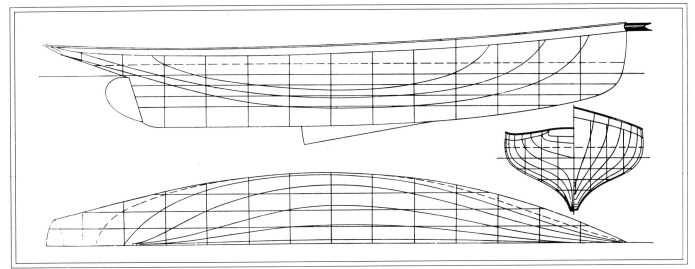

1 5 1

Edward Burgess was one of the first yacht designers to compromise between the traditional American and English types. Here is his successful 1885 America's Cup defender Puritan. *Her centerboard was retracted into a fairly deep lead keel, yet she still carried quite a bit of beam compared with the extreme cutters. The success of the cutter cranks can be gauged by comparing these lines with those of* Gracie *on page 139.*

ing with his brothers. Now totally blind, he sulked in his room for months; but through a great triumph of willpower, he returned to the shop and finished the boat with the help of his father, an amateur designer.

Although J.B. quickly developed remarkably sensitive hands that could "read" the shape of a yacht model or boat with the touch of his fingers, he needed human eyes when sailing, working at his lathe, and drawing lines. His eyes soon became those of his intense and frail younger brother, Nathanael. On the water, Nat guided J.B. around Narragansett Bay in *Meteor* in races and on expeditions to pick up lumber; ashore, he helped out in the shop. In 1860, when he was twelve, Nat took the offsets off a boat model shaped by J.B. They built the little boat they called *Sprite,* and accompanied by their father in another boat, the boys sailed the twenty-footer more than a hundred miles to New York to take a look at the massive new steamer, *Great Eastern,* which John Scott Russell had helped design and which had just arrived in the port. By 1863, J.B. had his own commercial boatbuilding firm in Bristol, and was turning out small racing boats for clients that included Edward Burgess's family.

After studying marine engineering at the Massachusetts Institute of Technology, Nat designed steam engines at a company in

Providence for nine years, meanwhile drafting plans for J.B. on evenings and weekends. In 1878, he went to work for his brother full-time. Ostensibly his job was to manage the yard's business side, in which J.B. had little interest, but inevitably he became deeply involved in design and construction while supervising a work force that numbered three hundred by 1880. During the eighties, the Herreshoff Manufacturing Company was one of the most respected builders of power yachts, steam launches, and torpedo boats, which went to the Russian, Spanish, British, and U.S. navies. J.B. and Nat became masters at building light, powerful engines (with a coil boiler invented by their brother James). The hulls were light and strong, with increasingly complicated composites of materials, including wood, iron, bronze, and steel. The best of these boats found themselves in races. One, *Vamoose,* a one hundred twelve foot steamer built in 1891 for William Randolph Hearst, the publisher, won a $12,000 cup in a race in which she made twenty-five knots — a very high speed before the coming of the internal combustion engine and the hydroplane after 1900.

From time to time, Nat drew up and built a sailboat — sometimes an iceboat for sailing in an especially cold winter, sometimes a normal sloop or catboat — and often a highly innovative response to an old design challenge of one sort or another. When

Nat Herreshoff took on a project, he never seemed to do it the same way as his predecessors. One example of his approach was *Shadow,* which he designed in 1871 and which, as we have seen, was the only boat to beat the invading cutter *Madge* ten years later. He had built her model as an exercise, but when his brother and father had a look, the design was used to fill an order for a doctor from New Bedford. The analytical powers of Nat Herreshoff's mind are exhibited in his description of this design: "My idea at the time," he wrote in his retirement, "was to shape the hull so the ballast would be lower, have the bilges practically out of water so as to get easy lines when the vessel is upright, and great beam that would give stability when heeled in a breeze." Later, he made a model improving on *Shadow* that, he claimed, appealed to Edward Burgess, who was a neighbor for a summer in the early 'eighties. "He fell quite in love with it," remembered Herreshoff, "and, in coming in, would say, 'I have come again to look at *the perfect model*'." Herreshoff was certain that this model turned Burgess away from cutter crankiness and inspired *Puritan* and Burgess's later compromise sloops.

Another of these boats was *Amaryllis* which, if you ignore Polynesian outriggers, was the first successful catamaran in history. As we saw in Chapter One, Charles II's contemporary, Sir William Petty, had experimented with catamarans in the seventeenth century, but the idea had not caught on, no doubt because the complicated materials and engineering required to build a strong multihull were still two hundred years in the future. *Amaryllis* was extremely fast. Though only twenty-five feet long, she could do twenty knots on a reach and eight upwind. In the end, she was too fast for her own good. After she conquered the New York Yacht Club's best boats at the Centennial Regatta of 1876, the type was promptly banned, thereby setting yacht design back at least a century. Late in his life, Nat said in a letter, "For the actual sailing, I enjoyed these craft more than any I ever owned." Despite the opposition of the sailing authorities, Herreshoff built several more catamarans for himself and others. He patented the carefully thought-out design and construction of these boats, which included an elaborate grid system to absorb the downthrust of the mast and a series of universal joints so the hulls could independently work over the waves. As the deep narrow hulls provided enough

resistance against leeway, they did not have centerboards. (When the catamaran finally gained the popularity it had long deserved, in the 1970s, it was only after another designer, Hobie Alter, built his first Hobie Cats without centerboards so they could easily be pulled up on a beach.)

But with the press of orders for steam vessels, Nat could not begin to concentrate on building sailboats until 1891, when he was forty-three. The immediate result was E.D. Morgan's *Gloriana,* which was based in part on a ballast-keel, cat-rigged cruising yawl called *Consuelo,* which Herreshoff had built for his own use in 1883. It was not his pattern to rest on his laurels. While he sailed in *Gloriana* in the summer of 1891, his mind was focused on an even more radical vessel with a tiny fin keel hanging independent of her rudder. This was *Dilemma,* which he built that fall. Like *Amaryllis* and *Gloriana,* in concept she was not original with Herreshoff, and he admitted as much; a fin-keeler had been sailed in Frontenac, Michigan, in 1881. But she probably was the first successful fin-keeler, and the company built more than a hundred of her sisters and cousins until the racing rules banned the type. It quickly reappeared in small racing boats like William Gardner's Bug, designed in 1907 and soon after enlarged by five feet to become the Star. But the fin keel was not used in the design of larger boats until Bill Lapworth put it on the Cal 40 cruising-racing sloop in the early 1960s.

The work of the Herreshoffs (the two brothers must be considered equally responsible) transformed the look of sailboats, at first racers and later cruisers. In 1893, the Herreshoffs in America and George Watson in England produced the first of the so-called "big class" of boats. Ninety feet on the waterline, they sailed for the America's Cup through 1903. Some of them were still sailing in England in the 1930s. The new look at first seemed ugly to people used to the short overhangs, modified clipper bows, and swooping sheerlines of the Burgess boats, and to the daintiness of the extreme five-and six-beam cutters. But most yachtsmen soon became used to the long, dangling ends and towering rigs of the new boats, whose designers were beholden to Herreshoff for looks and technology. In the hands of an artistic designer, this look could be breathtaking. Though not the champion of this fleet, the queen was universally regarded as *Britannia,* one of the most beautiful

152

*N*ot until he was forty-three, when he produced the watershed racing boat Gloriana *in 1891, was Nat Herreshoff called "the wizard of Bristol," but he had already made his mark in the design and construction of marine engines, power vessels, multihulls, and small cruising boats.* Vamoose, *which he designed and built for William Randolph Hearst, also in 1891, was the fastest steam yacht of her day.*

vessels ever built, which Watson designed for the Prince of Wales.

Nat Herreshoff was not that kind of designer. To him, efficiency and speed were beauty, not graceful profiles. The term "racing machine" was applied to his flat-sheered products, no doubt with his approval. After the 1903 America's Cup match, Sir Thomas Lipton paid Herreshoff a great compliment by saying in a fit of despair, "I don't want a beautiful boat. What I want is a boat to win the Cup — a *Reliance.*" Another item on the long list of Herreshoff improvements on other people's innovations, *Reliance* was a big scow that bore considerable resemblance to Bowdoin Crowninshield's design for the failed 1901 defense candidate *Independence.* But we shouldn't make too big a thing of this, as Crowninshield's

inspiration, of course, had been Herreshoff's own *Dilemma.*

Despite his engineering sophistication, Herreshoff began a design in the traditional way: first he drew a simple sketch showing the boat's dimensions and general shape, and then he quickly carved a half-model out of pine. In his biography of his father, L. Francis Herreshoff reported that it took all of two evenings to carve the model for *Reliance.* This was not the work of an artist. Nat Herreshoff was one of those geniuses who thought in the abstract language of mathematics and forces, yet could express himself in the language of three-dimensional shapes. Measurement rules, construction problems, displacement calculations, the flow of the water over the hull and keel — all were somehow inte-

The Parent of the Modern Scow

Nat Herreshoff's *Dilemma* is the parent of many modern one-design racing boats, foremost of which is the inland lake scow. This came about through her influence on the design of boats that sailed for the Seawanhaka Cup, a trophy for international competition in small boats put up by the Seawanhaka Corinthian Yacht Club and first sailed for in 1895.

In America, the first small-boat racing was in sandbaggers; but due to their increased complexity and expense they lost favor in only a generation. The sailing canoe became popular for racing, in the 1880s and 1890s, and in 1894 an American canoeist named William Willard Howard had such a fine time competing in canoes in England that he proposed that an American yacht club establish a trophy for international competition in what were called Half-Raters, which were about twenty-five feet long. Led by W.P. Stephens, the Seawanhaka Corinthian Yacht Club appropriated $500 for a trophy called the Seawanhaka International Challenge Cup for Small Yachts. As with the America's Cup, the Seawanhaka Rule and a match-race format were used.

At first, the boats that raced for the cup looked like small *Dilemmas;* Herreshoff himself designed a defense contender. In the first match, the American boat, designed by Stephens, beat an English challenger; but for many years thereafter a Canadian bridge engineer and amateur yacht designer named E. Herrick Duggan dominated the competition with a series of flat, shallow boats even more radical than *Dilemma.* One, *Dominion,* had a tunnel hull. Duggan eventually dispensed with the fin keel altogether and installed a centerboard (and later — shades of the *Jaght Schips* — bilge boards), relying for stability on his crew's weight on the windward rail of the flat, wide hull. Representing the Royal St. Lawrence Yacht Club of

Opposite is the "improbable object," the fifty-two-foot scow Outlook, *one of the first boats designed by Edward Burgess's son Starling, who later would draw the lines of three America's Cup defenders. Above, one of her descendants, a thirty-eight-foot Inland Lake A-Scow, flies away from the camera during the 1977* Yachting *magazine One-of-A-Kind Regatta, held on Lake Carlyle, Illinois. The fellow standing out over the water is a human boom vang keeping the boom from rising.*

Montreal, Duggan's "skows" (as they were dubbed) fended off challenges from Long Island, Boston, Connecticut, and Minnesota. The racing was intense and often bitter. In one year the challengers from Seawanhaka were accused of poor sportsmanship for increasing their weight, and therefore the boat's stability, by wearing sweaters soaked in water.

Though criticized in New York as "worthless boxes" that were as dangerous, expensive, and complicated as the old sandbaggers, this breed of boats became popular in other sailing areas. On Massachusetts Bay, Edward Burgess's son Starling, just out of Harvard, designed some "scows," as they had come to be called, to the simplest possible measurement rule: the maximum waterline length was twenty-five feet, and the maximum crew weight was eight hundred fifty pounds. Sail area was not measured. Burgess' *Outlook*, winner of the 1902 Quincy Cup, had these amazing dimensions:

Overall length: 52'	Waterline length: 25'
Beam: 16'	Sail area: 1800 sq.'

"This improbable object," writes Sam Merrick in his history of scows, "was built around a central steel truss which extended well above the deck. Much of her deck surface was cloth so the crew had to be careful not to step in the wrong places. Tacking meant going through a truss or hurdling it." Merrick rightly concludes that the effort to control freaks like *Outlook* exemplify one truth: "The story of sailboat design is a story of restrictions on excess — excess money, excess size, or one or more elements of the whole product." One of these efforts was made by Nat Herreshoff himself, who in 1903 produced the Universal Rule. It limited both overhangs and displacement, which under the Seawanhaka Rule had grown entirely out of proportion to waterline lengths.

Rule or no rule, similar eye-opening experiments were going on wherever people came across these enthralling boats, with their hair-raising speed and quick-trigger instability. The type caught on permanently on the relatively smooth waters of the small inland lakes of Wisconsin and Minnesota. Similar boats had been sailing there for years, but apparently what was needed to boost scow sailing was the example of Duggan's sophisticated, carefully engineered boats, refined through competition. Easterners were at first scornful of freshwater sailors. Answered Thomas Fleming Day in *The Rudder*, the foremost boating magazine at the turn of the century:

It has been the custom to decry western yachting and to picture fresh watermen as a lot of lubbers. But though they may be guilty of breeches of etiquette, hoist two flags on one string, fire guns on Sunday, and wear the names of their boats on their caps, when it comes to racing scows they know more about the game in one minute than we eastern people do in a month. It will be a bitter dose for the easterner to swallow to have to go to the west to learn what he fondly considers to be his own game, but if the west is to be beaten at scow racing, it can only be done by studying the fresh waterman's methods.

Soon after, Barnegat Bay, in New Jersey, became another scow center. Today, some of the best racing in America is done in these descendants of *Dilemma*. The Seawanhaka Cup, which inspired many match-race series between clubs and nations, eventually moved on to less freaky boats; in 1963, I helped defend it against Norway in a 5.5 Meter, a thirty-foot keel boat.

grated in the apparently simple, childish work of whittling a boat out of a block of wood.

Nat then drew detailed construction plans using his own formulas and rules of thumb for calculating the type and size of materials and supports. (These formulas later were part of a set of widely used scantling rules.) He experimented freely with construction and materials, which were cut and shaped on machines that he designed. Some of this work succeeded in the short run, but failed over time. The best example is his use of bronze, steel and aluminum in the Cup defenders of the 'nineties. This composite construction was light for its strength and smooth (before each race the crews would burnish the unpainted, bronze bottoms to a mirror finish). But while used with considerable ingenuity in terms of their strength, the various metals were installed with little or no concern about galvanic action, which in salt water was fierce. *Defender*, built in 1895, quickly became a huge floating battery. A U.S. Navy surveyor found her entirely corroded when he examined her in July of 1896, and she had to be rebuilt before she could be sailed again. Herreshoff learned his lessons, and it could be that his greatest accomplishment with *Reliance* was that she got through the summer with only one minor failure in her enormous, complicated rig.

If he had an advantage over most other designers then and since, it was that he built the boats he designed — which is another way of saying that he had absolute control over them until they were in the hands of their owners. Like J.P. Morgan, who was a steady client of the Herreshoff Manufacturing Company, he was a domineering man whose eye was always intent on his goal. L. Francis Herreshoff told of the last meeting between these two giants in their fields:

. . . A short time before Mr. Morgan's death, or in about 1912, J.P. invited, or perhaps ordered, Captain Nat to come down to see him. When in after years I questioned Captain Nat about that interview about all he would say was, "Mr. Morgan was such a strong-minded man that the doctors did not mind telling him he had but a short time to live, so he had me down to talk about old times." I can imagine, however, the conversation was not very lively as neither of them was ever a talkative person, and

the subject of how the Columbia *[owned by Morgan] beat the* Constitution *[in the 1901 Cup trials] was never a popular one with Captain Nat.*

While he was widely respected for his technical accomplishments — though some shared the Earl of Dunraven's opinion that he was too serious and businesslike about winning races — Nat Herreshoff was more admired than liked. He cared little for public relations. When he went into partnership with his brother, he stated that one of his goals was that the company's only advertisement would be the quality of its work; the other goals were to constantly improve his products and never borrow money (the inevitable corollary, never to deliver a boat before it was paid for, had already been promised by J.B.). He had no interest in satisfying the hordes of newspaper yachting columnists who inevitably flocked to Bristol while an America's Cup defense candidate was under construction. In 1901, after he refused to talk about *Constitution* because, he said, there was nothing to say, one rejected scribe sarcastically described him as "not the ideal boatbuilder of the whole-souled, hearty, hospitable variety encountered in marine novels." Herreshoff would not have known what to make of such a comment. His whole life was his work, as his son, L. Francis, suggested in the comment, "J.B. was human even if N.G. was too busy to be, and a mechanical genius is not meant to be human."

His endurance was itself machine-like. On his way to becoming the premier yacht architect and builder in history, Nat shrugged off exhaustion, typhoid, pneumonia, and rheumatism. He also shrugged off religion, even on his deathbed at the age of ninety. After Starling Burgess assured him of his resurrection after death, his only comment was, "Sometimes I think Starling talks a little foolish." He was much more responsive when Harold Vanderbilt and Olin and Rod Stephens (his successors as the major yacht designers) came to show him movies of the J-Class America's Cup boats. His mind still sharp, he quickly spotted and pointed out the most intricate technical details. "He was half a step ahead," remembered Rod Stephens almost fifty years later. "I shouldn't have been surprised; but I was."

The only thing that Nat Herreshoff apparently did not shrug off in his lifetime was World War I. After a career of building torpedo

In this historic painting by Frederic Cozzens, one of Nat Herreshoff's catamarans sails by two more traditional yachts. After his Amaryllis *cleaned up at the New York Yacht Club's Centennial Regatta in 1876, catamarans were banned from organized racing. The larger yacht,* Julia, *was designed as a centerboard sloop by George Steers, who produced* America, *but as yachting fashions changed she later became a keel schooner. The setting is the entrance to the harbor of New London, Connecticut.*

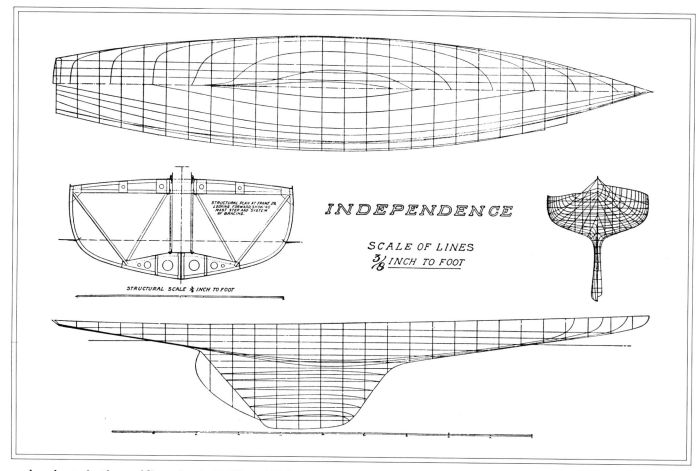

INDEPENDENCE

SCALE OF LINES
3/8 INCH TO FOOT

STRUCTURAL PLAN AT FRAME 29,
LOOKING FORWARD SHOWING
MAST STEP AND SYSTEM
OF BRACING.

STRUCTURAL SCALE 3/4 INCH TO FOOT

Although Thomas W. Lawson's Independence, *whose radical lines are shown at left, couldn't do anything right during her ill-fated America's Cup campaign in 1901, Nat Herreshoff concluded that her designer, Bowdoin Crowninshield (Captain George's great-grand nephew), was on to something. Two years later, Herreshoff produced another — and far more successful — scow-type Cup boat in* Reliance, *shown at right.*

and gunboats for the world's navies, in 1915 he told J.B. to refuse a large order to build warships for the Russians to use against his ancestral homeland, Germany. In his mathematical soul he felt a twitch of passion that originated either in pacifism or nationalism. Rarely if ever had he disagreed with his brother. The thunderstruck J.B. took to his bed and soon died. Outside owners took over; but in 1924 they were forced to auction the company off. By then, Nat was semi-retired, but construction work continued. In 1930 and 1934 the yard built its seventh and eighth Cup defenders, and there were several classes of small boats designed by Captain

Nat and his sons. His last design, a fifty-two foot yawl named *Belisarius*, was done in 1935, when he was eighty-seven years of age. He died in 1939.

Things weren't the same, and after doing some military work during World War II, the yard survived Nat by only a few years. Today, the surviving Herreshoffs in Bristol, including his grandson Halsey, a yacht designer and several-time America's Cup defending crewmember, keep a small but active museum devoted memory of one of the most extraordinary men and institutions in the history of the golden pastime.

VIII

Offshore Sailing

"In devising plans to make the
pleasure of a voyage complete then,
many cognitions were had last
winter, and these resulted in a beautiful
little sailing-boat; and once afloat
in this, the water was my road, my home,
my very world, for a long and
splendid summer."

e have been speaking much of racing here, and to it we will return soon and inevitably, since competition seems to be at the essence of the golden pastime. But let us reflect for a moment on less-extroverted sailing: on cruising both alongshore and out of sight of land. This is the story of dreamers and escapists like Roger North, who wrote of a cruise in the 1670s:

There was little remarkable in this day's voyage, only that I, with my friend Mr. Chute, sat before the mast in the hatchway, with perspectives and books, the magazine of provisions, and a boy to make a fire and help broil, make tea, chocolate, etc. And thus, we sat out eight whole hours and scarce knew what time it was. For the day proved cool, the gale brisk, the air clear, and no inconvenience to molest us, nor wants to trouble our thoughts, neither business to importune, nor formalities to tease us; so that we came nearer to perfection of life than I was ever sensible of otherwise.

That sublime state so near to perfection has been the goal of most cruising sailors, some in river voyages as unremarkable as North's, others in trips that verge on adventure and exploration. Without surveying the whole history of this branch of the golden pastime (that would take a thick volume), we will look at a few twigs that have sprouted from the limb.

At first, cruising was not much different from the gaudy life that surrounded the early yacht clubs and racing fleets. Wealthy people would build big steam yachts and take off on elaborate tours of Europe in search of art, princes, and game. If we believe the narratives that often trailed after these voyages, the yachts were little more than floating mansions or hunting lodges. Some were stages on which their owners, freed from the restrictions of an egalitarian social etiquette ashore, could strut as martinets.

Take, for example, J.H.W. Smyth-Pigott, the remarkably named Royal Yacht Squadron member who owned the cutter *Ganymede* in the 1840s. To quote a contemporary magazine, "for man-of-war efficiency, order, trim, and discipline" *Ganymede* was "the *beau idéal* of the English gentleman's yacht." Well, yes and no. As a guest, Mrs. N.M. Condy, reported in a scathing account of a cruise on her (safely published years later as a pamphlet), *Ganymede* was more like a lunatic asylum than a naval station. The down-Solent cruise in company with other Squadron yachts had hardly begun before the cook grimly announced that all the clean laundry had been left ashore. Using the Squadron's huge dictionary of flag-signals, Smyth-Pigott requested and received the commodore's permission to leave station, sailed back to Cowes, picked up the linen, and battered back through a storm to resume his appointed station. That problem solved, Mrs. Condy and the other guests were kept awake all night by the chickens caged on deck. "That bless'd old cock never will let any poor devil sleep after two o'clock," cheerfully explained the coxswain in the morning, "and the young'uns are larnin'!" A guest named Packem imaginatively addressed the problem by pouring gin into the chickens' corn ration, but instead of anesthetizing them, he only stimulated more and earlier racket.

Smyth-Pigott remained detached from the henhouse battle, no doubt because he was focusing his energies on preparations for the Sunday morning divine service, which, he insisted, must be strictly naval in discipline. A special church pennant must be flown from the mainsail gaff, which meant hoisting the mainsail regardless of the fact that the anchored *Ganymede* had no place to go. "I am convinced," wrote the impish Mrs. Condy, "he would have considered the whole ceremony imperfect had not this important piece of bunting been displayed to tell heaven what we were about." The enormous sail flopped from side to side, violently rolling the yacht under it. As Smyth-Pigott read a prayer for all at sea ("*Particularly* the Royal Yacht Squadron"), the crew and guests struggled against laughing and falling into each other. Finally, a sailor tumbled against the captain, whose hat flew overboard. His oaths awakened the chickens, which began to cackle and crow until the frustrated Smyth-Pigott gave up the charade and ordered the bos'un to pipe the crew below.

There was a more ambitious aspect of nineteenth-century cruising exemplified by the elaborate, famous voyages of Sir Thomas and Lady Anna Brassey in their one-hundred-seventy-foot, three-masted auxiliary schooner *Sunbeam*, the first yacht to sail around the world. Brassey was only thirty-eight when he launched *Sunbeam* in 1874, but he had already cruised extensively in smaller

Cruising has evolved into a popular pastime in areas that once would have been thought improbable. On page 160, a boat beats across Alaska's Prince William Sound. The first circumnavigation for pleasure (though the hard-nosed owner claimed he was on business) was by the Brassey family in their schooner Sunbeam, *in 1876-77. Lady Brassey's books about their voyages were best-sellers.*

vessels and had earned his master's papers. Over the next forty-two years he covered some half million miles in her, including twelve Mediterranean cruises, voyages to Canada and India, two round-trip passages to Australia, and the circumnavigation. A taciturn, Puritanical character — "the harder the struggle, the more persistent the effort," he once preached in a memoir — Brassey always went out of his way to deny that he was a pleasure cruiser: either he was on crown business or was conducting research for *Brassey's Naval Manual,* the widely respected survey of warships and naval policy that he published.

If *Sunbeam* was constantly on official business, you wouldn't have known it on board. His vivacious wife Anna was credited with inventing the type of gathering called the afternoon deck party, to which guests were ferried in rowing boats or the newfangled steam launches. She took the same spirit offshore. On *Sunbeam* when she left on her first voyage, in 1876, were the Brasseys, their four children, two dogs, three birds, a Persian kitten, a seven-hundred-volume library, thirty tons of extra equipment, four stewards, two cooks, a nurse, a stewardess, and a maid. While life below was blissful, Brassey ruled the twenty-three sailors and engineers with the priggish authority that only an amateur sea captain can muster, sometimes subjecting them to readings from his favorite books. Yet Brassey had some redeeming features. Well, he had at least one: though he rarely doffed his stiff collar and waistcoat, he was

a true sailorman. On one of the schooner's later voyages, a sailor struggling to reef a topsail loudly complained, "I wish the old bastard was up 'ere 'isself," only to be told, "The old bastard is up here." His companion on the footropes was elderly Sir Thomas.

Thanks to her owner's drive and her powerful steam engine, *Sunbeam*'s thirty-five-thousand-mile circumnavigation took only eleven months — probably a record for a yacht. On her return, Lady Brassey showed her journals to an editor who, entranced by her unpretentious writing style and keen powers of observation, published them as *Around the World in the Yacht Sunbeam*. It opened simply: "At noon on July First, 1876, we said good-bye to the friends who had come to Chatham to see us off . . ." Lady Brassey's chatty narrative is an irresistible combination of nursery story, adventure account, travelogue, and chauvinistic celebration of English values (the Emperor of Japan, she wrote, not only was out of place in western clothes, but had legs "that look as though they did not belong to him — I suppose for using them so little, and sitting so much on his heels . . ."). A kind of seagoing *Peter Pan,* the book became a best-seller both in Britain and the United States, and was followed by three more charming accounts of later voyages in which Lady Brassey admitted that she was no deckchair note-taker and concluded that, after enduring five gales in eleven days, she had become an accomplished sailor. On a trip to Constantinople in 1878, she mastered the sextant. She mastered the crew as well. "We on board the *Sunbeam* are like one large family," she wrote in *Sunshine and Storm in the East,* "some of the men having been with us for fifteen or sixteen years."

In 1887, during a canoe trip up a river in Borneo, Lady Brassey was bitten by a mosquito and contracted malaria. On September 14, as *Sunbeam* was entering the Indian Ocean on the way back from Australia, she died and was buried at sea. Brassey published her final journals as *The Last Voyage,* with his own grieving introduction, and his sadness was shared by a generation of American and British readers who had been introduced to the dream of ocean cruising for pleasure by this remarkable woman. The schooner carried her owner for another thirty years, and was not broken up until 1929, in her fifty-fifth year.

If Brassey had an American equivalent, he was Arthur Curtiss James, a mining and railroad tycoon and philanthropist (there is

a James Memorial Chapel at Union Theological Seminary, in New York City, where I have studied). Having obtained a master's license as a young man, he soon had a vessel to command, since, in 1893, when he was twenty-six, his father presented him with a one-hundred-thirty-three-foot schooner, *Coronet*. In 1895 and 1896, he sailed around Cape Horn to Japan to observe a solar eclipse, but unfortunately the decisive day was overcast (a humorist noted in the log, "We returned corona-less to *Coronet*"). James later voyaged extensively between the West Indies and Iceland in a brigantine. In 1910, when he was Commodore of the New York Yacht Club, he built the gorgeous two-hundred-sixteen-foot, full-rigged bark *Aloha,* designed by Clinton Crane and A. Cary Smith, in which he made a circumnavigation. James was not the only person to use science as the purpose of (or excuse for) a cruise. The Earl of Crawford sailed to Mauritius to observe a transit of Venus and three times went off on ornithological expeditions (three of the eight species that he discovered are named for him), and both William K. Vanderbilt Jr. and Prince Albert of Monaco conducted extensive oceanographic researches with their big steamers as vehicles.

Before the development of the racing machines of the 1890s, America's Cup yachts were known to take a cruise. In 1869, Thomas Ashbury broke off his nagging negotiations with the New York Yacht Club concerning the terms of the first challenge to take his *Cambria* to Egypt for the opening of the Suez Canal, through which she was the first non-royal yacht to make a passage. His successor at challenging for the Cup, Lt. William Henn, was distinctly a cruising type of sailor. He and his wife had already cruised some fifty thousand miles in the seven years they had lived aboard another boat. Their 1886 challenger, *Galatea,* was built and equipped for the same purpose, with thick rugs, heavy furniture, bulkheads hung with paintings and mirrors, and a menagerie that included a pet monkey named Peggy that was dressed in a sailor outfit and helped the crew with the running rigging.

Missionary work, too, played a part in the spread of privately-owned vessels across the seas. In the 1870s and 1880s, an English army officer turned priest named J.J. Curling served his enormous parish in Newfoundland in three yachts that he equipped or built personally for church work, and in later years the missionary-doctor Sir Wilfred Grenfell depended on yachts as well as fishing boats to carry him along the coast of Labrador.

But we should be careful not to make too much of serious business aboard cruising boats. As the story of another British sailor-clergyman, the Reverend A. van Straubenzee, suggests, the primary reason why people have bought cruising boats has been the search for pleasure. This late-nineteenth-century worthy was a former naval officer who (as a friend put it) "in spite of his stole and surplice, remained very much of a naval officer at heart." Upon his recovery from a serious illness, his grateful parish offered up a thanksgiving by presenting him with a large gift of cash. Instead of investing it cautiously, or using it to make his own gift to the needy, the vicar bought himself a champion fighting cock and a small cruising yacht in which he and his wife spent many hours of pleasurable escape from parish duties.

The people who pioneered in the kind of cruising that eventually caught on among the rest of us sailed very different types of boats from *Sunbeam* and *Aloha*. The most influential of them was a sailor-promoter named John MacGregor who, in a series of modest singlehanded voyages in small boats in the 1860s — and in the lively books that he wrote about his adventures — probably did more to popularize the pastime than any other man.

This son of a Scottish soldier was born in 1825 and almost immediately went to sea, being rescued from a burning troop ship when he was all of two months old. By the time he was fifteen, he had another two close calls with drowning and had developed a reputation for daring that earned him the nickname "Rob Roy," after the Scottish hero. MacGregor settled into an extroverted life whose variety was extraordinary even for the Victorian period, which knew few specialities. He climbed Mont Blanc, distributed religious tracts, illustrated a book on South Africa by David Livingstone, swam the waters where St. Paul was shipwrecked, wrote a treatise on eastern music, founded a society of shoeshine boys, was bugler in a volunteer regiment, helped with a school for slum boys, and despite his early experiences became a fanatical sailor and canoeist. In 1865 he designed himself a canoe named *Rob Roy* and paddled it a thousand miles on twenty European lakes. His lectures and book about his experiences led him to found the Canoe Club, of which (of course) he was Captain. Before long,

"Rob Roy" came to be a synonym for a canoe or small boat. MacGregor later assured a royal warrant for the club by charming the Prince of Wales into agreeing to be its sponsor. In 1866 he cruised the Baltic and wrote his second book, and in 1869 he paddled around the Middle East and wrote yet another.

MacGregor would be remembered solely as a canoe enthusiast if he had not gone off on a slightly different tack in 1867. The French Emperor Napoleon III, who like many people was fascinated by MacGregor's passionate propaganda in favor of small boats, scheduled a boat exhibition in Paris for that year (this was the original excuse for the 1866 Trans-Atlantic Race from New York). To MacGregor, the exhibition was a grand challenge. He built himself a new boat, a twenty-one foot keel yawl named (naturally) *Rob Roy*, sailed across the English Channel, and was towed up the Seine to Paris while distributing Protestant tracts to convert the Catholics. MacGregor returned buoyant with pride. "I feel I have performed a feat and no more need be added to it," he wrote in a letter. "It is worthy of the Captain of the Canoe Club and I am content." He fired off a long letter to the London *Times* describing his feat, and got to work telling everybody about it. "I am in extreme enjoyment," was his constant refrain, which he repeated on many lecture platforms; in the first year alone he earned £ 4,160 — the equivalent of about $20,000.

The story of the little yawl's successful voyage is recorded in MacGregor's *The Voyage Alone in the Yawl Rob Roy*, a wonderful little book that is the model of a good cruise story. Like Lady Brassey's books, it has a fast-moving, conversational prose style: here you are, the reader, on one side of a table in a cheerful cabin, sharing a bottle and some yarns with genial Rob Roy MacGregor, who sits in extreme enjoyment bursting with observations and anecdotes and good will — and milking every possible drop of excitement out of what little action there was. When the story gets thin, he breaks for short technical essays about the boat and how he handled her. Read, for example, MacGregor's inviting first paragraph:

It was a strange and pleasant life for me all the summer, sailing entirely alone by sea and river fifteen hundred miles, and with its toils, perils, and adventures heartily enjoyed.

*J*oshua Slocum may have been patronized by blue-blazer yachtsmen, but he accomplished one of the greatest feats of small-boat seamanship when he sailed his ancient Spray around the world in the closing years of the nineteenth century. He was fifty-one years old when he set out on this precedent-setting circumnavigation. Slocum and Spray *disappeared on a passage from Martha's Vineyard to the Caribbean in the fall of 1909.*

And the third, no less seductive:

In devising plans to make the pleasure of a voyage complete then, many cogitations were had last winter, and these resulted in a beautiful little sailing-boat; and once afloat in this, the water was my road, my home, my very world, for a long and splendid summer.

Who could resist it? The dream was always there, more or less buried in the souls of people drawn to the water; and now that Rob Roy MacGregor told people how to act on it, others followed after him. In 1869, one E.E. Middleton built a copy of the yawl and headed off to circumnavigate England clockwise, choosing that route because it was the most difficult one that he could imagine. Middleton was not bothered that he knew nothing about small-boat handling. That was a small inconvenience to Middleton, who had sailed to Australia and back on a square-rigger, had commanded soldiers in India, and was otherwise emboldened by that singular courage that seems a characteristic of lifelong oddballs. Among his curious convictions were that the earth was both flat and stationary, that all of society's problems would be solved if only the poor could read Aristotle's *Ethics,* and that what the world otherwise needed was his own translation, in pentameter, of the *Aeneid.* Middleton's attitude about life is fairly summarized in his declaration about navigating on this cruise: "To have known my way would have been quite disgusting." While he did allow himself to take sailing lessons for a few days, his itinerary around the British coast was somewhat haphazard as he was dedicated to sleeping and eating ashore. Instead of anchoring out, he had to enter a harbor each night, which required many hours of painful rowing against rushing currents. His book, *The Cruise of the Kate,* is an account of almost superhuman endurance as well as one of the greatest collections of curious opinions ever placed between two covers.

Sailors thrive on information, and they have gotten it from many periodicals (eight national nautical magazines were in print in the U.S. in the mid-1980s) and, especially, from books. MacGregor's book was the first of a genre of writing about sailing — part narrative, part instruction — that has remained popular ever since. Most successful books on cruising by Eric Hiscock, Lin and Larry Pardey, and other sailor-authors follow this formula. Another genre is the so-called "how-to" book which tells no stories but provides detailed advice on how to sail, navigate, or maintain a boat. As we have already seen, the early sailing manuals, such as *The Yacht Sailor* by "Vanderdecken," included full instructions on hiring and managing a professional crew. Later, the most popular how-to books were those that claimed to cover the whole territory of boating skills. The most enduring of these was Charles F. Chapman's *Piloting, Seamanship, and Small Boat Handling,* which was first published in 1922 and was still going strong more than sixty years later, thanks to its adoption as a textbook by the United States Power Squadrons, which ran boating courses in most waterfront towns and cities. Other types of popular how-to books were manuals on surviving storms and on choosing and equipping the right boat for fulfilling the dream of sailing off and across an ocean.

The books and exploits of MacGregor, Middleton, and another early singlehander named Richard McMullen were extremely influential. One indication is the fact that an Australian bought *Rob Roy* and had her shipped halfway around the world. The exploits of these pioneers — not all of them perfectly sane — succeeded in convincing a large number of people that the dream of sailing off in one's own little boat was not a fantasy but an exciting possibility. That the first influential cruising sailors ventured out alone should not be surprising, given the natural human tendency to project hopes and dreams on a single hero-like figure. In the one-hundred-twenty-odd years since the exploits of MacGregor and Middleton, solo sailing has remained the most romantic form of offshore cruising, often well out of proportion to the sensibility and practicality of the trip.

Without doubt, the best-known singlehander was a cheerful, somewhat disheveled Nova-Scotia-born sea captain named Joshua Slocum, who made the first solitary circumnavigation between 1895 and 1898 and wrote about it in a book that verges on being great literature. Slocum's *Sailing Alone Around the World* has deservedly remained almost continuously in print since it was first published in 1900. A seasoned merchant-ship captain, Slocum was fifty-one when he set out in a tubby thirty-six-foot sloop called

Women Voyagers

Beginning with Lady Anna Brassey, women have played a major role in cruising and other types of sailing. The Duchess of Westminster won a medal in the 1908 yachting Olympics, and twenty years later Virginie Hériot, a passionate French yachtswoman who owned a whole fleet of boats and cruised more than one hundred forty thousand miles in her short lifetime of forty-two years, won a medal in the 1928 games. But it is in offshore sailing that women have been most visible. In the 1930s, a Mrs. Strout and her husband made one of the first doublehanded circumnavigations, and later Susan Hiscock and her husband Eric sailed around the world twice in two different boats named *Wanderer,* about which Eric Hiscock wrote several important instructional and narrative books.

In 1952, at the very beginning of the offshore-cruising era, Ann Davison, an Englishwoman, sailed to the eastern United States from England via the Caribbean in a twenty-three-foot sloop called *Felicity Ann.* She was the first woman to cross an ocean singlehanded. The boat's builder recalled, "We told her that either she was daft or frightfully courageous." Davison's feat was widely publicized for its originality in *Life* magazine and other publications; but as a reader of her fine book on the voyage, *My Ship is So Small,* is quickly made aware, she had concerns other than records. Three years earlier, she lost her husband and almost drowned in a wreck of their big converted fishing trawler as they beat down-Channel on the start of a crossing. "What is courage?" she asks at the end of her narrative. "An understanding and acceptance," she answers; "but an acceptance without resignation, mark you, for courage is a fighting quality."

By 1973, six women had crossed the Atlantic solo; many more would join that list as each entry list for the London *Observer*'s Singlehanded Transatlantic Race would include

anywhere between three and a dozen women's names. The first singlehanded crossing of the Pacific by a woman was accomplished by Sharon Sites, who in 1969 covered the five thousand miles between Yokohama, Japan, and San Diego, California, in seventy-four days. Since then, a crew consisting entirely of women has sailed in the demanding Los Angeles to Honolulu Race as well as in the Southern Ocean Racing Conference, a major competition held annually off Florida.

Perhaps the most significant sailing accomplishment by a woman was made in the late 1970s by a New Zealand farm girl named Naomi James, who made a two-stop, two-hundred-seventy-two-day voyage around the world in a fifty-three-foot ocean racer. From time to time, she received some radioed advice from her husband, Rob James, a professional yacht skipper who was racing around the world; but in every other way the voyage was hers, and when she returned to Britain she was made Dame Naomi James.

Two developments in the 1980s promised to help more women participate in offshore and other sailing events. One was the arrival of new gear that eases the burden of handling sails for people with smaller physiques. The other was the long-overdue development of sailing and other athletic training programs for girls and young women, including the scheduling of the first women's yachting event in the 1988 Olympics.

Women sailors now follow in the wake of Lady Brassey and Ann Davidson on the race course. Here a Swedish crew races in the thirty-six boat fleet that sailed the first International Women's Keelboat Regatta, held in J/24s off Newport, Rhode Island, in 1985.

Spray, which he had rebuilt after he found her rotting away in a field. Many people believe he should have left her there. "My father," reported Nathanael Herreshoff's son L. Francis, "did not think much of the *Spray,* but he had great admiration for Captain Slocum's ability to go around the world in such a poor vessel." Slocum himself seemed to think her seaworthy, but he was the man who had sailed his family from Brazil to Massachusetts in a jerry-built sampan; and besides, he was broke and *Spray* was all he could afford.

Slocum fished commercially in *Spray* for a while, with no success — as he described it in his inimitable roundabout way, "I spent a season in my new craft fishing on the coast, only to find that I had not the cunning properly to bait a hook." Taking off without his chronometer because he lacked the money to have it cleaned and rated, Slocum sailed a roundabout route that totaled forty-six thousand miles. Along the way (if we are to believe his stories) he encountered all sorts of adventures, including shipwreck, attacks by Indians, and gales. Although everything in *Sailing Alone around the World* may not be perfectly true, Slocum's engaging, Huck Finn-like, irony-filled prose makes us want to believe it — and anyway, it's a great story.

The second solitary circumnavigation was not made until the 1920s, when a former farm boy named Harry Pidgeon did it in a self-built V-bottom thirty-four-foot yawl (he repeated the trick when in his sixties). Since the mid-1950s, an uncounted and probably uncountable number of people have sailed alone across oceans or around the world. Most of this activity has been non-competitive. The first pleasure boat (and only the second surface vessel) to make it through the Northwest Passage, in 1977, was the singlehanded ketch *Williwaw,* sailed by a determined yet philosophical Dutch circumnavigator named Willy de Roos, whose book *North-West Passage* can serve as a manual for enduring hard conditions. About fear he writes:

A man who understands a dangerous course of action must begin by accepting the prospect of living with anxiety. It is bad policy to avoid the feeling of anxiety by mentally minimizing the danger. It is better to remain conscious of the risk and to accept the fact that one is afraid.

If any one person brought about the boom in singlehanded voyaging — in fact, of ocean sailing in general — it was Francis Chichester, an Englishman born in 1901, and a full-blown romantic adventurer of the old school. Starting out in the early days of airplanes, he set records for long-distance solitary flights (for example, he made the first singlehanded seaplane flight from New Zealand to Japan) before taking up sailing in his fifties. When a war hero and sailor named Blondie Hasler proposed a singlehanded race for 1960 across the Atlantic from England to New York, Chichester helped organize it. The idea seemed crazy at the time, and only five entrants appeared. Chichester won in forty days in his forty-foot yawl *Gipsy Moth III.* Sponsored by a London newspaper, the *Observer,* the race was widely publicized, and when it was repeated in 1964, Chichester and other entrants were paid to file daily reports by radio to other English newspapers. (Comparisons with the circulation-boosting publicity of the 1866 Trans-Atlantic Race are inevitable. There is little new in yacht design *or* in public relations.)

170 Chichester's great moment came in 1966, when at the advanced age of sixty-five he set out in a fifty-four-footer — a very large boat for singlehanded sailing regardless of the sailor's age — to sail around the world, stopping only in Australia. He wanted to be the ninth yachtsman to round Cape Horn (which even Slocum had not dared to try), and he wanted to break the clipper-ship speed records. He succeeded in the first goal but narrowly failed in the latter. Britain was very much in need of heroes in those days, and when Chichester finished the voyage in June of 1967, the whole country came to a stop to watch in person and on television as he stepped ashore with shaking legs to be knighted by Queen Elizabeth II, who used the same sword that Queen Elizabeth I had presented to Sir Francis Drake. *Gipsy Moth IV* is now on permanent exhibit at the National Maritime Museum at Greenwich.

The publicity, the national fervor, and, it should be said, the commerical interest in Chichester's voyage attracted a new generation of English sailors looking for "firsts" of one kind or another. In 1968-69, this publicity-generated fad reached its nadir. On very short notice, the London *Sunday Times* announced that it would award £ 5000 to the fastest boat in a singlehanded non-stop race around the world. Unlike the sponsors of the *Observer* singlehand-

Singlehanded voyaging has been most popular in Britain and Europe thanks partly to free-spending commercial sponsors hungry for publicity. Francis Chichester, opposite, is the godfather of this trend. His solo voyage around the world in 1966-67 was headline news everywhere. A decade later, Naomi James, right, followed almost the same route and met with an even more enthusiastic reception.

ed race, the *Times* did not examine either the boats or the skippers for seaworthiness and strength. Of the eight boats that started, only one — Robin Knox-Johnston's thirty-two-footer *Suhaili* — finished. That her average speed was less than four knots suggests that this was a war of attrition, not a real contest. Of the others, all broke up or dropped out. One competitor, Donald Crowhurst, attempted a hoax by circling around in the South Atlantic instead of doing the circuit around the globe. His conscience got to him, and he jumped overboard and drowned himself before the fraud was discovered. Another, Nigel Tetley, actually led for much of the way in his trimaran; but, misled by Crowhurst's false reports into believing that he was losing, he pushed his boat so hard that she broke up only eight hundred miles from the finish. Though rescued, Tetley never recovered emotionally and committed suicide two years after the race.

A third competitor in the round-the-world race was a Vietnam-born Frenchman named Bernard Moitessier. The most experienced sailor of the eight, he was also something of a mystic, a man increasingly in tune with the big seas and the marine life of the Southern Ocean, and his mysticism won out over his competitiveness. After rounding Cape Horn in his brutally efficient steel ketch *Joshua* (named for Slocum), he did not turn north for the finish in England because, as he put it in his fascinating, introspective book *The Long Way,* "I am happy at sea, and perhaps also to save my soul." He continued on to the east to Tahiti, making a solo voyage one and one-half times around the world in ten months, most of it in the "Roaring Forties" of the Southern Ocean. Of all the voyages made under sail, this may well be the most extraordinary. After many years in the South Seas, Moitessier sailed to America only to see a freak storm blow *Joshua* onto a beach in Baja California, Mexico, in 1983 and all but destroy her. He was at sea again, in a new steel boat, sailing the Pacific in 1984 and 1985.

The *Times* race — which, I am happy to say, was never repeated — served as a watershed. Within ten years more than two hundred boats were sailing in the more sane *Observer* Singlehanded Trans-Atlantic Race (known by the acronym OSTAR), and five years after that a multi-stop round-the-world singlehanded race was under way. The equipment was stronger, the boats were faster and (usually) more seaworthy, and the sailors knew what they were in

for. There was also more money available from sponsors to pay the bills, including the salaries of the professional sailors. The wave of the future was forecast by a French naval officer named Eric Tabarly, who became entranced by the heroic loneliness of single-handed sailing in the 1960s. Although he won the *Observer* race to America in 1964, as well as several other long singlehanded races, Tabarly is most important for his technological daring. At one stage, he sailed a schooner whose external ballast was composed of spent uranium, which is more dense even than lead. In 1968, he turned up for the *Observer* race in a sixty-seven-foot trimaran, the first big multihull to race offshore, and although he did not finish — the boat was badly damaged in a collision with a freighter while he was below (an occupational hazard of solo sailing) — a precedent was set.

Besides Tabarly's ingenuity, the other major factor in the boom of singlehanded offshore sailing was professional sponsorship by companies looking for advertising in countries where television is non-commercial or where TV advertising of liquor and tobacco products is prohibited. Of these countries, France had the most interest in professional offshore racing thanks to Tabarly — a national hero because of his frequent triumphs over English sailors, à bas les anglais being as good a rallying cry as any in continental Europe. One of his crewmembers, Alain Colas, developed this appeal a step further. After winning the 1972 OSTAR in Tabarly's trimaran over a three-masted one-hundred-twenty-eight foot schooner called *Vendredi XIII,* Colas set a record for the fastest circumnavigation with an average speed of seven and one-third knots and then got to work planning for the 1976 *Observer* Race in a big way. He commissioned the design for an immense two-hundred-thirty-foot four-masted schooner, and to pay for her he not only recruited the resort combine, Club Méditerranée, as a sponsor but also made arrangements with newspapers and broadcast stations all over France to report his progress. This brilliant marketing ploy was, unfortunately, short-circuited by an injury to his leg that Colas suffered at the launching of *Club Méditerranée,* as the enormous vessel was inevitably named. He sailed the race and was beaten by a relatively small trimaran sailed by a Canadian, Mike Birch. The race sponsors very sensibly lowered the size limit to fifty feet, *Club Méditerranée* became a cruise ship, and, sadly, Colas and the trimaran were later lost at sea during a singlehanded race.

Colas's fate did not alter the fortunes of offshore singlehanded sailing or of multihulls. High-tech, corporately sponsored, professionally sailed monster catamarans and trimarans were racing across the Atlantic almost every year to try to break one record or another. Late in 1985, Chay Blyth capsized a big multihull near Cape Horn while attempting to shatter the New-York-to-San-Francisco record of eighty-nine days that had been set by the clipper ship *Flying Cloud* in 1854.

Returning to the 1870s, the pastime of cruising in small boats developed to the stage where a number of cruising sailors living or

working in London became interested in spending time together. Since the major yacht clubs of the day were interested only in racing, they took the time-honored step of forming their own club around their own special passion. In 1880, the Cruising Club was organized in a meeting in the Lincoln's Inn office of a young lawyer named Arthur Underhill. He was the first vice-commodore and secretary; the first commodore was the same Reverend A. van Straubenzee who had shocked his parish with the purchase of a fighting cock and a yacht. The name chosen indicates a radical departure from yachting tradition, for while the name "yacht club" reflects the members' interest in an object, "cruising club" shows interest in *doing* something. Here is how Douglas Phillips-Birt, the articulate and witty English yacht designer and yachting historian, described this first generation of cruisers:

A type of Englishman was taking to the sea who was well-educated, critical, amateur, and taking to it young enough to be relatively poor . . . The members of the club had small boats and the irreducible minimum of professional aid for the times — two paid hands, perhaps one, perhaps none but the man who looked after the boat while she lay on her moorings during the working week. It was the dawn of the amateur spirit in yachting.

In these boats, typically no larger than ten tons Thames Measurement, or about thirty-five feet in overall length, these early cruisers sailed either alone or with small crews. Many long cruises were made by father-daughter crews; in logs and reports, the fathers unabashedly praised their daughters for getting the boats through tough weather and making difficult landfalls. One of the most famous cruises in a boat of this kind was fictional — the English cutter *Dulcibella*'s zig-zag course in search of spies among the sand dunes and shallows of Germany's Frisian coast, as described by Cruising Club member Erskine Childers in his 1904 thriller *The Riddle of the Sands,* which was made into a superb film in the 1980s.

The Cruising Club was a social organization; but perhaps the most important role it played was as an educational forum for sailors who, unlike E.E. Middleton, wanted to be prepared for what they were getting into. From the beginning, it published a club newsletter — at first in a yachting magazine and later on its own — in which members summarized their logs, reported on lessons learned in seamanship and navigation, discussed yacht design and equipment, and described the challenges of sailing shorthanded. By the mid-1890s, soon before it was granted the royal warrant, the club had settled down in a permanent clubhouse where it kept a reference library of books and charts, and was publishing charts of popular cruising areas in a compact format for use in small cockpits and cabins. Like all good teachers, the Cruising Club established a standard of performance for its students to aim at. This was a prize for "the most enterprising, skillful, and successful cruise of the season." It was first awarded in 1882 for a canoe voyage to Spain, but ambitions fluctuated and the next year the winner had sailed all the way from Southampton to Falmouth. At first the prize was something useful — say, a pair of binoculars — but later there was the silver Challenge Cup, with smaller cups for second and third places. In 1930, one of the founders, Sir Arthur Underhill, could boast in his short history of the club that in fifty years of cruising in cold and rough weather and out-of-the-way places, the club had lost only one life at sea.

Since membership in the Royal Cruising Club was limited to three hundred, other active cruising sailors eager for the service that it provided formed other organizations that fulfilled the same purposes in varying ways. In London there were the Little Ship Club, which sponsored fortnightly lectures on seamanship and navigation (and in 1927 began to admit women as members), and the Cruising Association, which in 1926 had a library of charts and books large enough to take up seventy-six pages of small type in the catalogue. To the west, there was the Irish Cruising Club, which published sailing directions to the Irish coast. Up north, Scottish cruising sailors had the Clyde Cruising Club, which held cruises in company, offered courses in navigation, and gave examinations on seamanship, first aid, and piloting, much like the Royal Yachting Association's Yachtmaster training system of the 1970s and 1980s. In fact, just about everywhere one looked there was advice on how to fulfill the dream. Yachting magazines and instructional books by designer-authors such as Claud Worth, Maurice Griffiths, and Uffa Fox not only encouraged heading out there but recommended boats to buy and also knowledgeably and

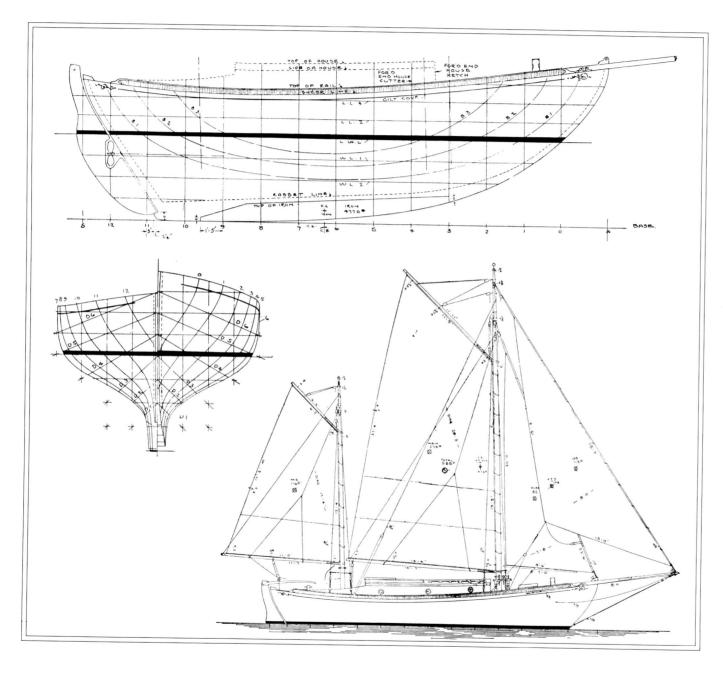

*A*mong the most enduring
designs for cruising boats is the heavy
double-ended "Colin Archer type,"
derived from seaworthy Norwegian pilot
boats and rescue vessels that Archer, a
proponent of the Wave Form Theory,
designed in the 1890s and early in this
century. In 1924, an American
designer, Bill Atkin, made minor
modifications on the type and turned
out a thirty-two-footer he called Eric,
shown here. Fifty years later, Atkin's
Eric, with a few modifications, became
the popular Westsail 32. Thomas
Fleming Day, right, was the first
American to promote offshore cruising
and racing in boats smaller than about
fifty feet.

artfully described how to sail them. The sea, they assumed, was now open to human exploration, even (or especially) for pleasure. But it was serious business, and we had to know our limitations. There was a *system* for cruising. Claud Worth delineated two categories — pastime and sport — for the system in the preface to his extremely influential 1910 manual, *Yacht Cruising:*

> *To sail from port to port by easy stages in picked weather is a most pleasant* pastime. *To make an open sea cruise in a seaworthy little yacht, neither courting unnecessary risks nor being unduly anxious as to weather, and having confidence in one's knowledge and skill to overcome such difficulties as may arise, is, to one who loves the sea, the most perfectly satisfying of all forms of* sport.

A Cruising Club member who followed the sea for sport was H.W. "Bill" Tilman — a grizzled old adventurer who had led an assault on Mount Everest in 1938, had parachuted behind enemy lines in World War II, and, in middle age, had taken up sailing into icy waters in search of cliffs to climb. He began an article in the 1969 edition of the club's journal, *Roving Commissions*, with these words about his plans for a cruise to the Arctic Circle:

> *For the summer of 1968 I had in mind Spitsbergen and possibly an attempt to circumnavigate it, a feat accomplished for only the second time by Commander Frank Worsley in 1919 in the one hundred fourteen ton brigantine* Island *with an amateur crew of twelve, losing his rudder and propeller in the process. But a Danish friend then suggested Scoresby Sound, "a most beautiful place, the biggest fjord in the world, with two big mountainous unexplored islands, Milnerland and Renland."*

That was a challenge. When his sixty-two-year-old pilot cutter, *Mischief*, hit a rock off Jan Mayen Island, at seventy-one degrees north, and, leaking badly, was trapped by ice, there was another challenge. After fighting the inevitable for two weeks, Tilman eventually gave up and abandoned ship. Two years later, he was sailing the Greenland coast in his new vessel. ("One is often asked what is the attraction of Greenland," Tilman wrote in his book *Ice with Everything,* "and the reply would be, where else would a man who desires both the hills and the sea want to go.") Tilman's "new vessel," seventy-one years old, was younger than her skipper. A few years later, Tilman, at eighty-five, was lost in the South Atlantic. And so the yarns continue.

In the United States, cruising under sail developed hand in hand with racing. We saw in Chapter Four how ocean racing began in December, 1866, when three millionaires sent their boats across the ocean for stakes of $60,000. Races of like grandiosity, but rarely of like insanity in terms of weather, were held from time to time. In 1905, another great trans-Atlantic race was sailed from Sandy Hook, New Jersey, to the Isle of Wight, and in it the one-hundred-eighty-five-foot three-masted schooner *Atlantic* — one of the handsomest yachts ever built — set a record for the U.S.-to-England crossing under sail of twelve days, four hours. (The record stood for seventy-five years, and was finally broken by Eric Tabarly sailing a trimaran with hydrofoils in 1980).

But all those contests were between gold-platers. When cruising became popular in America, it was in small boats enthusiastically promoted by boating magazines, the most important of which was *The Rudder,* edited by a firebrand named Thomas Fleming Day. Tom Day, L. Francis Herreshoff sniffed, "was a boatman at heart and not a yachtsman or racer." Which is to say that, like John MacGregor and the early English cruisingmen, he liked small, inexpensive, handy boats. Perhaps, too, Herreshoff was referring to Day's demeanor, which was blunt, to say the least. Any design that he thought flawed he excoriated as "worthless" or "dangerous." He called the people who ran the old, staid yacht clubs "grey-headed, rum-soaked piazza scows." While he criticized with exuberant scorn, he also complimented with exuberant praise. In his passion to get sailors out of sight of land, he proclaimed the sea as "our Great Green Mother" and a friend to be admired and trusted: "The danger of the sea for generations has been preached by the ignorant . . ." The true seaman, wrote Day, "knows that it never has or never will murder a vessel; that every vessel that goes down commits suicide." This breathtaking sanguinity led Day himself to take some amazing risks; not only did he sail his tiny twenty-six-foot yawl *Sea Bird* to Gibraltar in 1911, but the next year he took a small powerboat across the Atlantic.

In 1905 the three-master Atlantic *set a record for a trans-Atlantic crossing under sail that endured for more than seventy years. Pictured at the right are her skipper, Charlie Barr, crouching at the helm, her owner, Wilson Marshall, and a guest who also made the crossing, F.M. Hoyt. Sadly,* Atlantic *ended her days afloat as a tea shop and souvenir stand in a New Jersey river. After an attempt was made to get her sailing once again, she sank. Eventually, she was broken up. At least her whereabouts (no matter how humiliating they may have been) were known; most great yachts simply vanished into commercial service or onto a lonely reef.*

People thought his sponsorship of ocean racing even more irresponsible. In 1904, *Rudder* sponsored the first long-distance race for smaller boats, a three-hundred-thirty-mile test from New York City to Marblehead, Massachusetts. Of the six entries, none was longer than thirty feet in waterline length. Day's own *Sea Bird,* not much more than a glorified V-bottom dory that he designed (and thoroughly promoted for home building in his magazine), was only nineteen feet on the water. His first Bermuda Race, in 1906, attracted three relatively small boats, and the winner was a thirty-eight-footer. (The first race from California to Honolulu was held the same year.) Bermuda races continued annually through 1909 with small fleets consisting of bigger boats, and then a final last

*B*esides Tom Day, the list of offshore pioneers includes several other writers and publishers. The serious young man holding the boom at left is Alfred F. Loomis, heading off on a cruise to Florida. On the right is Bill Nutting, founder of the Cruising Club of America. Ironically, both Loomis and Nutting first made their livings writing about power boats in the 'teens. Only after World War I was there a sailing readership large enough for them to write exclusively about sailboats.

engine manufacturers that were springing up and fighting each other tooth and claw. With powerboat advertising, the magazines thrived (or at least survived); without it, they died. Since racing between powerboats, large and small, was widespread and well-publicized, not surprisingly Tom Day included a powerboat division in the race to Bermuda in 1908. In *Rudder* and its companion *The Cruiser,* Day published an increasing number of articles on boats with engines, and his competitors followed suit.

Boat and engine builders provided equipment for editors and writers to test, and these tests attracted more readers, and (of course) more advertising. In 1912, one manufacturer gave Tom Day a thirty-five-foot boat with a sixteen-horsepower engine to take from Detroit to St. Petersburg, Russia. With twelve hundred gallons of gasoline, a small sail, and stomachs of iron, Day and his two shipmates endured weeks of wild rolling on *Detroit* — whose very name was an advertisement for American engines. On the longest leg, from Vineyard Haven, Massachusetts, to Queenstown, Ireland, they never did worse than forty-three miles a day. Most important, they arrived safely, and so became walking advertisements for the dependability of the marine engine. In the same year as Day's adventurous powerboat cruise, a twenty-two-year-old *Motor Boating* writer named Alfred F. Loomis was given a runabout and told to head down the Inland Waterway to Florida to write stories and take photographs. He made it all the way around the horn of Florida, which in those days was not much less difficult than going to Russia. Seven years later, Loomis headed north in a twenty-six-foot open powerboat on a two-thousand, five-hundred-mile cruise to research a thirteen-part series of articles for *Motor Boating.* The series provided the first cruising guide to the New England coast.

Between those two adventures, during World War I, Loomis and some other young men who knew a bit about boats were assigned as Navy officers aboard submarine chasers. The subchasers were one-hundred-ten-foot-long cigars with small crews and large areas of water to cover, the closest thing to a small boat that the Navy could provide. If their pre-war experiences had hinted that the sea — if not quite as chummy as Tom Day had exuberantly promised — could at least be handled by amateurs in small boats, subchaser duty drove the point home. The young lieutenants and ensigns

gasp in 1912 with only two entrants, the winner being the quintessential yachtsman Harold Vanderbilt in his Herreshoff schooner *Vagrant.*

One reason why the early Bermuda races lost their original small-boat spirit was that Tom Day became distracted by the growing popularity of small, moderately-priced powerboats. The development of the small gasoline engine attracted to boats many people who were fascinated by the new automobiles. Most important for Tom Day and the editors of *Yachting, Motor Boat, Motor Boating,* and the other boating magazines, there was plenty of potential advertising from the large number of powerboat and took their boats to the Mediterranean and then, after the armistice, brought them back, making the last leg from Bermuda into a well-publicized race.

One of those subchaser officers was a young midwesterner named William Washburn Nutting, who had learned how to sail on an Indiana lake. In love with the very idea of salt water, he made his way east in 1907 and knocked around a bit in New York before finding his way onto the staff of *Motor Boat* magazine. He bought a twenty-eight-foot cutter in which he made several mistake-ridden cruises (including a singlehanded voyage to Newfoundland) that he described with apparently scrupulous honesty in articles in the magazine. Subchaser duty expanded his horizons and his confidence. In his short history of the subchasers, *The Cinderellas of the Fleet,* Nutting bragged, "Nobody except a handful of small-boat enthusiasts would have believed it possible for [the subchasers] to live out some of the dirtiest weather that ever flayed the western ocean."

Something very original was going on here. That amateurs could safely navigate the high seas in small boats was a radical idea. We take it for granted now; but, until about 1916, it went against the ancient dogma, stretching back thousands of years, that the only people fit to manage a boat offshore were professionals. Charlie Barr and the other men who handled the first great ocean racers were professionals, and so was Joshua Slocum. Now there were lawyers, writers, and businessmen banging across the Gulf Stream in command of warships. And so Nutting, Loomis, and the others returned to civilian life eager to go back to sea for pleasure. Loomis went off on his long powerboat cruise and soon after took a small yawl to Panama, learning how to sail along the way. His book about the voyage, *The Cruise of the Hippocampus,* became an instant classic, and he went on to a long and distinguished career as the writer of the best non-fiction prose about boats that has ever been published.

Bill Nutting scratched together the cash to pay for a new forty-five-foot ketch, *Typhoon,* designed by a young Long Island sailor named William Atkin and built in Nova Scotia by Casey Baldwin, who supervised Alexander Graham Bell's experiments with hydrofoil-equipped powerboats. In the summer of 1920, Nutting, Baldwin, and another man sailed *Typhoon* to England. The reason

May 1917

Cents

MOTOR BOATING

The wartime cover from Motor Boating *magazine, left, hints at the risks that the young pleasure sailors took when they went offshore in small naval vessels. The experience opened up a whole new world of possibilities for the generation of sailors who came home from World War I with a lot of salt water already wrung out of their socks. The three* Yachting *covers, right, suggest how those possibilities became actualities. Photographs did not appear regularly on* Yachting's *covers until the 1960s.*

July, 1927   35 Cents a Copy

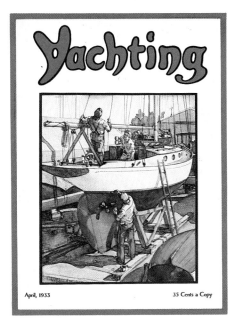

April, 1933   35 Cents a Copy

September, 1939   50 Cents a Copy

why suggests the new spirit. Wrote Nutting in his book, *The Track of the Typhoon,* "I had a little vessel built according to Atkin's and my own ideas of what a seagoing yacht should be and we sailed her across the Atlantic and back again for the fun of it." *(For the fun of it!)* Over there, he was warmly received by English yachtsmen, among them the aging Earl of Dunraven and Claud Worth, an officer of the Royal Cruising Club. Safely returning to New York, Nutting found that his trip was not universally admired. He defended himself in his book about the voyage:

Many people who seem not to realize that size is the least important element in the seaworthiness of a vessel, felt that by looping the Atlantic in so small a boat we had taken too great a chance. . . . Now, apart from the question of the risk involved, which is largely a matter of personal opinion, I feel that what American yachting needs is less common sense, less restrictions, less slide rules, and more sailing.

With the assurance of a person who has been there and back,

Nutting asked rhetorically, "is 'Safety First' going to become our national motto?" He went on:

In this day when life is so very easy and safe-and-sane and highly-specialized and steam-heated, we need, more than ever we needed before, sports that are big and raw and — yes — dangerous.

In 1924, while following his precept that a full life demanded danger, Bill Nutting was lost at sea west of Greenland; but before he died he found a way to institutionalize his philosophy. In 1921 and 1922, he began to meet regularly with his sailor friends over bootleg liquor in a Greenwich Village speakeasy in New York called Beefsteak John's. They discussed their adventures and dreams and, inevitably, a club was formed. In February of 1922, Nutting sent out invitations to help launch "a sort of American equivalent to the Royal Cruising Club." The thirty-six charter members of the new Cruising Club of America included sailors from Boston and New York and points in between. The burgeoning boating

The Cruising Powerboat

Beginning in the 1880s, powerboat design went through a series of interesting stages that have led it full circle to the present day. A century or so ago, power yachts were steam-driven, and came in only two types: big luxury yachts like J.P. Morgan's *Corsair,* which, as we have seen, served more or less as a combination of second home, entertainment center, and personal retreat; and boats called "launches," which varied in size from about thirty to about ninety feet, and which shared the characteristics of high speed and very small accommodations. Stuffed to the rails with steam engines, their coal bins, and the professionals who stoked and ran them, the launches provided fast, high-visibility transportation to and from work, summer homes, and the luxury yachts. For some reason, 1884 was the year of the launch in New York. After that year, nobody claiming to be a millionaire would be caught dead without one.

The greatest change in powerboat design was brought about by the development of lightweight and compact internal combustion engines around 1890, when the first motor boats to be used regularly appeared for launch duty at Hamburg, Germany. Engines and speed quickly became a mania. In America and Britain by the first years of the century, big and small yachts powered by gas engines regularly raced for trophies and large bets, and in 1905 more than a hundred small "speed launches" turned out for a race off Monaco. The first competition for the British International Trophy for powerboats smaller than forty feet — usually called the Harmsworth Trophy in honor of its donor, Sir Alfred Harmsworth — took place in 1903, with the winning average speed being all of nineteen and one-half miles per hour. Two Clinton-Crane-designed American boats named *Dixie* won the trophy in 1907 and 1908, and *Dixie II* later did thirty-six and six-tenths miles per hour over a measured mile.

The first small cruising powerboats were little more than commuters with some engine space given over to accommodations. The development of light, compact gasoline engines quickly made boating accessible to the middle class.

Those were displacement boats; they went through the water rapidly, but they still went *through* the water. For years, engineers had tried but failed to develop gas engines powerful yet light enough to lift the boat out of the water, to make the hull plane (literally skim across the water like a wood plane slicing off a thin sliver of pine). As far back as 1872, the Reverend C.M. Ramus had come up with an idea for a hull shaped like a double wedge "to cause the ship to be lifted out of the water." He submitted his plan to the British Admiralty, which couldn't do anything with it. A generation later, Sir John Thornycroft and an American named William Henry Fauber filed patents on similar ideas; but the engine had not yet been built that could do the lifting. Finally, in 1908, the year Fauber's first patent was granted, the Isle of Wight boatbuilder S.E. Saunders brainstormed on Fauber's idea to produce the first hydroplane. Four years later, his *Maple Leaf IV,* whose bottom was built with five ledges or steps, brought powerboat speed to a level that is surpassed today only by sophisticated high-performance pleasureboats. (One of the men who worked on this breakthrough speedboat was a young Cowes shipwright named Uffa Fox, a design genius who in 1927 would come up with the first planing sailboat, an International 14 dinghy named *Avenger,* which is the grandfather of every planing dinghy in the world today.) T.O.M. Sopwith, who would later twice challenge for the America's Cup, won the 1912 Harmsworth Trophy in *Maple Leaf IV* with a speed of more than fifty miles per hour, and reached more than fifty-seven miles per hour the next year. The speed record leapt to ninety-nine miles per hour in 1930, one hundred sixty miles per hour in 1950, and almost three hundred miles per hour in 1970.

As we have seen, powerboats became popular in the United States very suddenly in the first decade of the century. These were displacement boats; but lessons learned on engines and hull shapes between 1910 and 1920 quickly led to a new fleet of powerboats for pleasure use in the 'twenties and 'thirties. Most carried outboard or small inboard engines and were used as runabouts, launches, or fishing boats, although there were some stock cruisers built by the likes of Elco, ACF, Richardson and Chris-Craft. After World War II, with more money and leisure time available, builders such as Chris-Craft, long the largest company in the boating business, began mass-producing cruisers in the twenty- to forty-foot range. These boats, while comfortable on the relatively flat water of lakes, bays and rivers, pounded very badly in the chop of big lakes and coastal waters.

The problem of combining a planing hull with a smooth ride and decent accommodations was eventually solved in a variety of ways, two of the most successful of which were discovered in the 1950s by C. Raymond Hunt, a New Englander who until then had been best known for his cruising sailboats, but who had studied the literature of powerboat design and, as a part-time lobster fisherman, spent considerable time in motorboats. One of Hunt's inspirations was a thirteen-footer that combined high speed, reasonable comfort in a seaway, and a large interior space. This became the famous Boston Whaler. While boxy-looking from above, the Whaler has a complex bow shape that permits some seakindliness.

Hunt, a genius who seemed to go to the essence of things, also came up with the so-called constant-deadrise deep-V hull. Instead of having V-shaped forward sections followed by flat after sections, as most fast powerboats had since the 1920s, this design's deadrise — the angle of the bottom from the keel to the topsides — is the same from bow to stern, exactly twenty-four degrees. Rather than slapping down on the waves, the deep-V hull usually slices through them. A series of longitudinal strips, or strakes, along the sides of the V affords some lift and some grip on the water to a hull that rides higher on the V as speed increases. An advantage of this design is that it permits the hull to be beamy at the deck line, which means that good accommodations and a large cockpit can be fitted, which was not the case with old-fashioned narrow hulls that were good in a seaway. A Florida yacht broker named Dick Bertram took up Hunt's new design in 1960 and began building a thirty-one-footer, the beginnings of the Bertram Yacht Company. Dick Bertram, a former racing sailor, also won a string of offshore races with these boats, and he was followed in both racing and boatbuilding by others, notably Don Aronow, creator of Cigarette, Magnum, Formula and Donzi powerboats, and by Miami engineer and yacht designer Jim Wynne, inventor of the stern drive. Since the 'sixties, the deep-V hull has been the norm for the design of most of the world's powerboats under forty feet.

But many powerboats in the thirty to sixty foot mid-range of things continued to be designed with traditional vee-bottom lines, although Bertram Yacht and the C. Raymond Hunt design firm — the constant-deadrise pioneers — continued to develop deep-V boats as large as eighty-five feet. In this mid-range there returned in the 1960s the displacement hulls of old in the form of so-called "trawler" yachts. These were diesel yachts for slow, comfortable cruising, and their popularity has held, due in part to the high cost of fuel. Another throwback to the displacement and semi-displacement hulls of old is the Maine lobsterboat, which began to be seen in yacht-finish versions in the 1970s and continues to enlarge its share of the powerboat market.

On the upper end of things, a new luxury yachtbuilding boom began in the 1970s and accelerated in the 1980s, so much so that it resembles the opulent era of the steam yachts a hundred years before. After World War II, any luxury yachts that were visible were either leftovers from the 1920s and 1930s or were converted military vessels. But in the 'fifties a new fleet of large luxury yachts began to be

Ray Hunt's design of the deep-V hull, shown above in a Surf Hunter 25, allowed powerboats to go into rough water at high speed, thereby opening up many new bodies of water to cruisers using relatively small boats. At the other end of the spectrum are the "megayachts," like Malcolm Forbes's one-hundred fifty foot, $15 million Highlander, seen here sliding under the Brooklyn Bridge. Like many luxury yachts in the 'eighties, she is often used for business and, therefore, many of her expenses are tax-deductible — a tactic that J.P. Morgan probably would have deplored (but would have taken advantage of).

184

built, principally by the several Feadship yards in Holland. These yachts were big, expensive, luxurious and showy; but by the standards of the "megayachts" of the 1980s they seem small and ordinary. In 1963, a Dutch yard launched a one hundred six foot luxury yacht for Henry Ford II that was the biggest and grandest thing that had come along in the postwar years. *The Macmillan Book of Boating* described *Santa Maria* thus: "The grandeur of the Ford yacht makes it a contemporary equivalent of George Crowninshield's *Cleopatra's Barge,* and is evidence that pride of boat ownership has not waned between 1817 and the present day."

A one-hundred-six-footer, by the mid-1980s, was a relatively modest machine. In 1985, there were forty large luxury yachts under construction in yards throughout the world, most of them bigger than one hundred fifty feet. The new opulence these yachts typically represent includes worldwide cruising capability; speeds above twenty knots with sophisticated diesel power and sometimes gas turbines; decorator-designed quarters that make use of such materials as marble, glove leather, rare woods, and solid gold; and office suites equipped with satellite communications equipment that make it possible for their owners to keep up with business while enjoying cruising grounds that may be half a world away.

The megayacht — so called — although anticipated by the large power yachts of the 1950s, 1960s and 1970s — seems to have established an especially gilded niche in the golden pastime in the 1980s.

185

1980s, Thomas J. Watson Jr., of the IBM family, cruised to both Arctic and Antarctic waters. Watson's friend and sometime crew-member, a Bermuda-based CCA member named Warren Brown, made Arctic and Antarctic cruises within a year's time. Sailing a sixty-four-foot sloop, *War Baby,* that he had bought from Ted Turner, Brown voyaged in 1984 to Spitzbergen, following in the wake of the Royal Cruising Club's Bill Tilman. A few months later, Brown sailed with Watson to Antarctica.

Second, club membership is limited to people who have proven themselves both as sailors and as agreeable shipmates. In the 'thirties, the CCA membership committee came up with two questions that would test those qualities: first, as to technical qualifications, "Would you be willing to loan your yacht to the candidate for a cruise of several days?"; second, as to sociability, "Would you enjoy the company of the candidate, glass in hand, in the cabin of a small yacht?" That is to say, members should be competent to handle both breeze and rum.

The third similarity between the two clubs is that they both serve an educational function. Like the English club, the Cruising Club of America quickly and early furthered its educational aims by assuming the authority to judge seamanship. Its Blue Water Medal, which has become something like a Medal of Honor for cruising sailors, is awarded for "the year's most meritorious example of seamanship, the recipient to be selected from among the amateurs of all nations." It was first presented in 1923 to a plucky but barely competent French tennis player named Alain Gerbault, who took all of one hundred days to sail singlehanded from Gibraltar to New York in a ratty old cutter. (Gerbault went on to finish a circumnavigation in much better style.) For a while, winners were typically people who made well-planned family trans-Atlantic passages; recent Blue Water Medalists include some remarkable voyagers, among them Harry Pidgeon, Eric Tabarly, Hal Roth, Willy de Roos, H.L. Tilman, Bernard Moitessier, Sir Francis Chichester, David Lewis (who was the first person to circumnavigate the Antarctic and the first to sail around the world in a multihulled boat), and Marvin Creamer (who sailed around the world without using a compass or any other navigational instrument, relying on astronomy and his wits to find his way).

As additional stimulus to education, CCA meetings are occa-

John Alden, left, was the most successful designer of racing-cruising boats in the 1920s and early 'thirties, basing his designs on traditional fishing schooners. In the early years of ocean racing and long-distance sailing in the United States, these sturdy vessels could be found everywhere — for example, at the start of the 1923 Bermuda Race, right. Alden was a tireless promoter of long-distance sailing and, not coincidentally, of doing it in boats that he designed.

business was well represented. The first commodore was Nutting, a boating magazine editor, and the second was Herbert L. Stone, the publisher of *Yachting.* Boating writers Thomas Fleming Day and W.P. Stephens were elected as honorary members, and yacht designer John Alden and builder Casey Baldwin were also among the founders.

In many ways, the CCA modeled and continues to model itself after the early RCC. First, its members are adventurous. As the club's motto, "Nowhere is too far," suggests, members habitually sail to far-off parts of the world. Far northern areas are especially favored, I suspect, not because these sailors like cold weather but because they do not enjoy crowded harbors. In the 1970s and

*T*hough it was initiated two years after the first Bermuda Race, in 1925, and though most of its course is near shore, the British Fastnet Race is usually considered the most demanding ocean race in the world. In this dramatic painting, the converted pilot boat Jolie Brise *approaches the lonely light off the Irish coast that gives the race its name. This was the first race, and* Jolie Brise *won it. In the 1932 Bermuda Race, she and her crew rescued all but one man from a burning yacht.* Jolie Brise *is still sailing.*

sions for members to gam and yarn to their heart's content. A superb semi-annual journal, the *Cruising Club News,* provides a forum in which they can tell each other about their experiences and the lessons learned.

There is some irony here: people presumably dedicated to individualistic, solitary pastimes where personal satisfaction is the highest reward gather in a club to award a prize, of all things. The real and sustaining strength of groups like the Cruising Club of America, the Royal Cruising Club, and all the other organizations of cruising sailors lies less in trophies than in the intangible bonds of community between people who consciously take life-threatening chances. It is a truism that people who take risks are usually able to learn something vital about themselves, if they open themselves up to that possibility. Outside of the religious journey and deep psychological introversion, no activity offers as many opportunities for spiritual insights as does prolonged exposure to the elements. For many people, this experience occurs in late youth. When Herman Melville wrote in *Moby Dick* that "a whaleship was my Yale College and my Harvard," he was referring to the time when adolescence slips into adulthood, a place or event or ceremony that initiates people into the world in some memorable way that may be both painful and joyous.

Having experienced that moment of initiation, many people naturally enough want to relive it. They may write about it, as Melville did in his early novels and as Richard Henry Dana did in *Two Years before the Mast.* Or they may rehearse the discovery in the company of friends, as former schoolboys and schoolgirls do in alumni and alumnae associations. Or they may go back for more, as many sailors seem to do, for cruising is one of the few activities that can be as refreshing and eye-opening the one hundredth time as it was the first time. There are always new lessons to learn, storms to be surprised by, harbors to discover, hardships to overcome. For many, there is somewhere that is too far; for a few, literally nowhere is too far to go in order to relive those first stirrings in the heart on encountering risk and adventure, and to enjoy the fellowship of people with the same dream. *Cruising Club News,* it should be noted, was first published in the 1940s not to record successful pleasure cruises but to keep members of the American cruising community in touch from the heaving decks of navy ships

and the bloody dirt of battlefields far from home.

The one characteristic that has made the Cruising Club of America profoundly different from most other cruising clubs has been its sponsorship of races. As we have seen, since well before Thomas Fleming Day used races to pull small boats out of sight of land, American yachtsmen were more likely than their English cousins to compete hammer and tongs offshore. Almost immediately after the formation of the CCA, Herb Stone and other members got to work organizing a race to Bermuda for 1923. There were twenty-three entries, many of them sturdy fisherman-type schooners designed by a Bostonian named John Alden, so called because they looked much like the schooners used for fishing off the New England coast. Alden himself won the race in his fisherman-type *Malabar IV.*

Finishing sixth on corrected time was a yawl called *Memory,* owned by Robert N. Bavier. There were those who were surprised she finished at all. One of the New York 40 class of one-design inshore racing yachts designed and built by Nathanael Herreshoff to his Universal Rule, she had long ends and a tall jib-headed, gaffless rig, which, though long used in small boats (it was also called the "Bermudian rig" because it was frequently seen in Bermuda), was very new to big boats. The jib-headed rig was a product of the same engineering and aerodynamic research that produced the Eiffel tower and Guglielmo Marconi's radio antennas (for this reason, it was also called the "Marconi rig"). At first, its main appeal was that, by raising the rig higher, it brought the sails inboard — no more long "widow-maker" bowsprits and long overhanging booms. In time, it was also proven to be more efficient than the gaff rig. Of two ocean-racing yachts with the same waterline length, the one with the jib-headed rig needed less sail area and, therefore, a smaller crew to sail as fast as the gaff-rigged boat.

Although the CCA did not officially sponsor the 1923 Bermuda Race, most of the members took part, and beginning with the next race in 1924 it was an official event of the Cruising Club. By then, the club's constitution had been ratified. Its article entitled "Object" included the development "of suitable types of cruising craft." Ever since, that object has been the keystone of the CCA's continuing interest in racing, despite continuous and sometimes bitter protest by some members who think that a cruising club has

189

no business involving itself in competition. Many Royal Cruising Club members agreed with the dissenters, and when some British sailors decided that if the Americans could race across the rough waters of the Gulf Stream they could jolly well compete offshore, they had to run the race on their own since Claud Worth and the other RCC officers thought the idea dangerous. A gale might blow up, Worth argued, and because of the competitive pressures, sailors might not heave-to as they should. "These conditions might not occur once in a dozen races," he warned, "but the magnitude of possible disaster should be taken into account." Undiscouraged, the racers chose a course down the coast of Cornwall, across the Western Approaches to the Fastnet Rock lighthouse and back, and the first Fastnet Race was held in 1925. The Ocean Racing Club (eventually to be given a royal warrant) was born spontaneously during the awards dinner.

In the 1930s, both the Royal Ocean Racing Club and the Cruising Club of America developed their own racing handicap rules that, it was hoped, would encourage the construction of boats that were both seaworthy and fast. The rules did that; they also encouraged a certain amount of rule-beating, the excesses of which were typically penalized by rule alterations. What happened in the late nineteenth century soon happened again: the shapes of all boats — not just those for racing — came to be determined by the demands of rating rules. Even the shapes looked vaguely familiar, the Americans often tending toward relatively beamy centerboarders and the British sailing narrow deep-keel boats. This sameness in design was most apparent after one-design, or "stock," cruising boats began to be built out of fiberglass in the late 1950s. The advantage of fiberglass is that it is easy to maintain. One of its disadvantages is that setting up the molds to build a fiberglass boat is extremely expensive. Therefore, in order to keep the per-unit costs down and still provide boats for people who were tired of caulking seams, builders had to produce boats for a wide market. All this meant that stock boats tended to look like whichever custom boat was doing well in the distance races that received so much attention in the yachting magazines, regardless of the owner's intended use of the boat. For a long time, there was little conflict between these various trends. Between the rating rules, offshore race courses, the occasional gale, and a widespread consensus about what a good boat should look like, most boats that appeared on starting lines for long races were seaworthy. "Dual-purpose" boats they were called, and dual-purpose they often were. Crews lived aboard in comfort, and they sailed across oceans to get to races. Although they might be raced with ruthless aggression, these boats usually were built and equipped with an eye toward longevity, safety, and cruising comfort.

Still, there could be variations in shape and type in custom boats, for the rules provided elbow room both to meet local conditions and for experimentation. For example, in the early 1930s, the young New York designers Olin and Rod Stephens broke the monopoly of the fisherman-types with a series of jib-headed, deep keel, relatively narrow boats, beginning with the yawl *Dorade*, whose extraordinary performance in 1931 — when she won a Trans-Atlantic Race and the Fastnet Race — earned the Stephenses a tickertape parade up lower Broadway. Twenty years later, after people began to sail extensively in the thin waters of the Bahamas and needed shoal-draft boats, the Stephenses produced a beamy centerboarder called *Finisterre*, which won three Bermuda Races in a row under Carleton Mitchell. The other great designer of cruiser-racers of the day, Philip Rhodes, had equal success with deep boats as well as centerboarders. In the early 1960s, the Californian Bill Lapworth and the Bostonian Dick Carter were able to improve speed and reduce displacement by using Nat Herreshoff's old trick of separating the rudder from the keel. After each of these successes, there was a shift in the look of stock cruising boats.

In the late 'sixties, a single rule called the International Offshore Rule was developed for the large international fleets that were flourishing on both sides of the Atlantic and in Australia. The IOR boats that were spun out through the mid-1970s by Olin Stephens, James A. McCurdy (Rhodes's former righthand man), and a generation of younger designers that included Douglas Peterson, a Californian; German Frers Jr., an Argentinian; and Ron Holland, a New Zealander living in Ireland, were widely respected for their speed and seaworthiness. Gradually, however, the pressures of competition coupled with the growing popularity of ocean racing led to boats that were as controversial as the "out-and-outers" of a hundred years before. With light, beamy, and shallow hulls, they

With her young designer, Olin Stephens, at her helm and his brother and partner Rod at his left hand, Dorade *goes through her paces for the photographer. A development of the racing boats of the 'twenties, she could not have been more different from the Alden fisherman schooners, with her low, narrow hull and all-inboard rig.*

If yachting history means anything, it is that there is little new in yacht design. In the 1980s just as in the 1880s, there were extreme out and outers intended only for racing, and then only in smooth conditions. Left, a Swedish boat competing in an Admiral's Cup regatta off the Isle of Wight, where America won her races, broaches wildly out of control as her crew watches helplessly. The photographs on this page show two extremes in modern boats. Upper, modern out and outers have an excess of complication on deck and a bare minimum of comfort and privacy below deck. These boats were built to be raced on, not cruised in. Lower, a breed of comfortable, relatively fast cruising boats developed alongside the skinned-out racers. On the left is a J/40; on the right is the main cabin of an O'Day 40. The contrast between the upper and the lower photographs is dramatic.

looked like racing dinghies with keels stuck on, and when the wind piped up, were just as enthralling and challenging to sail. However, with their light displacement (intolerant of added weight in stores and gear), skimpy interiors, and unforgiving hull forms, they were hardly seaworthy boats for offshore sailing.

As this type of racing-oriented boat appeared, the old dual-purpose boats of the 'sixties all but disappeared from the new-boat market. People who wanted only to cruise were soon served by builders producing traditional-looking boats designed years before by Bill Atkin and Colin Archer, or by some younger designers who worked on the same themes of heavy displacement and long keels. The most successful of these was the Westsail 32, a stubby, ponderous, but visually appealing fiberglass version of an ancient Colin Archer, Wave-Form-Theory design. It could not sail to windward very well, but it *looked* like a cruising boat, and its builders mounted an ingenious and, for a time, highly successful public relations and advertising campaign that banked on that amorphous quality and on dreams of sailing idylls in the South Seas. These heavy double-enders were slow (who cared?); but they were safe. They were designed and built to be sailing buoys — hove-to or left to ride out a gale they were almost impregnable — and for voyagers, perhaps with families aboard, they were ideal vehicles for the great adventures of distance cruising.

On the racing circuit, there finally came the gale that Claud Worth had warned about. On August 13, 1979, a force ten, sixty-knot storm smashed the fleet of three hundred boats that was crossing the Western Approaches in the Royal Ocean Racing Club's Fastnet Race. Some one hundred boats rolled over completely; at least another hundred were knocked down until their masts were in the water. Five boats sank and twenty-four were abandoned. Most astonishingly, in a sport whose fatalities since the tragedy of the 1866 Trans-Atlantic Race could be counted on the fingers of two hands, fifteen sailors drowned or died of exposure in the cold waters between England and Ireland.

The 1979 Fastnet Race disaster grabbed the world's headlines, at least partly because it was so anomalous: this was, after all, a pleasure-boat race, yet people died out there. More important in the long run, it shocked the sailing community into a thorough rethinking of the sport. Yacht clubs and sailing groups that had taken safety for granted immediately began to sponsor off-season seminars and lectures on safety at sea. Sailors began to examine their emergency equipment and clothing with the care of mountain climbers heading off to the Himalayas. And researchers began to look into the dynamics of how boats work — not with the traditional goal of making boats sail faster, but with the intention of making them sail more safely. Technical studies proliferated and rating rules were altered; but at first they seemed to have little effect, and while a Fastnet-level death toll was not repeated, boats that started races often did not finish them. Storms hit boats racing in the 1984 race from Sydney, Australia, to Hobart, Tasmania, and in the 1985 Fastnet Race. In each race, half the fleet retired. Perhaps dropping out was a sign of maturity; no boat owner would possibly want "another Fastnet." However, it was more likely a

1 9 5

After a long absence from larger boats, centerboards returned in the 1950s in fast, seaworthy racing-cruising boats that could win races, cross oceans, and also cruise in shallow waters. The thirty-eight-foot yawl Finisterre, *opposite, set the trend. This Sparkman & Stephens design won three straight Bermuda Races, 1956, 1958, and 1960 — a remarkable feat in a sport with as many variables as ocean racing has. Her cruises provided plenty of material for her talented owner, Carleton Mitchell, to write about in wonderful articles for* National Geographic. *In the crew portrait, Mitchell stands at the helm. The man with his hand on a winch is Dick Bertram, who developed the Bertram line of powerboats using Ray Hunt's deep-V design.*

symptom of unchecked development brought about by a combination of intense competition, wealthy and ambitious owners, and crafty designers and manufacturers of boats and gear who had at their fingertips an array of fragile space-age materials for hulls, sails, and lines that would have made Nat Herreshoff, were he alive, green with envy. Unfortunately, the boating industry was not large enough to thoroughly test many of these materials before they went offshore, and it was only in full-scale destruction testing on the open ocean that people had a chance to see how they worked.

While some failures were dramatic and sometimes well publicized, in the long run this leading edge of the sport at the grand prix level was doing everybody else a favor. In 1986 alone, there were two round-the-world races — one for singlehanded sailors, one for crewed boats — whose participants would be depending on Kevlar sails and hulls, titanium winches, complicated rigging, and other high-tech equipment first tried out on ocean racers in Admirals' Cup competition in England or Southern Ocean Racing Conference events off Florida. In the middle of the ocean, they would be grateful for the lessons learned from those early failures.

Racing sailors were not the only ones to benefit technologically. With thousands of boats out cruising, some in small inland lakes, some along the shorelines of oceans, some around the world, demands for accurate navigation and reliable rigging were wide-

Long-Distance Races

A wide variety of long-distance races have come and gone over the years. Here is a brief summary of the races longer than three hundred miles that were being run in the mid-1980s. In addition to these, there were cumulative points championships for "maxi-boats" (approximately eighty feet in length) and for smaller boats participating in the Admiral's Cup (in Britain), Southern Cross Cup (Australia), Clipper Cup (Hawaii), Onion Patch Trophy (Newport and Bermuda), Southern Ocean Racing Conference (Florida and Bahamas), and Sardinia Cup (Italy) competitions.

For Fully-Crewed Boats

Around the world (27,000 miles): Whitbread Round-the-World (quadrennial, first race 1973-1974)

Trans-Atlantic (2500-3000 miles): U.S. to Europe (occasional, first race 1866).

Britain: Fastnet Race (605 miles, biennial odd years, first race 1925)

To Bermuda (635 miles): Newport, Rhode Island-to-Bermuda (biennial even years, first race 1904); Marion, Massachusetts-to-Bermuda Cruising Race (biennial odd years, first race 1977)

U.S. East Coast: Annapolis, Maryland-to-Newport, Rhode Island (473 miles, biennial odd years, first held 1947); Marblehead, Massachusetts-to-Halifax, Nova Scotia (357 miles, biennial odd years, first race 1905)

To Hawaii: Transpacific Yacht Club, Los Angeles, California-to-Honolulu (2225 miles, biennial odd years, first race 1906); Victoria, British Columbia-to-Maui, Hawaii (2380 miles, biennial even years, first race 1967)

Australia (630 miles): Sydney, Australia-to-Hobart, Tasmania (annual, first held 1945)

Caribbean and Gulf of Mexico: St. Petersburg-to-Ft. Lauderdale, Florida (400 miles, annual, first held 1959);

Miami, Florida-to-Montego Bay, Jamaica (811 miles, occasional, first held 1961)

California and Mexico (1000 miles): Los Angeles or Long Beach to La Paz, Cabo San Lucas, or Mazatlan (annual)

Mediterranean (613 miles): Middle Sea (occasional, first sailed 1968)

For Doublehanded Crews

Round-Britain (2100 miles, quadrennial, first held 1966)

For Singlehanded Crews

Around the World (27,000 miles, several stopovers): BOC Round-the-World Singlehanded Race (occasional, first held 1983-1984)

Trans-Atlantic (2800 miles): *Observer* Singlehanded Trans-Atlantic Race (quadrennial, first held 1960); Route du Rhum, France to Caribbean (biennial, first race 1978); various others, Europe to America.

The Admiral's Cup is a series of races ending with the Fastnet Race, involving three-boat teams from each entering country. In this 1985 start, all the boats are flying sails made from brown Kevlar cloth, most of them on light, highly adjustable fractional rigs that demand the crew's full attention if they are to be kept upright. The International Offshore Rule is used in Admiral's Cup competition. Another handicapping system that encourages less light, tricky boats is the International Measurement System, which became increasingly popular as owners tired of the expense and sensitivity of IOR boats.

spread and serious. At the same time as the new techonology was improving gear for racing, cruising equipment was undergoing extraordinary advances. For example, Loran navigational devices that cost upwards of $5000 in 1972 were one-tenth that price and many times more easy to use in 1985. With them, navigators could pinpoint a position to within fifty yards. Soon, more than a dozen satellites circling the globe would be providing an automatic navigational system available almost everywhere on earth. On deck, sophisticated self-steering devices took much of the tedium out of steering, and roller-furling and roller-reefing gadgets greatly reduced the physical strain of sail-handling. Crews could be both

smaller and less muscular. Those two advances alone promised to extend a sailor's active on-deck life span by a good five years.

If there was a lingering problem with these fascinating and revolutionary advances, it was the one that seems to accompany all technological progress: a positivistic conviction on the part of the user that in the equipment lies salvation. In other words, there was a loss of every sailor's best friend, a good dose of humility. When Thomas Fleming Day described the sea as benign ("every vessel that goes down commits suicide"), he belied thousands of years of experience by professional seamen. His faith in the human ability to conquer all was echoed by some survivors of the 1979 Fastnet

Deaths are few in yachting, so the fifteen fatalities in the 1979 Fastnet Race came as a shock. Left, I steer Toscana, a forty-seven-foot sloop, down the face of a great sea on the morning of the Fastnet storm. The wind speed and air and water temperatures were all in the sixties. Opposite, twenty-four yachts were abandoned by their crews during the storm. This boat, Ariadne, twice rolled over completely. The second time, a crewmember was swept overboard, and the rest of the crew left in a life raft; three of them died during a rescue attempt by a small freighter. The Fastnet disasters led to an international re-examination of the goals, techniques, and equipment of offshore racing.

Race disaster. "I feel a little like Noah," said the race's winner, Ted Turner, with a grandiosity that was appallingly inappropriate. "I knew that the flood was coming, and I had a boat ready that would get me through it."

In their delight at taking over the sea from the professionals, amateurs would have benefited from a healthy inoculation of awe of the kind expressed, for example, in a fairly typical cruise narrative of the 1870s, George H. Hepworth's *Starboard and Port: The Nettie Along Shore:*

Such sailing as that was worship. I think my better nature is never more completely stirred than when I am gazing upon the broad deep, the most wonderful part of God's creation.

Or, more profoundly, in Lord Byron's famous verse from *Childe Harold's Pilgrimage:*

Roll on, thou dark and blue Ocean, roll!
Ten thousand fleets sweep over thee in vain;
Man marks the earth with ruin, his control
Stops with the shore; upon the watery plain
The wrecks are all thy deed, nor doth remain
A shadow of a man's ravage, save his own
When, for a moment, like a drop of rain,
He sinks into thy depths with bubbling groan,
Without a grave, unknell'd, uncoffin'd,
and unknown.

IX

The Bottom Line II: The America's Cup, 1920–1983

"Young man, I don't want you to feel like we're putting any undue pressure on you. I don't want you to feel like you have to dominate them at the start. Just as long as you're comfortably ahead."

fter an eleven-year hiatus that, as we saw in Chapter Six, was partly due to disagreement about the size of boat to be used, Sir Thomas Lipton challenged for the America's Cup for the fourth time, the match to be held in September of 1914. It was, of course, not held then; *Shamrock IV* was en route to New York when on August 5 her crew intercepted a German radio transmission about a war that had just started. She continued on and spent the next six years high and dry in an American shipyard. When the match was finally held in 1920, it had a radically new flavor that reflected important developments in the pastime: the boats were commanded by amateurs. Before describing the match and its successors, let us look at the state of amateur sailing at that time.

By the end of the nineteenth century, amateur sailing was fairly popular in Europe, Britain, and especially the United States. All but inevitably, many of these sailors could not resist the natural human instinct to compete in order to test the merits of both their boats and themselves. Racing is a sociable act, and racing sailors tend to be extroverts. They require meeting places as well as facilities for mooring their boats and storing their gear, so on the heels of racing came yacht and sailing clubs. Many clubs were (and are) extremely simple — not much more than a cottage with some storage rooms and a pier jutting into an anchorage. Others have been more elaborate, with a big clubhouse (often called a "casino") that might have formal dining facilities, a marina, a swimming beach or pool, and tennis courts. Volunteers or paid hands supervised the races, which were run under idiosyncratic club rules until regional and national yachting associations began to systematize racing and handicapping.

The local yacht clubs of the early twentieth century performed three important functions that guaranteed the perpetuation and eventual expansion of sailing. The first was the assumption of the role of sailing instructor, which until then had been the job of a parent or a professional seaman who was a family retainer. A youngster no longer had to be from a wealthy or sailing family in order to learn the sport. In a summer, one college student working in a yacht club junior program would teach more children how to sail than could dozens of professional seamen in a decade.

The second role that the yacht clubs assumed was as promoters

of racing. The most important committee in many clubs was the race committee, which handled the logistics of starting and finishing races and hearing protests about violations of the racing rules. Many clubs also sponsored races for the younger sailors in their sailing programs. In Marblehead, Massachusetts, the Pleon Yacht Club was devoted exclusively to junior sailing. Inevitably, local racing led to inter-club racing. Beginning in 1921, the best sailors under the age of eighteen met at a national junior championship regatta; many future international champions were first exposed to high-pressure competition at these championships. In 1924, the first championship for women was held, and by 1985, the United States Yacht Racing Union sponsored nineteen national championships.

The yacht club's third function was to select or sponsor boats for these new sailors to use. Since there were few small pleasure boats in the early days, a club would commission a yacht designer to come up with a fast daysailer that met its unique needs and sailing conditions. To keep costs down and to ensure equal speed when racing, the boats would be built from the same design, which is why they were called "one-designs." Many of these boats are still sailing; you can spot them by their anachronistic appearance (some have gaff rigs) and colorful names, which usually have something to do with the club that sponsored them.

The language used to describe this process is suggestive. People talked — still talk — of "growing up in" a particular class of boat "at" a particular yacht club. In the 'thirties, my father grew up in Atlantics at the Cold Spring Harbor Beach Club. The club, which is at the head of a deep, quiet harbor near an old whaling town on Long Island, near New York City, was founded in 1921 to meet the leisure needs of the first generation of suburban summer people. "The objects of the Club," the founders stated in the constitution, "are to provide and maintain for its members a clubhouse and grounds and facilities for bathing and other out-of-door sports." As the name indicates, there is a nice beach and there have always been tennis courts (two white circles in the club burgee represent tennis balls). Soon after the club was founded, Bowdoin Crowninshield, George Crowninshield's great-grandnephew, was commissioned to design and build a twenty-foot sloop with the spanking new marconi (or Bermudian) rig; the class was called the Beach

One-design dayracing has taken many forms. Before World War I, some racing was done in large daysailers with minimal accommodations, like the Nat Herreshoff-designed New York Yacht Club 50s. Nine of these seventy-two footers were built in 1913 after being commissioned from The Herreshoff Manufacturing Company by J.P. "Jack" Morgan, Jr. They were sold to the partners in the Morgan bank. This kind of racing boat being somewhat expensive, people with smaller budgets looked elsewhere — for example, to the Bug Class, right, a keel boat designed in 1907 by William Gardner, who turned out the lines of the record-breaking schooner Atlantic.

Club One-Design. Around 1930, some members looking for a larger boat for adults to race came to like a powerful thirty-one-foot sloop designed by Starling Burgess called an Atlantic, which was being built in Germany. The Atlantic fleet was formed, and is still there in Cold Spring Harbor. In 1932 my grandfather bought one and he and my father raced together every weekend. In 1958, when I was fourteen, my father allowed me to take his Atlantic out for a sail; it was one of the high points of my young life. He was still racing Atlantics in Cold Spring Harbor in the mid-1970s, and many of his opponents were men he had sailed with and against as a boy forty years earlier. Every now and then somebody loans me an Atlantic so I can go sailing with my boys.

Today, when transporting boats and sailors is so easy, yachting has national and international communities; but in the first half of the twentieth century most sailing was extremely localized. A racing sailor of my father's generation could easily spend his or her entire sailing career — a lifetime, in fact, since it is a pastime that can be enjoyed from youth into old age — within the confines of a single class of boats in the same harbor. Many people still limit their horizons to the outer entrance buoy; each yacht club has an old-timer who knows every rock by name and can sail the race course blindfolded, but who would be completely lost in the neighboring harbor. Not until the 1920s did people (and then only a handful) begin to regularly ship small boats abroad for international racing; and it wasn't until the 1950s and 1960s when national and international one-design classes began to predominate over club boats, and when interstate and inter-regional highway systems were developed in America and Europe, that large numbers of people made a habit of traveling away from their home harbors to race in other areas.

The Seawanhaka Corinthian Yacht Club, around the corner from us in Cold Spring Harbor, was the first American club to get interested in international racing in smaller boats. As we saw in Chapter Seven, it played a key role in the development of American yacht design through the influence of Seawanhaka Cup competition. It attracted many of the members of the first generation of top-flight amateur international racers. Having honed their skills in local racing, these people traveled far afield to other classes and sailing areas. Less ambitious sailors would follow their accomplishments in the yachting magazines. The best of them, and the ones with the best connections, sometimes ended up aboard the America's Cup boats. A gifted sailor and part-time yacht designer named Sherman Hoyt was Seawanhaka's best-known contribution to international sailing; he saved the America's Cup in 1934. Another great sailor of that day was the Bostonian Charles Francis Adams, skipper of *Resolute* in the 1920 Cup match and, later, after a tour as Secretary of the Navy, of the almost-defender *Yankee.* In other circles he was known as the heir of a great New England name: his great-grandfather and great-great-grandfather were Presidents of the United States. (This kind of lineage runs in the sport; in 1893, a reporter for the Boston

Herald counted six descendants of signers of the Declaration of Independence either sailing or watching a race on the New York Yacht Club Cruise.)

Since few owners of the big hundred-footers would trust their vessels to anybody but horny-handed professional sailors, amateur racing was nurtured in small boats, which until the 1930s meant boats shorter than about seventy feet. As there was more small-boat racing in the United States — probably because the middle class burgeoned there first — people like Hoyt and Adams became more prominent earlier than amateurs in England. Adams was in command of *Independence* when he was in his thirties.

The first boat to be raced regularly in international competition was the Six-Meter, a keel sloop about thirty-five feet in length designed to the International Rule, which was drawn up in Europe in the years after *Reliance* in an attempt to develop some seaworthy racing boats to replace the skimming dishes. The Sixes had two appeals for wealthy and not-so-wealthy owners: they were relatively small, and thus were inexpensive and could be shipped easily in freighters; and the rule allowed some design differences, so an owner could feel that he had something that was unique. Between 1920 and the mid-1950s, some of the best international racing was held in Six-Meters on Long Island Sound and in Bermuda, England, Scotland, and Scandinavia, and many America's Cup sailors were alumni of the Sixes. The class died out around 1955 due to increased costs, but made a revival in the 1970s and 1980s, partly due to its similarity in shape and performance to the Cup's Twelve-Meters, another product of the International Rule. Both boats are narrower, heavier, and quite a bit slower than more modern designs of comparable size. It may be just those differences that help to keep them alive — an indication that yachting has not lost its traditional, healthy contrariness.

Around the time the Six-Meters began to grow, the Star Class appeared and quickly became one of the standards of sailing excellence. Inspired by the turn-of-the-century skimming dishes, this twenty-two foot keelboat was an enlarged version of a seventeen-footer called a Bug, designed by William Gardner in 1907. Carefully modernized over the years, the Star is one of the most sophisticated and demanding of all racing boats. Its alumni have played important roles in the America's Cup, and two former world champions, Bill Ficker and Dennis Conner, have defended it three times. Another older class that became widely popular and served as a spawning ground for top international sailors is the sixteen-foot Snipe which, because it is a centerboard boat, has been sailed just about anywhere there is water — on South American rivers, Asian rice paddies, and Kansas reservoirs.

While popular in the 1930s, one-design racing grew enormously after World War II. With the coming of more leisure time, vast highway systems, good trailers, and strongly-built wooden and fiberglass boats that could take the punishment of long-distance trailering, the focus shifted from indigenous local classes with a handful of boats to huge national and international classes. The toughest competition was in world championships and the Olympic Games, in which the Scandinavians excelled. The greatest skipper in the history of the yachting Olympics was a Dane named Paul Elvstrom, who set a record by winning four straight gold medals between 1948 and 1960, and, in his fifties, came back in the Tornado catamaran in 1984 to narrowly miss winning the third-place bronze medal. In the 1984 games, boats representing the United States set another record by winning gold or silver medals in every class. When forty-nine-year-old Bill Buchan, from Seattle, won the gold medal in the Star Class and his son, Carl, won the gold in the Flying Dutchman Class, they were the first parent-child dual medal winners in different events in Olympic history.

Ironically, the most important one-design class, a one-hundred-thirty-pound, fourteen-foot, singlehanded dinghy called the Laser, was not at the Olympics. Its builder and its sailors believed (probably accurately) that they would not benefit from the near-professional intensity of Olympic competition, which had severely limited the growth of other classes. Designed in 1970 by a Canadian boating writer and amateur yacht designer named Bruce Kirby, the Laser became the training ground for the next generation of racing sailors. There was hardly a skipper or crew in the 1983 America's Cup and 1984 Olympics who had not won his spurs in the intensity of Laser racing. In concept, there was little new about the Laser. It was simply a highly refined, well-built development of the first planing hulls that the Englishman Uffa Fox designed in the late 1920s. Kirby, like Fox, specialized in designing boats for the International 14 class, whose rules allowed some flexibility in

*O*n these pages are two of the late twentieth century's most significant contributions to yachting history: two "people's boats" that can challenge even the most accomplished sailor and yet be afforded by almost anyone. Opposite is the sailboard, little more than a surfboard with a sail. These boards are being sailed by the husband and wife team of Scott and Kathy Steele; Scott Steele won a silver medal for the United States at the 1984 Olympics. On the left, sailed by her designer, Bruce Kirby, is the Laser, a simple, easily handled, and fast dinghy intended primarily for singlehanding in sheltered water. Kirby has also designed a Canadian challenger for the America's Cup.

shapes and rigs. Such openness in class rules always tends both to produce fast boats and to further a designer's education by providing an opportunity for experimentation.

In the 1984 Olympic fleet for the first time was the sailboard, a boat of such originality that it deserves a place alongside *America* and *Gloriana* as one of the great designs in yachting. In an essay on the history of yacht design since the 1920s, Olin Stephens praised the sailboard as "one of the most important and innovative trends." That the boat looked like a surfboard with a sail was not surprising, since the sailboard was invented by two California surfers, Hoyle Schweitzer and Jim Drake, in the late 1960s. Fast, fun,

and inexpensive, windsurfing (as it was first called since Schweitzer and Drake called their creation the Windsurfer) was so radical that it took a while to catch on. At first it was popular only among California surfers and the European jet-set, but windsurfing soon became a major sport around the world with more than half a million boats launched by the mid-1980s. A professional sailboard racing circuit (the first yacht racing for pay since the days of the big class in England) was financed by boatbuilders looking for publicity, resorts looking for customers, and beer companies looking to latch onto the sexy, athletic image of sailboarding. While professional racing was significant, the sailboard's greatest contribution was that it was the closest thing to an everyperson's boat that yachting had ever provided.

In America, and sometimes in Britain, the amateurs who sailed one-design boats were not the gentlemanly "corinthians" of the nineteenth century. Yachting for them had become a sport to be worked at, not a pastime to be enjoyed. They were especially keen students of sailing's theoretical underpinnings. Sailing theory was not a new subject; recall Sir William Petty's work that led to the first European catamaran back in the 1660s. What was different now was that, with the modern airplane, aerodynamic theory had taken an enormous leap. The boating magazines were filled with long speculations about what it was that really made a boat sail to windward, and how a crew could make her do better. The earliest, and perhaps most influential person in this area was Manfred Curry, a sailor and aerodynamicist who was born in the United States but did his work in Germany. His book *Yacht Racing: Aerodynamics of Sails and Racing Tactics,* first published in English in 1928, was not the first book about racing, but it was by far the most technical. In it, Curry reported in vast detail about tests that he had performed on sails both in wind tunnels and on the water. His recommendations on racing tactics were based on discoveries that he had made about how one boat's sails affect another's. His term "the safe leeward position" quickly entered the vocabulary of thousands of sailors. In the 1950s, when I was getting serious about sailing, I kept *Yacht Racing* by my bedside, and every year I read a boy's novel called *Curry Was Right,* by Charles G. Muller, in which the hero becomes a racing champion after he applies Manfred Curry's lessons to his small boat.

Far away from the local clubs, in exotic boats and places described in lavish detail in the boating magazines, lay the world of the big America's Cup boats. They were not untouched by the rise in amateurism. The great shift would wait until the 1930s, when the smaller Bermudian rigs did not demand the huge crews that only a tyrannical professional captain could handle; but hints came as early as the turn of the century.

In England, the first big yacht to be consistently commanded by an amateur was the royal racing yacht *Britannia*. The Prince of Wales had commissioned this very lovely G.L. Watson cutter in 1893 after he heard that the Earl of Dunraven was building the big

Valkyrie II. Except for the war and a few years when she was in other hands, *Britannia* raced season after season under royal colors until the death of King George V in 1936, when she was intentionally sunk. As Prince or King, neither of her two owners, Edward VIII and George V, was able to be aboard for more than a handful of races each year, and even when they were they were not competent to be captain. (For Edward, the yacht served mainly as an escape from shore responsibilities; he often sat through races reading his newspaper.) It would hardly do to have a professional in command, so talented amateurs were asked to be in charge. Major (later Sir) Philip Hunloke had the longest tenure, from 1921 through 1935.

The professionals did not always approve of amateur authority on board; at the least, they wished to be consulted. Nevertheless, Hunloke preferred to manage on his own. In his 1929 book on *Britannia*, the yachting writer Brooke Heckstall-Smith, who often sailed in the royal racing yacht, described a confrontation between a professional skipper and Hunloke over whether or not the spinnaker should be doused:

> I remember an incident in one race . . . when a good old soul, an old-fashioned skipper, was in the Britannia, and that skipper had formerly been in a yacht in which he gave all the orders. We were running before the wind and the old skipper said, "In spinnaker." "I did not give the order to in spinnaker," said Major Hunloke, as he was then; "haul the spinnaker out again." "In that case," said the old skipper, "I had better go below." "Yes," said Major Hunloke, "by all means, and stop there." And the old man disappeared down the forecastle hatch. I must say, however, to the old fellow's credit, that he soon appeared on deck again, smiling as ever!

If the issue was not substantive, it concerned the chain of command. "I'll follow no amateurs' judgment again on a big job," Captain Edward Sycamore was heard to mutter after the 1901 America's Cup match, when *Shamrock II*'s tactics were decided by an afterguard of gentlemen, which apparently had trouble making up its collective mind.

The same criticism was made after the 1920 match. Sir William

*I*n 1911, the Bug was enlarged to twenty-two feet, and the new boat was called the Star. By the 1930s, Star boats were raced in harbors all over the world in extremely tight competition. The class eventually became one of the handful in which sailors with the greatest ambitions competed. The Star skipper on the right is Bill Buchan, a Seattle, Washington, contractor who won the class's gold medal at the 1984 Olympic Games. In the same regatta, his son Carl won the gold medal in the Flying Dutchman Class.

The royal racing yacht Britannia *was designed in 1893 by G.L. Watson and had a long, successful racing career under Kings Edward VII and George V until 1935. Here she is sailing by the Royal Yacht Squadron fleet at Cowes in her favorite conditions — a good, strong breeze of wind leaning her over into a wide river of foam. In the photo at right, Charles Francis Adams, the first amateur skipper of a Cup defender, steers* Resolute. *Standing behind him is a uniformed professional — making this photo a perfect image of the transition between professionals and amateurs aboard the big yachts.*

Burton and his amateur afterguard on *Shamrock IV* quickly won two races and were within a day of taking the Cup, but then lost three straight at least partly due to indecisiveness about sail selection and tactics. They had been lucky, however. Adams was forced to drop out of the opening race when *Resolute*'s throat halyard broke and the immense gaff came down (that was one of the very few times when a defender has broken down); and, in the second race, *Shamrock IV* was first to catch a building wind. When the luck evened out, *Resolute* was unbeatable, to the intense disappointment of many Americans who rooted for Lipton. In all Cup history, only two other boats — *Endeavour* in 1934 and *Liberty* in 1983 — have blown a two-race lead. However, *Shamrock* has one singular distinction: she was without doubt the ugliest vessel ever to compete for the trophy. "Something like a cross between a tortoise and an armored cruiser," was how Alfred F. Loomis described her gratifyingly unique combination of snub bow, square stern, slab topsides, and reverse sheer.

The main criticism of English yachting at the time was not that it was too amateur or too professional, but that it was incompetent. In 1930, after Lipton was whipped for the fifth and last time and went home muttering, "I canna win, I canna win," some Britons blamed the whole mess on the wealth of Harold Vanderbilt and the other American defenders. "No," an English journalist (probably Brooke Heckstall-Smith) demurred anonymously. "Our failures in the America's Cup . . . cannot be attributed to the 'Almighty Dollar,' for if we had but looked astern we would have discovered that we were towing a host of foolish conventions, traditions, and personal differences far heavier than any bucket ever made." He had plenty of detailed criticisms: too often good amateur skippers like Hunloke were not considered because of some old personal antipathy; too often modern equipment, like good winches, was not used because of an anachronistic view of seamanship; "in this country we cannot part with the old regime which is painfully senile." While these specifics were important, the writer had one general criticism: unlike the Americans, the British refused to take yacht racing sufficiently seriously. Here he was criticizing the view enunciated by Dunraven that sailing should not be conducted in a business-like way:

. . . Anyone who has given a thought to the American sportsman's viewpoint must know perfectly well that your American never does anything half-heartedly. He is never lukewarm. Mr. Bobby Jones takes his golf very seriously; Mrs. Helen Wills-Moody has made lawn tennis her life's study; and Mr. Harold Vanderbilt does not exactly go boat-sailing because summer is the closed season for fox-hunting.

Indeed. Harold Stirling "Mike" Vanderbilt's attitude about games might best be called cut-throat. He was a many-time national champion in bridge and, later, in contract bridge, which he invented, and he won many yacht races near and offshore (*Vigilant*, the Herreshoff schooner in which he won the 1910 Bermuda Race when he was twenty-six, was later my great-uncle Nat Ayer's *Queen Mab*). In him were combined the technical competence of a General Paine, the judgment of character of a J.P. Morgan, the managerial skills of an Oliver Iselin, the ruthless competitiveness of a John Cox Stevens, and the wealth of . . . well, a

Vanderbilt. He steered a boat well enough; but if he did not have the sailing ability of a Charlie Barr, he could find people — Sherman Hoyt, Olin Stephens — who did. In 1930, in the first match sailed off Newport, which his family had helped make a major resort for the rich, he sailed *Enterprise,* the "mechanical boat." Each position on deck and each seaman's shirt was numbered; when sails were set or doused, numbers, not names were called. The five-person afterguard was a small model of the modern American corporation, with helmsmen delegated for every wind condition and point of sail, and with committees assigned to deal with every foreseeable problem. Once Starling Burgess had tuned the tricky duralumin mast that weighed one-third less than her competitors', once the crew had sorted out all their numbers and the boat's tricky rigging, once the afterguard began to click together — in short, once all the parts were in place, *Enterprise* was unbeatable.

Yet for all his fanaticism about efficiency, Harold Vanderbilt was no clockwork sailor. As he neared the finish line at the end of the fourth and final Cup race, he felt the pain of eighty-year-old Thomas Lipton. In *Enterprise'*s log book he wrote:

> *Our hour of triumph, our hour of victory, is all but at hand; but it is so tempered with sadness that it is almost hollow. To win the America's Cup is glory enough for any yachtsman; but why should we be verging on the disconsolate?*

Lipton went home to be elected to the Royal Yacht Squadron, from which he had been blackballed many times because he was a "tradesman." Then he died. Vanderbilt would have two more hours of triumph before the decade was over.

When Thomas Sopwith turned up in *Endeavour* in 1934, for the first time since James Ashbury came over in 1871 the challenger was all-English: English owner, English designer, English builder. In Sopwith, the Royal Yacht Squadron had a challenging owner of unprecedented ability and dedication. As a successful airplane manufacturer, he understood the technology and had the cash — almost half a million dollars — to pay for the sophisticated rigging and innovative sails that he dreamed up. He was a good helmsman, and in Charles Nicholson he had a good designer. Whether he was

*S*kipper Harold Vanderbilt, with the pipe, and designer Starling Burgess pause for a smoke and a chat during the tense America's Cup summer of 1934, when their Rainbow, right, came close to being eliminated by Yankee in the trials and then beaten by Endeavour in the Cup match. The struts on Rainbow's boom were part of a sophisticated system that allowed the boom to be bent to shape the sail properly. The tackles on deck were used to trim sails and running backstays. The sheer size and power of the J-Class yachts is obvious. Rainbow was probably making more than ten knots when the picture was taken.

a good enough organizer and had a stable enough head was an open question. Somehow, he got into a position where his professional crew struck for higher wages before sailing across, and he ended up with a crew of yachtsmen volunteers who were plenty skilled but perhaps not sufficiently strong to bring him full confidence. He made some mistakes during the races that to this day cannot be explained as anything else than caused by panic.

In the new *Rainbow,* Vanderbilt was lucky to be in the match at all. He had barely squeaked by *Yankee* and Charles Francis Adams in the trials, and then only because the other boat had problems

2 1 4

The Traveling Circus

War years excepted, racing in yachts of a hundred and ten feet and larger was popular in England from 1893 right up to the last year of J-Class racing in 1937. While America's Cup boats came out to play only in Cup years, the "big class," as it was called, was hardly ever inactive in England. Year after year, as many as half a dozen gigantic cutters would be found racing in Britain, moving from race week to race week — Cowes to Plymouth to Falmouth to Penzance, up the Irish Sea to the Clyde in Scotland, back to the south coast, and often across Channel to La Rochelle. The racing season might stretch from May into September, longer than the Americans raced; if the yachts went to the Riviera for the winter, they might be either racing or sailing to and from races for seven or eight months a year.

The length of the season was not all that was unique about the big-class competition, as the American pharmaceuticals tycoon Gerard B. Lambert was amazed to discover when he took his one hundred thirty-five foot J-Class sloop *Yankee* to race in Britain in 1935. He was used to racing in a rather staid and distant manner, far from land in open water in the same general area, regatta after regatta. The only award he could expect for winning at the end was a trophy. The British, on the other hand, raced in what he called "a traveling circus." In his fascinating book about the trip, *Yankee in England,* Lambert described

In this classic photograph made by the famous Beken of Cowes, Herman Andréae eyes the competition while he steers his big-class yacht Candida. *Big-class racing usually was this close, and the boats were always driven this hard. Note the small, solitary winch; the British were firm believers in the value of strong backs assisted by a very limited number of mechanical aids.*

it with the air of an anthropologist analyzing a strange and wondrous culture:

Now note, please, this startling fact. In England the regattas for the large class are run for the benefit of the spectators, hence the race committees consider it their obligation to arrange the races so that they may be properly viewed by the public. The natural question arises, why do they do this? The answer is logical and simple, namely, that for the most part the public pay for promoting the races. A series of regattas are held along the coast of England and the town holding the regatta furnishes large cash prizes to be paid to the various winners. The theory is that crowds are attracted to the town to witness the regatta and that it pays the town to do this. On the other side of the balance sheet, we have the yachtsmen who receive these large cash prizes, and in making up their budget for the operation of the yacht they take these figures very definitely into account. A good seaman can bring in prizes sufficient to make a major contribution towards the total expense of running the yacht. A further item enters into the calculation of the owner. As most people know, the crew on the yacht are paid a special fee in case of a win. The healthy check received, when the winning flag is obtained, goes a long way to make prize money for the crew less of a burden. The element of cash runs constantly across the path of yachts during a season. . .

Lambert first noticed this approach to racing when the 1934 Cup challenger, Thomas Sopwith's *Endeavour*, crossed the finish line at Harwich:

As she finished, Mrs. Sopwith was at the wheel and she steered Endeavour *close into the pier, missing it by scarcely a hundred feet and affording the sightseers a wonderful picture. We were beginning to realize that we had an audience before which we must perform. Let me say at once, that the idea was not distasteful. There is no particular reason why yacht racing should be conducted in the exclusive distances of the open sea, and all of us could feel a normal and somewhat stimulating pleasure in realizing that so many thousand people were interested in our sport in a friendly way and were enjoying our efforts.*

Ever eager to copy the customs of his English relatives — his mother was a daughter of Queen Victoria — Kaiser Wilhelm II sponsored race weeks for the big class on the Baltic, but English boats rarely attended. His own schooners named *Meteor* (one of which was the former Cup challenger *Thistle*) were regulars on the circuit, though he tended to stay ashore for the longer races. "The Kaiser's very fond of giving these 'ere long races," said one of his English professionals, "but he takes precious good care he don't sail in 'em himself."

The Kaiser's yachting disappeared with the beginning of World War I, but it wasn't until 1937 that the last big class races were held in England and the United States. All the American J-Class yachts were broken up by 1941 so their millionaire owners could make symbolic donations of lead and aluminum to the Allied cause. Most of the English boats survived. One was *Shamrock V*, which in 1986 was purchased by the American Lipton Tea Company and brought across the Atlantic for a triumphant tour of maritime museums before settling down on permanent exhibition at the Museum of Yachting, in Newport, Rhode Island. Another was *Endeavour*, which Gerard Lambert had seen performing for the crowds at Harwich that June day in 1935. After sitting for many years in the mud of the Medina River near Cowes, she was bought by a young American named Elizabeth Meyer, who began the expensive job of bringing her back to sailing condition.

with equipment. After two races in the 1934 Cup match, Sopwith's *Endeavour* had been clearly proved to be the faster boat; she had simply sprinted away from *Rainbow* like a rabbit passing a turtle. It was embarrassing. Well behind at the last turning mark in the third race, Vanderbilt turned the wheel over to his alternate helmsman, Sherman Hoyt, and went below certain that he would be the first man to lose the America's Cup. In the same situation, other skippers would have kept the helm either to relieve their crews of the responsibility or to play the soul-satisfying role of martyr. But the self-disciplined Vanderbilt had an organization chart on which Hoyt usually steered when the genoa jib was set in light air. With considerable cunning, and aided by Sopwith's poor navigation and lack of confidence, Hoyt succeeded in luring his opponent into twice tacking away from the finish line. *Rainbow* never tacked and won the race by three minutes, having gained ten minutes on the fifteen-mile last leg.

The next day was a lay day. Vanderbilt made two major changes, pouring tons of ballast into *Rainbow* and asking his old opponent, Frank Paine, designer of *Yankee* and son of General Paine, to come aboard to trim the new circus-tent-size parachute spinnakers that neither he nor Hoyt were comfortable with. *Rainbow* won the fourth race to even the match at two races each, partly because she sailed faster under spinnaker and partly because of Vanderbilt's aggressive tactics. Sopwith protested him for once refusing to give way, but the New York Yacht Club would not hear the protest because Sopwith had not raised his red flag promptly, as the rules required. The public debate over this decision was heated — "Brittania rules the waves and America waives the rules," was one commentary. Mike Vanderbilt had a reputation for hardnosed if not reckless sailing, and there were those who felt that he had been in the wrong and should not have been protected by his own yacht club's reliance on a technicality. But several months later, the race committee chairman said that since the committee had seen *Endeavour* commit a foul before the start, they would have been compelled to disqualify her first, making the protest moot. *Rainbow* went on to take the next two races, the clincher when Hoyt once again bluffed Sopwith into making the wrong move.

After winning a match that, by all rights, he should have lost, Harold Vanderbilt made sure that he would not be caught in a slow boat when Sopwith returned in 1937. Like Charlie Barr in 1903 and Bus Mosbacher in 1967, he followed a match won against a faster boat by turning up for the next match in an invincible boat — the extraordinary *Ranger,* which, in her one and only summer, sailed in thirty-four races and won thirty-two of them by an average margin of seven minutes, four seconds, or more than a mile. In her crew were three young veterans of the small-boat racing wars: Arthur Knapp Jr., a former national junior sailing champion and world champion in the Star Class; and Olin and Rod Stephens, who had been racing Six-Meters since the 1920s. This experience bore fruit, and *Ranger* was the first big yacht to be sailed like a small one.   ·

The best of all the big-class yachts, *Ranger* was also the last of them. After World War II, boats that had seemed small to J.P. Morgan in 1907 now seemed enormous, especially in financial cost. After almost twenty years of desultory discussions about Cup challenges, the New York Yacht Club in 1956 changed the deed of gift for the fourth time, now to allow the much smaller sixty-footers in the Twelve Meter Class and to permit a challenging boat to be shipped to the site of the match instead of making the long voyage on her own bottom.

Though the decision to switch to boats one-half the size of the Js was obviously realistic if the Cup were ever again to be contest-ed, it was a sad one. No Twelve-Meter — in fact, no sailing yacht built after World War II — could equal a J in grace, power, and efficiency. The big class was the last vestige of the golden age of yacht racing; there would be faster boats, yes, and more sensible ones, but there would never be racers like the Js and the big-class machines. Born several years after the Js were taken apart, my friends and I all but worshipped them. We memorized just about every word of Harold Vanderbilt's book about the 1934 and 1937 matches, *On the Wind's Highway,* and when we sailed out into Cold Spring Harbor in my father's thirty-one foot Atlantic we played out the adolescent fantasy that we were in *Ranger* racing an imaginary *Endeavour II.* One of us took the helm and played Mike Vanderbilt, another was Olin Stephens at his right hand, and the third was Rod Stephens running around on the foredeck setting spinnakers. Some kids dreamed that they played for the Yankees; we dreamed that we were J-Class sailors.

A thing that did continue in the nine Twelve-Meter Cup matches since the eclipse of the Js was the theme of good management, strong leadership, and good design. The 1958 match was a runaway by the third *Columbia* to defend. Steered by a Six-Meter champion, Briggs Cunningham, she destroyed the English *Sceptre,* the last Royal Yacht Squadron challenger. Six years later, *Sovereign,* representing the Royal Thames Yacht Club (the old Cumberland Fleet), was humiliated by the defending *Constellation.* All the other Twelve-Meter matches were between the New York Yacht Club and Australians.

Australians had shown interest in the Cup long before, in 1889, when a Sydney naval architect named Walter Reeks stopped off in New York to inquire about a possible challenge. Concluding that the cost would be too great and the challenger might not even be able to survive the delivery passage half-way around the world. Reeks went home and recommended that the idea had little merit. It took smaller boats, the new deed of gift, and a stubborn communications tycoon named Sir Frank Packer to bring the first Aussie challenge, in 1962.

This was the second of three America's Cup summers for a talented American, Emil ("Bus") Mosbacher, Jr., a real-estate developer who many years before had been a champion junior and Six-Meter skipper on Long Island Sound. In 1958, he was helmsman of the trials runner-up, *Vim;* in 1962 and 1967 he was skipper of *Weatherly* and *Intrepid*. He had much in common with Vanderbilt — fierce competitiveness, technical aptitude, strong leadership ability, and a serious businesslike attitude about racing sailboats. And he was a better helmsman as well. Off the water he was personable and approachable; but in competition he was as tense as a tightly wound clock and sometimes lost seven pounds of weight during a three-hour race. According to Willie Carstens, a talented professional sailor who served under both, the younger man was Vanderbilt's equal in some departments. The influence was direct. Mosbacher readily conceded that the aggressive tactics he used in *Vim* and *Weatherly,* each slower than her competitors, came straight out of Vanderbilt's two books. "I didn't invent 'tailing', the tactic of driving a match-race competitor away from the starting line by hanging your bow on his stern. Vanderbilt wrote all about it in *On the Wind's Highway.* We realized in 1958 that we had a slower boat and that we had to win starts. We did it by taking many risks we got away with." In the one-on-one, only sometimes civilized warfare of match racing, the start is almost everything. Win the start and you've won half the battle; win the start and sail between your competitor and the wind, and hope he isn't *too* fast. Like Charlie Barr in the 1901 match and Vanderbilt in 1934, Mosbacher did it brilliantly.

Yet that vital aggressiveness created a problem: it could lead to fouls. Back in 1901, the New York Yacht Club's Cup committee did not find it contradictory to throw Charlie Barr out of the same race in which he won their selection to defend. The racing rules were not vital then. But thanks partly to Harold Vanderbilt, whose reaction to the 1934 controversy was to rewrite and recodify yacht-racing's rules, people had become sticklers for the rules. "I always had in the back of my mind a reminder not to do anything that would allow the selection committee to believe that I was not reliable," Mosbacher said in an interview in 1980. "I did not want to take unnecessary risks." Neither did he want the selection committee to be surprised by his tactics: "So much of what you do is not so much what you think you *should* do in the circumstances as it is what you think the educated observers *think* you should do."

It takes considerable self-discipline to be able to sail two races at once — your own race and the one that a selection committee

On the wind's highway," Ranger *pulls away from the fleet in one of the last races that the J-Class ever sailed, during the New York Yacht Club Cruise after the 1937 Cup match. She flies her eighteen thousand square-foot parachute spinnaker. The pole projecting from her bow is a sprit to catch the enormous sail should it collapse and keep it from being dragged under the hull. The third boat, probably* Endeavour, *flies an old-fashioned balloon spinnaker, which looks tiny compared with the parachutes. It was a winning margin like this that led Harold Vanderbilt to fear that he had killed off J-Class racing forever with his superboat.*

expects of you. It also takes a great deal of independence. Mosbacher's boats were always that; they were *his* boats, in which he was in complete charge without any second-guessing by a manager in a spectator boat. In 1962, his opponent, Jock Sturrock, skipper of *Gretel,* was subject to this kind of supervision from Packer, who, like many autocratic entrepreneurs who buy Cup boats, became jealous whenever the spotlight shifted from himself to his crew. The traditional solution to this problem is for the jealous owner to keep public control as long as possible. Packer accomplished this very efficiently; not only did he postpone naming Sturrock as skipper until the eve of the match, but he changed navigators on the morning of the first race. Strange as it may seem, *Gretel* went out for the America's Cup — the first formal race she ever sailed — with a crew of twelve men who had never before sailed together. She lost, but not by much considering that Mosbacher forced her over the line early and that she broke some equipment and was flying the wrong mainsail. That afternoon, Mosbacher realized that Alan Payne, *Gretel's* designer, had put together a very fast boat using American equipment and the model test tank at the Stevens Institute of Technology, in New Jersey. The American skipper knew that if he made any mistakes *Gretel* would beat him.

The challenger was best on upwind legs; with the powerful jib-sheet winches that Payne had installed, she could beat *Weatherly* during the long duels in which, tack after tack, the boat behind is always trying to find clean wind, and the boat ahead is always trying to dirty the wind up. Mosbacher won the starts but surprised the spectators by refusing to be drawn into these duels. Instead, he sailed off a little way. "We knew when we made the decision we would have to live with it," Mosbacher said later. "Our strategy worked out perfectly. Can you imagine the howl that would have gone up if it hadn't?" *Gretel* never took the lead on a windward leg. She did pass *Weatherly* on a reach to win the second race and almost caught her on another reach in the fifth race, in which Mosbacher, like Vanderbilt and Hoyt in 1934, duped Sturrock into sailing a longer, slower course. Man conquered technology once again.

Other than the New York Yacht Club's deep sigh of relief, the match had two major effects. To prevent another foreign designer from taking advantage of American technology, as Payne had done, the club interpreted the deed of gift to require that each boat

not only be constructed in her country of origin, but also carry equipment made there. As the best sails and sailing equipment in the world were made in the United States, this interpretation severely cramped the challenger's style. Second, when the Australians next challenged in 1967 with *Dame Pattie,* Mosbacher was not about to be caught in another slow boat. A small, wealthy syndicate (including Harold Vanderbilt) paid for, Olin Stephens designed, and Mosbacher supervised the layout of the amazing *Intrepid,* which lost only one race all year. Mosbacher was in firm control; he even turned down the designer's normal request to supply a project engineer for the boat because, as he firmly put it, "We were not going to have somebody who was not going to sail telling us what to do." Equipment alterations that year totaled the relocation of one small winch. The sail inventory may have been one of the smallest in Twelve-Meter Cup history; "I knew what I wanted. We used all Hood sails and there were no experiments."

Crew loyalty was a vital component in Twelve-Meter racing after 1958, since everybody was a volunteer. Like Dennis Conner after him, Mosbacher had a steady core of able, committed sailors in his team. Their relationship becomes clear in a story that he has told about *Intrepid's* first sail after she was launched. As she approached a buoy, he told the crew to set the spinnaker on an easy "bear-away" maneuver as he gradually bore off to a run. The crew disagreed. They wanted to do a "tack-jibe" set — the most difficult maneuver in the repertoire as the spinnaker is hoisted while the boat comes about and then jibes. Mosbacher had his doubts, but eventually agreed; "If you're going to delegate responsibility, you've got to learn to live with it." He tacked around the buoy and jibed, and instantly the spinnaker was up and pulling. "You know, there's something special about that crew," he remembered somewhat wistfully in 1980. "Here it is thirteen years later and this morning I talked to Vic Romagna and I see Billy Kelly and Toby Tobin and Bizzy Monte-Sano all the time, and we're trying to find Buddy Bombard's phone number . . ." Four years later, in the line of Stevens and Morgan and Vanderbilt, Bus Mosbacher was elected Commodore of the New York Yacht Club.

Three years after *Intrepid's* great 1967 season, she was back in a Cup match, surprisingly enough as the slower boat. Tank tests had led Britton Chance Jr. to redesign her with a bigger hull and smaller keel. The tank also led — misled, it turned out — Olin Stephens into putting the same features on the new *Valiant.* Under Bill Ficker, a former Star Class world champion, the older boat won the defense trials against *Valiant* and *Heritage.* The latter boat was designed, built, outfitted, owned, and commanded by Charley Morgan, a Floridian who was no relation to the banking Morgans and who had made a small fortune building fiberglass sailboats for the expanding sailing population of the 'sixties. When Ficker came up against Sir Frank Packer's new Payne-designed *Gretel II,* which had beaten Baron Marcel Bich's *France* in the first international challenger trials in Cup history, he found himself in the same position Mosbacher had been in back in 1962. Like Mosbacher, he took chance after chance.

Luckily, the Australians made enough mistakes in the first race to hand it to the Americans. In the second race, Ficker took a risk at the start, coming in late and fast between *Gretel II* and the committee boat. Martin Visser, the challenger's starting helmsman, luffed hard. Just after the starting gun fired, *Gretel*'s bow hit *Intrepid*'s port side. The defender shot ahead but was gradually ground down and beaten. After the inevitable protest was heard, the New York Yacht Club's race committee (which was standing there watching the whole incident) disqualified the Australians. The uproar was world-wide, with *"Gretel Robbed!"* being one of the tamer headlines in the Down-Under newspapers. Packer offered a delightful if somewhat skewed simile: "An American skipper protesting to the New York Yacht Club race committee is like a man complaining to his mother-in-law about his wife."

Against this onslaught of critical publicity, defenders of the decision sounded more legalistic than fair-minded: "It's rule 42.1 and it's basic as hell!" exclaimed George Hinman, who, as a former New York Yacht Club Commodore, was hardly considered neutral by a press eager to support the Australians. Although most experienced sailors from many countries were sure that *Gretel* was at fault, the yacht club's Cup committee at one stage considered resailing the race. They went so far as to ask Bob Bavier, the President of the North American Yacht Racing Union and an official of the International Yacht Racing Union, for his opinion. As Bavier put it with typical forthrightness in a column in the New York *News,* his opinion was that "The Australians deserved to lose at

the hearing just as much as they deserved to win on the race course. They simply don't know the rules."

The controversy over the foul blinded people to the fact that Ficker's action was a sign of desperation. If *Intrepid*'s timing had been slightly off and she had reached the committee boat four or five seconds earlier, the Australians would have had every legal right to do what they did, and the disqualified skipper would have been Bill Ficker. No sane and experienced sailor would take such a risk unless his or her boat was slower than the competition. Later, Ficker ignored some of the so-called "rules" of match racing by not covering *Gretel* tack for tack and by setting different sails. Like Mosbacher and Vanderbilt, he knew that some "rules" are only guidelines. The Australians eventually won one race legally. If they had known Rule 42.1, they would have won two races. If, like Ficker, they had been confident that *Gretel* was faster than *Intrepid* and had sailed as aggressively as the defender did, they could easily have won the series.

Three times the Australians had challenged, and two of those three times they had turned up in Newport with the faster boat and proceeded to self-destruct on the race course. For a long while in the Cup summer of 1974, it looked as though the Americans, at last, were the ones who were self-destructing.

First, the test tank convinced Britton Chance Jr. to take a big chance on a new boat called *Mariner.* She looked very odd. She had a tiny keel and rudder and an underbody that was squared off aft where there was usually a taper. While *Mariner* turned out to be as slow as she was strange-looking, she made three important contributions to the America's Cup. One was the way that her syndicate took advantage of the U.S. income tax system when raising money for her construction and upkeep. By channeling funds through a non-profit educational institution, her donors enjoyed the same tax deductions that they received when giving money to more traditional charities such as a hospital or church. This approach made fund-raising a good bit easier than it had been, and it quickly became standard operating procedure for Cup supporters. Her second contribution was her skipper, the colorful Georgian Ted Turner, who had no success whatsoever with *Mariner* but who, after he was fired in mid-August, promised to be back. Her third contribution was her second skipper, Dennis Conner, another Star

world champion, who did a little better with her after she was rebuilt to look somewhat more normal. Conner stayed around a lot longer than anybody had expected.

Besides *Mariner,* the other new boat was Olin Stephens' *Courageous,* commanded by Bob Bavier. Her arch-rival was *Intrepid,* back to her 1967 form and sailed by yet another Star world champion, Gerald Driscoll. (Not to belabor my point, but I must report that Driscoll's tactician, Bill Buchan, had himself won two Star world championships.) As the two Stephens Twelves fought it out bow to bow all summer, neither skipper won much acclaim. Conner, after he took over from Turner, quickly proved himself to be the most aggressive starter and tactician in Newport; but he was on *Mariner,* which hadn't a chance. "How can we get Conner onto one of those boats?" one frustrated committeeman asked. "Don't worry, one of the syndicates will find a way," a colleague replied.

One of the syndicates did find a way. After the Cup committee eliminated *Mariner* from the trials, Bob McCullough, manager of *Courageous,* asked Conner to join him and the crew for dinner at

the mansion where they were living. When the meal was over, the crew went off by themselves with McCullough and Bavier. The subsequent conversation, described in Conner's book, *No Excuse to Lose,* provides a revealing look at how Cup syndicates are run:

. . . After the meeting McCullough, Bavier, and a couple of syndicate members asked me into the study, and Bavier said that the crew had met and had decided to ask me to sail with them.

I was honestly surprised and said, "I'm flattered."

There was silence, and I could see that Bavier was a bit uneasy. After a moment, McCullough said, "Not only are we asking you to come aboard Courageous, *but we want you to steer the boat at the start, too. We want you to start the boat."*

I leaned forward with my eyes popping out of my head and said, "Start the boat!" with a little squeak in my voice. I was really excited. After a few moments, I asked if I could steer the boat on the way in from the race the next day to get the feel of her.

McCullough said, "We want you to start the boat tomorrow."

"Tomorrow?" I said, shocked.

"Yes, tomorrow," he said. He then leaned over me — he's very tall and commanding — and he said, "Young man, I don't want

Maxiboats are racing yachts designed to the top limit of the International Offshore Rule. Usually about eighty feet long, they carry two dozen crew members in a worldwide series of races held everywhere there is water deep enough for them to sail in. Unlike the smaller IOR boats, they have good accommodations, but a large part of the boat is set aside for extra sails, tools, and work benches, since equipment weakens quickly under the huge loads of sailing at high speeds for long periods of time. Most maxis carry sophisticated electronic equipment, including computers for evaluating data about the boat's performance that is measured by various boat- and wind-speed indicators. The best organized boats are supported by large professional crews using trucks and shipping containers to stow and transport extra gear. The annual cost of maintaining a maxi may be as high as $750,000. The boats themselves cost more than $2 million. This is the kind of sailing that a James Gordon Bennett would aspire to.

you to feel like we're putting any undue pressure on you. I don't want you to feel like you have to dominate them at the start. Just as long as you're comfortably ahead."

So I said, "Thanks very much," and went back to my rented house and told my wife the good news. I had a little trouble sleeping that night. Here I was thirty-one years old and about to start a boat I'd never sailed in the final trials of the America's Cup.

The confused organization in *Courageous*'s afterguard was every professional skipper's bad dream. Bavier was skipper but only steered downwind. Ted Hood steered upwind, and Conner was starting helmsman. Neither Hood or Conner had been on board at the beginning of the summer. Who was in charge at any given moment may have been clear on paper, but it wasn't in the boat's cockpit. Mistakes were made, races were lost, morale plummeted. After a few days, on the morning of the last day of the trials, McCullough fired Bavier and named Hood as skipper and Conner as tactician and starting helmsman. *Courageous* won that race from *Intrepid* in half a gale of wind. "They had sailed *Intrepid* to at least ninety-five percent of her potential," Conner said about her crew, "and had almost beaten us, who, new to *Courageous*, were getting no more than about eighty-five percent out of a better boat." That was a situation that usually applied to a slow Cup defender and a fast challenger, not two defense candidates. *Southern Cross*, the Australian challenger, was fast; but after she lost two reasonably close races, her panicky owner, Alan Bond, nullified any speed advantage she might have had by switching crewmembers, gear, and sails around, and *Courageous* beat her fairly handily in races three and four to win the match that ended a long, angry summer.

So far in this chapter, I have stressed the involvement of skilled, serious amateur sailors in America's Cup racing. By the mid-1970s a whole new type of sailor had appeared. Neither a pure amateur nor a professional in the old-fashioned sense of the word — a person directly paid to sail a boat — this sailor was noteworthy both for sailing skill and for making a living in the boating business. Racing boats was part of the job. This was certainly not new. For years Rod Stephens and other yacht designers had been sailing and racing on the boats that they had helped produce. Too, Bob

Bavier as publisher of *Yachting* magazine had done a great deal of on-the-job sailing. But what was different about the new expense-account sailing was that the focus shifted from preparing and writing about boats to winning races.

Manfred Curry was right; sailboat racing is a complicated sport. By the mid 1970s, if the sport was to be played successfully at the very top level in the grand prix events — the America's Cup, the Olympics, the Admiral's Cup — its sophisticated gear, and especially the sails, demanded the full attention of specialists. There were plenty of specialists available once young, talented sailors found that as sailmakers they could simultaneously pursue their favorite pastime and make a decent living. Just about every serious racing boat had at least one sailmaker on board not just to trim and repair the sails that his company had made, but to steer and make tactical decisions as well. Very occasionally, an extremely talented sailor who was not in the boating business would surface as a skillful skipper for an owner; Dennis Conner, a San Diegan in the drapery business, is the best example. Before long, the yachting press came to identify the hot racing boats not by the names of their owners but by the names of their skippers.

By the mid-1980s, the heightened technology and increased pressures of competing for the America's Cup, as well as the demands of the Olympics and top-flight ocean races, had altered the traditional idea of amateurism (or, to use the old term, Corinthianism). The undisputed fact was that sailors who did not work on their equipment and skills full-time or close to full-time for months or even years before these events were at a disadvantage. The authorities and individuals who financed these campaigns made sure that was not the case. Inevitably, the question was raised as to who was and was not an amateur, and authorities struggled for definitions. By 1985, the rule of thumb in the United States was that anybody was a professional who was paid to race a sailboat or who raced for cash or a prize worth more than $300. There were many ways to disguise being paid to sail a boat. For example, a sailmaker might simultaneously be taken on as a crew-member on a Twelve-Meter and hired as a full-time consultant to develop sails for the boat. He would receive paychecks only between races; when the boat was racing, only his living expenses would be paid. The United States Yacht Racing Union, the nation-

Olin and Rod Stephens

The heirs to Nathanael Herreshoff as the most successful yacht designers of their time were the brothers Olin J. Stephens II and Roderick Stephens Jr., whose careers stretched from the 1920s into the 1980s. With Olin drawing lines and Rod supervising rigging and construction, they were responsible for a fleet remarkable in both its variety and its success: six America's Cup defenders; the popular Lightning and Blue Jay one-design classes; a full-scale replica of *America;* in the 1930s, the first ocean-going sailboats to take full advantage of the jib-headed rig; in the 1950s, *Finisterre,* which won three consecutive Newport-to-Bermuda Races; in the 1960s, the first big boats to use the fin keel and separated rudder; in the 1970s and 1980s, the winners of the first two Whitbread Round-the-World Races; and many distinguished cruising boats, power and sail, stock and custom-built. Rod also helped to create an amphibious landing craft called the DUKW, which played an important role in World War II and for which he was awarded the Medal of Freedom.

The Stephens brothers were drawn to boats early. In 1922, sailing into the harbor of New Rochelle, New York, in his yawl *Hippocampus,* the yachting writer Alfred F. Loomis was met by two inquisitive, towheaded boys in a rowboat. He invited them aboard for a look. Many years later, he recalled that they were "young lads, eager, silent lads. What they were thinking as they fingered her heavy standing rigging or peered into her bilge they never told me." Olin and Rod were then fourteen and twelve years old and wild about boats. Their father, a successful businessman, encouraged and supported them in their enthusiasm, sailed with them on the family cruising schooner, designed by Bowdoin Crowninshield, and in 1927 bought them a Six-Meter to race in the highly competitive Long Island Sound fleet. Both boys knew what they wanted,

which was to design, build, and sail yachts, and they dropped out of college because it did not further those aims. In 1929 Olin saw his first design launched, a twenty-two-foot keel sloop commissioned by Drake Sparkman, a yacht broker who soon went into business with him.

Like most successful yacht designers, the Stephenses burst upon the scene with a boat that they themselves commissioned and sailed. This was *Dorade,* a fifty-two-foot yawl that their father paid for (the price was $28,000), Olin designed, Rod helped build, and all three of them raced to England in 1931 with four other men. *Dorade* won the race by the whopping margin of two days on elapsed time and then won the Fastnet Race. While she looked odd next to the hefty fisherman-type schooners designed by John Alden that were popular at the time, she was not a radical boat;

Above, in a photograph taken in the early 1920s, the towheaded Olin and Rod Stephens are seen cruising around a harbor with friends, examining visiting yachts. Four decades later, Olin was sailing with skipper Bus Mosbacher in the revolutionary Twelve Meter Intrepid, *and Rod was engaged in his favorite task — improving a*

piece of sailing gear — on another America's Cup defender. Widely respected for their integrity and humanity as well as for their technical brilliance, the Stephens brothers remained among the leaders of international yachting at ages well beyond those at which most people would have retired.

her narrow, handy hull and simple jib-headed rig reflected lessons that the brothers had learned sailing Six-Meters. Although some old-timers mourned the demise of the grand old days of husky hulls and mammoth gaff rigs, the logic behind *Dorade* had an immediate appeal to anybody who could not afford a gang of professional sailors in the Great Depression.

Dorade launched the brothers' careers. While Olin turned out the hulls, Rod took charge of their rigging with a passion for detail, functionality, and ultimate safety. To give two examples: in his *Dorade* days he invented a ventilator that scooped up air while filtering out sea water (it has been called the "Dorade vent" ever since), and his written instructions on the proper use of a cotter pin in a turnbuckle — to many people a simple concern — went on

for several paragraphs. While both brothers had strong opinions about what was and was not seamanlike, they were hardly closeminded. Elsewhere in this chapter I have quoted Olin's praise of the sailboard, and Rod, in his chapters on rigging for a book that I edited in 1985 on the design of offshore cruising boats, was extremely receptive to some new ideas in rigging and hardware.

While other designers — Philip Rhodes, Charles Nicholson, William Tripp, James McCurdy, William Lapworth, and German Frers (who was trained at Sparkman & Stephens) — would have their successes, the brothers Stephens earned and kept a reputation as the top designers of racing boats larger than forty feet. The trademark Sparkman & Stephens hull was born of their sailing experience and their extensive model testing in the towing tank at Stevens Institute (a legacy of John Cox Stevens' inventor-brother Edwin): moderate in beam, displacement, and length, with good stability and a fairly large, flexible, and easily handled sailplan. When extreme dinghy-type boats with complicated rigs began to win races in the mid-1970s, Sparkman & Stephens fell from its position of leadership, partly because the brothers, for all their interest in speed, could muster up no enthusiasm for boats that seemed to run contrary to their experience of safe offshore sailing.

Rod Stephens continued to play an active role at Sparkman & Stephens and sailed frequently, learning how to windsurf while in his late sixties. Olin Stephens retired from Sparkman & Stephens in 1978, leaving a young designer named William Langan in charge, and moved to New England, where he developed computer programs for yacht designers. He spent his summers in a house that he designed, on the top of a mountain in southern Vermont, looking down on a mass of rolling hill tops that, when the fog came in, could easily be mistaken for mounds of ocean waves.

al governing body of sailboat racing, appointed a committee on eligibility to rule on this sticky issue on a case-by-case basis. The complication of the task may be estimated by the eight-page, single-spaced report that the committee wrote on thirteen cases it considered in 1985 alone. Many of these involved payments for services and living expenses made by multi-million dollar syndicates to skippers and crews of America's Cup challenge candidates on their pricey way to Perth to try to win the Cup back from the Australians.

Though on a smaller scale, Olympic competition, too, was intense. A three-year Olympic campaign, including the cost of a $20,000 boat, might have a budget as large as $100,000. To cover their expenses, many sailors set up small tax-exempt foundations to attract donors. The national authority's Olympic Yachting Committee, on which I served for several years, was able to provide some funds to the top crews. In the dying days of the pure amateur, there was little money to work with — the committee's budget in 1977 was less than $50,000 — but more funds were made available with the burgeoning intensity (and commercialization) of competition. In the first six months of 1984 alone, the committee spent almost $500,000 on coaching and international travel, which sometimes involved shipping boats by air to distant regattas. Most of that money came from yachting's share of funds derived from commercial sponsorships of amateur sports.

Were these new subsidized sailors professionals? "Semi-professionals" is probably the most accurate term; but the point is moot. The relevant issue was how a sailor approached the sport, not the source of his or her income. Many years ago, the Earl of Dunraven pointed out that some people approached sailing in a business-like way. Ted Turner, the television and sports magnate who may well be the last truly amateur sailor to have competed for the America's Cup, made Dunraven's point when he said in 1976 that, whether or not they earned money from sailing, some people were changing the sport by racing yachts in a *professional-like* way, as though it was the only thing they cared about.

The most successful sailmakers were Ted Hood, from Marblehead, Massachusetts, and Lowell North, from San Diego, California, each of whom had world-wide systems of lofts. Also a yacht designer, Hood was best known for racing offshore. North was a multi-time Star Class world champion and Olympic medalist who had recently become involved in ocean racing, where his sails had quickly ended Hood's domination. In their 1977 Cup campaigns, each used an approach that echoed Conner's comment about the vital importance of getting everything possible out of a boat: launch the boat early and sail, sail, sail. While some money was spent on model-testing, the tank had been considerably discredited by the bad information it had provided in 1970 and 1974 (remember *Mariner*?), and it was generally agreed that rather than search for incremental improvements on the hull design of *Courageous,* clearly the fastest Twelve in existence, the major effort should be to experiment with rigs, sails, and rudders. Hood and North launched their boats in 1976 and, working on either coast, devoted months to full-scale testing, sometimes against other Twelves, sometimes against on-board computers into which were fed the predictions of the boats's optimum performances. Hood sailed his *Independence* until Marblehead Harbor froze up in January of 1977, while in southern California North was taking *Enterprise* ten to fifteen miles out into the Pacific in search of wind.

When they got to Newport in 1977 for the summer-long series of defense trials, they began a cat and mouse game in which each hid from the other his newest developments in sails and gadgets. For a while, it looked as though they were actually trying to lose races. Meanwhile, Ted Turner was winning race after race in the three-year-old *Courageous,* which ostensibly was serving as Hood's trial horse. Although many stiffnecked people predicted that Turner would never be selected to defend because of his unpredictable and sometimes outrageous behavior ashore, the New York Yacht Club Cup committee — which now included Mosbacher, Cunningham, and Bavier — was more impressed by the gutsy aggressiveness shown by Turner and his young tactician, Gary Jobson, than by North's and Hood's constant tinkering with technology. The bottom line was Turner's near-sweep of the final trials. As one committee member said, "Turner selected himself." In the 1977 Cup series, he easily beat Alan Bond's *Australia,* which had won a complicated set of defender trials that included the old *Gretel II* as well as French and Swedish yachts.

Although Dennis Conner was disappointed that nobody asked him to sail on one of the 1977 defense candidates, he probably

understood that he was too talented to be the number-two man. Within a few months after the last race, he was given almost a free hand by the well-financed syndicate that had supported North and *Enterprise*. During one hundred fifty days of tuning and practicing at Newport in 1979 and at San Diego during the winter and spring of 1980, Conner tested more than one hundred sails on the older boat and the new Sparkman & Stephens-designed *Freedom*. In the trials, *Freedom* won forty races and lost only four, destroying Turner in *Courageous* and Long in *Clipper*.

The Cup match was not so easy, primarily because an old calculated design risk by the Australians finally paid off. Close followers of the Cup's history had developed the theory that a challenger's best hope was to turn up with a boat that was especially fast in one particular weather condition; if that condition prevailed, she had a good chance to dominate the defender, which had to be a good all-weather boat in order to survive the long summer of defense trials. The condition to aim at, said the experts, was lighter than ten knots; that's what the wind tends to blow at Newport in September. Granted, the challenger would lose in stronger winds, but if history was any indication, she probably would lose then anyway. The best defense of this theory was *Gretel II*, a good light-air boat that would have beaten the lumbering *Intrepid* in 1970 had her crew been as talented as her designer.

The introduction of trials for the challenge candidates complicated things to some extent, since there tends to be a good breeze at Newport in August; but *Australia,* designed for light air, was well enough sailed in both 1977 and 1980 to handle the rougher conditions. In 1980, she appeared for the match looking quite a bit different than she had during the trials, sporting a rule-beating hooked mast that provided one hundred feet more sail area — which can make quite a difference in light air. Her designer, Ben Lexcen, had borrowed the idea from the otherwise undistinguished British boat *Lionheart.* With this rig, she was faster than *Freedom* in soft winds. Dispensing with traditional match-race covering tactics, Conner and his tactician, Dennis Durgan, sailed as they would in a fleet race, caring little for the other boat as they hunted down puffs and favorable wind shifts. This strategy worked so well in the first race that they spurted out to a ten-boat-length lead after only eleven minutes of sailing. *Australia* was lead-

229

The Other Bottom Line

America's Cup competition has never come cheap. In the 1970s, the most expensive campaigns were the three-to-six-million dollar challenges of the Australians, who had to ship boats and crews halfway around the world. U.S. sailors soon found out how well-off they had been before they lost the Cup in 1983: with shipping and extremely expensive research into keel shapes, the budgets for the 1987 American challenging syndicates were as high as ten and perhaps twelve million dollars each.

Where does all the money go? One of the most detailed accountings available is the one for Lowell North's unsuccessful 1977 defense candidate, *Enterprise,* whose expenses totaled one and one-half million dollars. Considering inflation, this probably was less than the estimated six hundred thousand dollars that Harold Vanderbilt singlehandedly spent on *Ranger* in 1937 and greater than the one hundred thousand dollars that went into *Vigilant* in 1893.

ENTERPRISE BUDGET, 1976-1977

Research and design	$375,000	25%
Hull construction	300,000	20
Shipyard, crew housing, and transportation	220,000	15
Spars and rigging	165,000	11
Sails	100,000	6
Winches	60,000	4
Trial horse	65,000	4
Shipping	50,000	3
Administration	50,000	3
Insurance	35,000	2
House rental	25,000	2
Boat storage	25,000	2
Electronics	12,000	1
Tenders	10,000	1
Miscellaneous	8,000	1
Total	$1,500,000	100%

Corporate sponsors began picking up much of the cost of America's Cup and other expensive racing boats in the 1980s. In exchange, the boats became temporary floating billboards, flying sails that the racing rules would not allow them to use in the races themselves. This is Australia II, *the 1983 Cup winner, in the guise of a beer commercial.*

By 1980, that budget was paltry thanks to the development of even more sophisticated electronic instruments, the use of multiple trial horses, and the arrival of sails made of space-age materials like Mylar and Kevlar — a new mainsail alone cost seven thousand dollars. Even after donors were allowed to deduct their gifts from their income for tax purposes, money became increasingly hard to come by. To make up deficits, Cup managers and fund-raisers did something that might have appalled J.P. Morgan and Harold Vanderbilt: they opened themselves to commercial ties. At first, they simply accepted what were called "in-kind services" — free T-shirts, foul-weather gear, shoes, automobiles, and other equipment provided by manufacturers looking for promotion. In 1980, the winning boat, *Freedom,* was given goods of this sort whose retail value was estimated at three hundred thousand dollars. However, that was hardly sufficient, and soon Russell Long, the young skipper of *Clipper,* was saying with considerable prescience, "The future of the America's Cup rests in the hands of corporate sponsors." His boat's own name reflected financial support given the syndicate by Pan American Airways, whose clippers flew some of the first long-distance routes. When practicing off Newport, she sometimes flew a spinnaker that carried the highly visible logo of a rum distiller (international rules did not allow commercial logos in actual races). Before the 1987 match, American challengers vied for the attention (and cash) of companies that made and sold high-prestige goods. By the summer of 1985, the syndicate closest to the New York Yacht Club had three official corporate sponsors, Cadillac, *Newsweek* magazine, and the Amway Corporation, each of which donated up to one million dollars. Even the New York Yacht Club got into the act. To cover the considerable expense of running the trials and races, it trademarked the image of the America's Cup and licensed its use to corporations.

Another cost consideration was that of the crew. This was not a problem in the old days, when boat construction did not begin until the winter before the match so that the designer could take full advantage of the test tank. Launched in the spring, the boat had weekend drills until vacations liberated the bulk of the crew, who then sailed or worked on the boat almost every day until she was excused from the trials in August or won the match itself in mid-September. At most, a working man would take a summer-long leave from his job. But the regimen changed with Dennis Conner's long *Freedom* campaign leading up to 1980. "The days when a New York stockbroker will leave his business for a month or two to race in the America's Cup are over," observed Halsey Herreshoff, a grandson of Captain Nat and a crew member in many Cup campaigns. "To compete now will require time — a lot of it." Herreshoff recalled that, in 1958, he and the other crew members on *Columbia* had had only fifteen days to prepare for the first race.

Now, preparing for the Cup summer was a full-time workup of as much as two years. Day after day, twenty-two sailors were needed to handle the defense candidate and trial horse during sail-testing. Budgets were stretched to cover their living expenses; after the definition of "amateur" was expanded by yachting authorities, they were provided with modest incomes. (Another development was that they were not all male; a talented young woman named Christie Steinman became one of the navigators in Conner's campaigns.)

ing the second race when the time limit expired, then won the rematch. Conner actually gave the start away in the third race so he would have room to maneuver; he won by less than a minute. The wind blew hard enough in the last two races for *Freedom* to come into her own and to nullify the advantage of the hooked mast; it was so new the Aussie sailmakers were still experimenting with mainsails. Once again a fast challenger scared the daylights out of the defender. Once again only highly unorthodox tactics

kept the match from running its full seven-race limit — or from being lost altogether.

Conner almost immediately went to work preparing for the 1983 match. He placed the highest priority on developing a fast light-air boat. For almost ten years, U.S. designers had been content to make minor modifications on the shape of *Courageous*. Now it appeared that more basic research in the test tank and greater risks were necessary. By the end of 1982, his syndicate had

launched a total of three new Twelves, one of them a radically small light-air boat, *Magic,* designed by a Dutch yacht designer named Johan Valentijn. She had not worked out. Valentijn was a talented man with an interesting history. While at Sparkman & Stephens, he had worked on IOR designs; later he had co-designed *Australia* with Ben Lexcen and designed *France III* for Baron Bich. Nervous that his freelancing ways were violating the spirit of the deed of gift, the New York Yacht Club after the 1980 match required that a designer henceforth be a national of the country that the boat represented. Valentijn chose a U.S. passport and ended up designing Conner's eventual defender, *Liberty,* which was another modification of the *Courageous* theme. (The rules about equipment that had been made after *Gretel* did so well with American equipment in 1962 were dropped for the very good reason that the thorough internationalization of the boating industry had made it meaningless.)

And then the most extraordinary event occurred: the Australians won the America's Cup in 1983. They did it the way that Conner feared they would, by developing a faster boat.

Sometime in 1981 or 1982, Lexcen learned from work in a Dutch test tank that a radically new type of keel would produce a faster Twelve-Meter. The drawings of this appendage seemed childish. The keel was short, thin at the top, and wide at the bottom, and it sprouted little wings on either side. It looked like a normal keel that has been turned upside down and married with an airplane's tailfins. The keel succeeded because it increased stability by getting the ballast lower and increased lateral plane when the boat was heeled. As *Australia II* proved, a boat whose hull is carefully designed around the characteristics of such a keel is very fast in almost every condition, on almost every point of sail. With it, a boat heels less, turns quicker, and makes less leeway than a boat with a normal keel.

The challenger had other advantages besides the keel. Her sails were thought to be the best at Newport, and she was well and confidently sailed by her skipper, John Bertrand, a North Sails loft owner and an Olympic medalist who was sailing in his fourth Cup match. This was the fourth match also for her owner, Alan Bond, who had settled down considerably since 1974 to become a hard-driving but better-organized syndicate leader.

When *Australia II*'s great speed advantage became obvious during the challenger trials, the New York Yacht Club's America's Cup committee assiduously pursued every means of getting her disqualified. One approach it took was to declare that the keel had actually been illegally designed by Dr. Peter van Oossanen and the other Dutch engineers with whom Lexcen worked at the Netherlands Ship Model Basin, whose use by the Australians had been specifically approved by the Cup committee. At one stage that summer, the *Liberty* syndicate manager, Ed du Moulin, telegrammed van Oossanen asking for help with *Liberty*'s keel using words that apparently were intended to encourage the Dutchman to admit that he had designed the Australian keel. The ploy, if that was what it was, failed to the loud glee of Alan Bond and spokesman Warren Jones, whose summer-long public relations campaign against the New York Yacht Club was unceasingly aided by the Cup committee's remarkable aptitude for shooting itself in the foot. That "Keelgate" was the episode's most popular nickname suggests, with its reference to the Watergate investigation of Richard M. Nixon, how badly the authorities handled the issue of the winged keel.

Besides claiming that the challenger violated its own very new rule about the nationality of the designer, the Cup committee also protested the keel on the grounds that it twice violated the Twelve-Meter measurement rules. First, in the language of the rules it was a "peculiarity," and boats with peculiarities should not be rated by measurers. Second, the boat's measured draft should be the depth of the tips of the winglets, not of the keel bottom. Since the winglets were reported to extend below the keel, and the keel was near Twelve-Meter maximum depth, this would have resulted in a major increase in *Australia II*'s rating. Her sail area would have had to be reduced to make her a Twelve-Meter again; of course, that would have made her a slower boat.

Both counterattacks failed. First, it was revealed that the Australians had patented the keel before the Cup summer. Since then, however, a Dutch aerodynamicist named Joop Slooff has claimed that, while it is conceivable that he and Lexcen came up with the idea simultaneously, he himself suggested it to van Oossanen during a professional conference sometime in the late 1970s and later conducted a computer analysis that led to the model testing that in turn led to the final keel design. (How pleasing it is that this mystery focuses on the Netherlands, where yachting was born!)

Second, although the keel was unusual, it had been tried over the years and was hardly a peculiarity. As some members of the Cup committee knew full well, Olin Stephens had experimented with winglets while working on *Intrepid* back in the 'sixties but had dropped the idea when the test tank showed that they created considerable resistance. (During the 1983 brouhaha, Stephens, by then retired from his firm, publicly congratulated Lexcen on the ingenuity of the keel.) When the Cup committee was finally told on August 26 that the International Yacht Racing Union's Keelboat Technical Committee, which had jurisdiction over the Twelve-Meter rules, had the year before actually *approved* the idea of winglets on request by the British challenger, its house of technicalities finally collapsed.

Throughout all this messy dispute, the keel itself was never seen except by the Australians. Maybe that fact explains some of the Cup committee's fury. Like their predecessors in 1887, who were confronted with the unknown of *Thistle*'s secret keel, some of the New York Yacht Club's spokesmen seemed less concerned with the substance of the matter than with the challenger's unwillingness to snap to and show all. Who owned the Cup, anyway? Unbelievably, even after the August 26 revelation some committee members revealed a belligerent unwillingness to accept the political reality that, regardless of dark whispers about Australian trickery and self-satisfied claims of American moral superiority, *Australia II* could not be kept from racing without bringing the Cup in pieces down on the New York Yacht Club's shoulders. In their fine book about the 1983 match, *Upset,* Michael Levitt and Barbara Lloyd described how late this stubborness hung on: only two hours before the American defenders and the Australian challengers were to meet to discuss the ground rules for the match, scheduled to begin a day later, the Cup committee was still seriously debating whether to hold the match at all.

Above all, there was fear that the America's Cup would finally be *lost.* While *Liberty* won the first two races, there was little doubt which was the faster boat, especially in light air and on a square run. In the second race, despite the fact that *Australia*'s mainsail came apart at the head and was never fully hoisted, she was beaten by only a minute and a half. She easily beat Conner in the third race; but in the fourth race Conner sailed about as perfectly as any Cup skipper ever has — and still won by less than one minute. Ahead three to one, *Liberty* was favored to win the fifth race and the match in what looked like her type of breeze. But the unthinkable occurred for a defender: before the start, a jumper strut collapsed aloft and then the replacement broke, and her crew was unable to shape her mainsail correctly on port tack. *Australia II* won by almost two minutes. If not intimidated by his opponent, Conner clearly was wary of her; as in 1980, he sailed his own race and took what many observers thought were great risks. After the fifth race, in which he went off in search of wind only to see it get to Bertrand first, he was harshly and publicly criticized by Gary Jobson, who had been a losing tactician in the defense trials. Through a combination of luck and good sailing, the Australians had come back from a two-race deficit to tie the match at three races apiece. It was a remarkable performance. They called a lay day to rest and check their equipment for weaknesses. Then a race was started but abandoned in a calm, and the Americans asked for a day off to take out one thousand pounds of ballast, which allowed them to increase *Liberty*'s sail area for the expected light air.

Not just the sail area was increased. The pressure on Dennis Conner became enormous. For years people had joked about the fate of a losing U.S. defender: his severed head would be placed in the empty America's Cup case in the trophy room of the New York Yacht Club. Charles Francis Adams in 1920, Harold Vanderbilt in 1934, Bus Mosbacher in 1962, Bill Ficker in 1970, and Conner himself in 1980 had all glimpsed the sharp edge of the executioner's sword. On the eve of the seventh and last race of the 1983 match, Conner now had his head upon the block.

Conner had brought much of the pressure upon himself over the previous two years by inflating his job and mission far beyond realistic expectations. Part of the problem was his passion for detail. "Give yourself no excuse to lose" is how he summarized his approach in his book, which his opponents studied as though it were his psychological profile. His instinct was to supervise every aspect of any project he took up, almost to the point of fanaticism (and sometimes beyond it). Objectively, as he awaited the start of the rubber race he had no excuses at all; he had sailed extremely well against a boat whose brilliant design could not have been anticipated. But Conner had somehow gone beyond a normal, professional concern with details to an obsession that led him to identify himself personally not only with his boat (which he had helped design) but also with patriotic mission. At one stage in *Liberty*'s campaign, he made a remarkable and telling statement. "I have three hundred million Americans to represent," he said. "I have a lot to think about, and I don't want to let them down." This was the skipper of the New York Yacht Club's defender talking. The sailors who preceded him would have been astonished by such a claim. They had found it difficult enough simply to represent the two thousand members of the yacht club, but here Conner was claiming to be a yachting equivalent of the President of the United States. A declaration of such grandiosity suggested that in 1983 Conner was having trouble keeping things in perspective. Like Crowninshield's voyage to save Bonapartes, like Morgan's marriage to Mimi Sturges, like the Earl of Dunraven's attack on the honor of Oliver Iselin, Conner's self-assigned role fairly glowed with self-sacrifice and the anticipation of martyrdom. In that way, he violated perhaps the most important precept of the business-like and professional approach to yacht racing that, as we have seen, kept the America's Cup in New York for more than a century: exciting and challenging as it might be, the job of sailing a boat in the America's Cup is, after all, just a job.

John Bertrand was not carefree; but he had less at stake. Even if he lost the seventh race, the fact that he had gotten this far would always be held to his credit. Perhaps Bertrand's greatest advantage in these nerve-shattering last hours was that, unlike Conner, he was able to focus on the job at hand without having to cart around any unnecessary baggage. He was the beneficiary of a brilliant campaign organization on traditional American lines assembled by Bond and Warren Jones. The aggressive, noisy public relations campaign that these two men led against the yacht club's anti-keel maneuvers and, later, against Conner himself, kept the pressure on the defender while easing it on the challenging helmsman. Behind this smoke screen, Bertrand calmly concentrated on preparing himself and his boat and crew.

On September 26, twelve days after the series began, the trophy was finally won in a race that sailors will be analyzing for years.

Televised all over America and Australia, it was watched with breathless expectation even by people to whom sailboat racing had always seemed a bore. Conner won the start, for once was on the correct side of a wind shift, and led by twenty-nine seconds at the first mark. He gained some on the next leg, a reach, lost some on the following reach, and then pulled out to what seemed like a commanding fifty-seven second lead at the second windward mark. Ahead lay a run and a final beat.

But it was *not* a commanding lead. At some time during the match, a member of Conner's afterguard was quoted as saying that, on a square run before a light wind, *Australia* could gain a minute and a half. Here *Liberty*'s lead was less than one minute. Perhaps that is why Conner, instead of covering Bertrand, once again sailed off in search of wind. It didn't work. *Australia* did not gain those ninety seconds; she gained seventy-nine, and rounded the last mark twenty-two seconds ahead. On the final leg, Conner did all that was left to him to do. Tack after tack, forty-seven tacks in all, he tried and failed to force *Australia*'s crew into making a mistake. The challenger crossed the finish line to a bedlam of horn blasts from the spectator fleet, a salute whose power had been building for more than a century.

Down in New York, in the baroque clubhouse of the New York Yacht Club, the bar was filled with men staying in touch with the race by telephone reports shuttled in from the pay phone in the corridor. Soon after the worst news was reported, a phone call from Newport triggered prearranged plans to pack the Cup up for the next day's presentation ceremony at the old Vanderbilt mansion, Marble House, where there was an exhibit of the America's Cup mementoes of Harold Vanderbilt. The Brink's truck arrived a few minutes before eight in the evening, and the glass case was removed. The long bolt that held the Cup to the table was undone, and the padded box that had stood in readiness all these years was brought out.

It would not be let go without ceremony. A hundred or so people gathered around it in the small trophy room a few steps from the bar. Some gave speeches and some wept. One member unthinkingly poured a bottle of champagne into the bottomless trophy, and it slushed out onto the rug. And then the guards moved in and hefted the wooden case. The America's Cup was gone.

*A*n era ends in a moment that, for one hundred thirteen years, had lived in the dreams of Cup challengers from James Ashbury onwards: John Bertrand and Alan Bond, Australia II's owner, take possession of the Hundred Guinea Cup.

A Selected List of Sources Consulted

Listed below is an extremely pared-down list of published books and articles consulted, omitting most sources that are mentioned in the text. In addition, the New York Yacht Club's collection of scrapbooks and boating magazines, going back to the 1840s, has been an invaluable resource. Readers interested in pursuing yachting history in greater detail will find a microfilm of the scrapbooks on file at the Mystic Seaport Museum, in Mystic, Connecticut.

GENERAL

Burke's Peerage.
Dictionary of American Biography.
Dictionary of National Biography.
Drummond, Maldwin. *Salt-Water Palaces.* New York: Viking, 1980.
Gavin, C.M. *Royal Yachts.* London: Rich and Cowan, 1932.
Hofman, Eric. *Steam Yachts.* Tuckahoe, N.Y.: De Graff, 1970.
Johnson, Peter. *Boating Facts and Feats.* New York: Sterling, 1976.
National Cyclopedia of American Biography.
Phillips-Birt, Douglas. *The History of Yachting.* New York: Stein and Day, 1974.
Richey, Michael W. (ed.). *The Sailing Encyclopedia.* New York: Lippincott & Crowell, 1980.
Robinson, Bill. *Legendary Yachts.* 2nd edition. New York: McKay, 1978.
Rosenfeld, Morris, William H. Taylor, and Stanley Rosenfeld. *The Story of American Yachting.* New York: Appleton-Century-Crofts, 1958.

Rousmaniere, John and the Editors of Time-Life Books. *The Luxury Yachts.* Alexandria, Va.: Time-Life Books, 1981.
Schoettle, Edwin J., (ed.) *Sailing Craft.* New York: Macmillan, 1928.
Stephens, William P. *Traditions and Memories of American Yachting.* Camden, Me.: International Marine, 1981.
Wallace, William N. *The Macmillan Book of Boating.* New York: Macmillan, 1964.
Whipple, A.B.C. and the Editors of Time-Life Books. *The Racing Yachts.* Alexandria, Va.: Time-Life Books, 1980.

YACHT CLUB HISTORIES

Dear, Ian. *The Royal Yacht Squadron, 1815-1985.* London: Stanley Paul, 1985.
Fairchild, Julia F. and Arthur M. Crocker. *Cold Spring Harbor Beach Club.* New York: Cold Spring Harbor Beach Club, 1964.
Guest, Montague and William B. Boulton. *The Royal Yacht Squadron.* London: Murray, 1903.
Parkinson, John, Jr. *The History of the New York Yacht Club.* 2 vols. New York: New York Yacht Club, 1975. (Index published 1983)
---. *Nowhere is Too Far: The Annals of the Cruising Club of America.* New York: Cruising Club of America, 1960.
---. *The Seawanhaka Corinthian Yacht Club: The Early Twentieth Century, 1897-1940.* New York: Seawanhaka Corinthian Yacht Club, 1965.
Phillips-Birt, Douglas. *British Ocean Racing.* London: Adlard Coles, 1960. (Royal Ocean Racing Club)
---. *The Cumberland Fleet: Two Hundred Years of Yachting.* London: Royal Thames Yacht Club, 1978.

Stephens, W.P. *The Seawanhaka Corinthian Yacht Club: Origins and Early History, 1871-1896.* New York: Seawanhaka Corinthian Yacht Club, 1963.
Underhill, Arthur. *A Short History of the First Half-Century of the Royal Cruising Club, 1880-1930.* London: Royal Cruising Club, 1930.

EARLY YACHTING

Casson, Lionel. *Ships and Seamanship in the Ancient World.* Princeton: Princeton University Press, 1971.
Clark, Arthur H. *The History of Yachting, 1600-1815.* New York: Putnam's, 1904.
Fraser, Antonia. *Royal Charles: Charles II and the Restoration.* New York: Knopf, 1979.
Massie, Robert K. *Peter the Great: His Life and World.* New York: Knopf, 1980.

GEORGE CROWNINSHIELD

Crowninshield, Francis B. *The Story of George Crowninshield's Yacht Cleopatra's Barge.* Boston: privately published, 1913.
Ferguson, David L. *Cleopatra's Barge: The Crowninshield Story.* Boston: Little, Brown, 1976.
Hilen, Andrew, (ed.) *The Diary of Clara Crowninshield: A European Tour with Longfellow, 1835-1836.* Seattle: University of Washington Press, 1956.

J.P. MORGAN

Canfield, Cass. *The Incredible Pierpont Morgan: Financier and Art Collector.* New York: Harper & Row, 1974.

Jackson, Stanley. *J.P. Morgan*. New York: Stein and Day, 1983.

Satterlee, Herbert L. *J. Pierpont Morgan: An Intimate Portrait*. New York: Macmillan, 1939.

Sinclair, Andrew. *Corsair: The Life of J.P. Morgan*. Boston: Little, Brown, 1981.

OTHER FIGURES

Cochran, Thomas C. *Railroad Leaders, 1845-1890*. Cambridge, Ma.: Harvard University Press, 1953. (John Murray Forbes and Charles J. Paine)

Conner, Dennis and John Rousmaniere. *No Excuse to Lose*. New York: Norton, 1978.

Dunraven, the Earl of. *Past Times and Pastimes*. 2 vols. London: Hodder and Stoughton, n.d.

Herreshoff, L. Francis. *An L. Francis Herreshoff Reader*. Camden, Me.: International Marine, 1978. (Charlie Barr)

Leslie, Anita. *Francis Chichester*. New York: Walker, 1975.

Seitz, Don C. *The James Gordon Bennetts*. Indianapolis: Bobbs-Merrill, 1928.

Turnbull, Archibald Douglas. *John Stevens: An American Record*. New York: Century, 1928.

THE AMERICA'S CUP

Dear, Ian. *The America's Cup: An Informal History*. New York: Dodd, Mead, 1980.

---. *Enterprise to Endeavour*. New York: Dodd, Mead, 1977.

Leather, John. *The Big Class Racing Yachts*. London: Stanford Maritime, 1982.

Levitt, Michael and Barbara Lloyd. *Upset: Australia Wins the America's Cup*. New York: Workman, 1983.

Morris, Everett B. *Sailing for America's Cup*. New York: Harper & Row, 1964.

Rousmaniere, John. *America's Cup Book, 1851-1983*. New York: Norton, 1983.

Thompson, Winfield M. and Thomas W. Lawson. *The Lawson History of the America's Cup*. Boston: privately published, 1902.

Thompson, Winfield M., William P. Stephens, and William U. Swan. *The Yacht America*. Boston: Lauriat, 1925.

YACHT DESIGN

Chapelle, Howard I. *The History of American Sailing Ships*. New York: Norton, 1935.

Fox, Uffa. *Seamanlike Sense in Powercraft*. Chicago: Regnery, 1968.

Gribbins, Joseph. "Ray Hunt: New England Archimedes." *Nautical Quarterly* 25 (Spring 1984), 37-47.

Heckstall-Smith, B[rooke]. *The Britannia and Her Contemporaries*. London: Methuen, 1929.

Herreshoff, L. Francis. *Capt. Nat Herreshoff: The Wizard of Bristol*. New York: Sheridan, 1953.

Herreshoff Marine Museum Chronicle 1-13 (1979-1985).

Kinney, Francis S. *You are First: The Story of Olin and Rod Stephens of Sparkman & Stephens*. New York: Dodd, Mead, 1978.

Merrick, Sam. "Digging up Scow Roots from the Developmental Years, 1895-1904, When the Scows were Conceived." *NCESA Reporter* 13, no. 1 (Summer 1977): 3-21.

Morris, E.P. *The Fore-and-Aft Rig: A Sketch*. New Haven: Yale University Press, 1927.

Robinson, Bill. *The Great American Yacht Designers*. New York: Knopf, 1974.

Stephens, Olin J. II. "Trends in Yacht Design, 1920-1986," in John Rousmaniere (ed.), *Desirable and Undesirable Characteristics of Offshore Yachts*. New York: Norton, 1986.

CRUISING AND OCEAN RACING

Doherty, John Stephen. *The Boats They Sailed in*. New York: Norton, 1985.

Heaton, Peter. *The Singlehanders*. New York: Hastings House, 1976.

Henderson, Richard. *Singlehanded Sailing: The Experiences and Techniques of the Lone Voyagers*. Camden, Me.: International Marine, 1976.

Londsdale, the Earl of and Eric Parker, (ed.) *Cruising*. The Lonsdale Library, vol. 15. London: Seeley, Service, 1933.

Loomis, Alfred F. *Ocean Racing: 1866-1935*. New York: Morrow, 1936.

Rayner, D.A. and Alan Wykes. *The Great Ocean Yacht Race*. London: Peter Davies, 1966.

Rousmaniere, John. *"Fastnet, Force 10"*. New York: Norton, 1980.

Teller, Walter. *Joshua Slocum*. New Brunswick, N.J.: Rutgers University Press, 1971. A revised edition of the same author's *The Search for Captain Slocum*. New York: Scribner's, 1956.

Credits